LAST O
OF THE
LOST CAUSE

> *Maj. R.J. Moses, C.S., will pay $10,000, the*
> *amount of bullion appropriated to 2.M. Dept. by Sec.*
> *War to Maj. R.R. Wood.*
> *By order of 2.M.Gen.*
>   *W.F. Alexander, Maj. and Ass. to 2.M. Gen.*
>
> *5 May, 1865, Washington*

The Civil War Memoirs of a Jewish Family
from the "Old South"

Raphael Jacob Moses, Major, C.S.A.
1812-1893

Compiled, Edited, and Expanded
by
Mel Young

University Press of America, Inc.
Lanham • New York • London

Copyright © 1995 by
University Press of America,® Inc.
4720 Boston Way
Lanham, Maryland 20706

3 Henrietta Street
London, WC2E 8LU England

Library of Congress Cataloging-in-Publication Data

Moses, Raphael Jacob, 1812-1893.
Last order of the lost cause : the true story of a Jewish family in the
'Old South' / Raphael Jacob Moses ; compiled, edited, and expanded
by Mel Young.
          p.   cm.
Includes bibliographical references.
1. Moses, Raphael Jacob, 1812-1893. 2. Jews--United States--
Biography. 3. United States--History--Civil War, 1861-1865--
Personal narratives, Jewish. 4. Confederate States of America.
Army--Officers--Biography. I. Young, Mel. II. Title.
E184.J5M668   1995   973.7'82--dc20   95-23904 CIP

ISBN 0-7618-0080-8 (cloth: alk: ppr.)
ISBN 0-7618-0081-6 (pbk: alk: ppr.)

⊖™The paper used in this publication meets the minimum
requirements of American National Standard for Information
Sciences—Permanence of Paper for Printed Library Materials,
ANSI Z39.48—1984

DEDICATION

This book is dedicated to those millions of persons,
throughout the world, living, long since passed,
and to those of future generations who can point with pride,
head held high, and declare,
from the words of Raphael Jacob Moses:

•••

"You can point to your ancestry and show the Wisdom of
Solomon, the Poetry of David, the Music of Miriam, and the
Courage of the Maccabees."

•••

Contents

Part II: The War Years, 1861-1865

RAPHAEL JACOB MOSES
1812-1893

Introduction

With the evacuation of Richmond by the Confederate Government in April 1865, President Jefferson Davis and the senior cabinet, government, and staff initially established a temporary capital at Danville, Virginia. With Federal columns of the Army of the Potomac moving toward that region, President Jefferson Davis and several key Confederates moved south, through North Carolina and South Carolina and into Georgia, avoiding the Union Army of Tennessee, under General Sherman, operating in the central and eastern Carolinas.

By early May 1865, realizing the war was lost, the major units of the Confederate Army had surrendered, General Robert E. Lee having surrendered the Army of Northern Virginia to General U.S. Grant at Appomattox, Virginia, on April 9, 1865, and General Joseph E. Johnston surrendering the Army of Tennessee to General Sherman at Durham Station, North Carolina, on April 26, 1865.

Individual Confederate soldiers, groups of soldiers, and small units were trying to walk, ride, or move in groups back to their homes. They were in tattered uniforms, hungry, and mostly penniless. General Johnston requested of President Davis that 250,000 rations be obtained to be distributed to these discharged soldiers.

A final meeting of the Confederate Government was held at Washington, Wilkes County, Georgia, on May 5, 1865.

Present were President Jefferson Davis; Secretary of War, General John C. Breckenridge; Postmaster General John H. Reagan; Quartermaster General A.R. Lawton; I.M. St. John, Commissary General, and Major Raphael J. Moses, at that time assigned as Commissary Officer for the State of Georgia.

These are the events leading up to Major Raphael J. Moses being present; and, the fascinating events of a bizarre episode of history.

THE LAST ORDER OF THE CONFEDERATE GOVERNMENT

Maj. R.J. Moses, C.S., will pay $10,000, the amount of bullion appropriated to Q.M. Dept. by Sec. War to Maj. R.R. Wood.

May 5/65   By order of Q.M. Gen.
Washington   W.F. Alexander,
                   Maj. and Ass. to Q. M. Gen.

AVERY - "THE HISTORY OF THE STATE OF GEORGIA"
1850 - 1881, N.Y.C. 1890

The receipt for the bullion follows:

Washington, May 5, 1865.

Received from Maj. R.J. Moses three boxes estimated to contain
$10,000 in bullion. This has not been weighed or counted, and is to be
opened before two commissioned officers and a certificate of contents
made, which certificate is to be forwarded to Maj. R.J. Moses, and by the
amount certified to the undersigned is to be bound.

R.R. Wood, Maj. and Q.M.

Raphael Jacob Moses was a remarkable person in
many other ways. He was a successful businessman. He was
a well recognized attorney, orator, and member of the Georgia

State Legislature. He was a devoted family man to his wife, Eliza (nee Moses). He was a caring husband and, to the 12 children they had, he was a sensitive father. Together, Raphael and Eliza would have the pain of infant deaths, the pleasure of marriages, and the trial of war and Reconstruction.

He was a man who proudly acknowledged and defended his Judaic heritage. To a critic, he published, "... You honor me. You call me a Jew." To a grandson, he wrote, in explaining this heritage, "... [it has] the wisdom of Solomon, the poetry of David, the music of Miriam, the courage of the Maccabees."

His is a true story set in the Old South of his family from 1812 to 1893, from Charleston, South Carolina, to St. Joe and Apalachicola, Florida, to Columbus, Muscogee County, Georgia, in 1848.

The lives of Raphael and Eliza Moses were changed forever, with the advent of the Confederacy and the Civil War. The Moses family gave their all to the cause and were true to their Southern heritage.

Major Moses, now 53 years old and his war service ended, returned to Columbus, Georgia, his fortune very much depleted, his family and household suffering losses of family and status. He began to rebuild.

However, the Confederate military service of the three sons of Raphael J. Moses provides an insight to the strong family determination. Three sons of Moses were of military age. The youngest, Raphael Moses, Jr., served in the Confederate Navy. The middle son, Albert Moses Luria, served in the infantry. The eldest, Israel Moses Nunez, also referred to as "Major," served in Parker's Battery of Virginia Artillery.

The eldest surviving son, Israel Moses, was born in 1838, in Florida, was later given the name Nunez, and as such is carried on the Confederate military files as Israel Moses Nunez. The middle son was born Albert Moses in 1843, and his father later changed his surname to Luria. Thus, he appears in the military records as Albert Moses Luria. Interestingly, the only son to carry the Moses family surname was the youngest, Raphael J. Moses, Jr., called Lea or Lee, born in Florida in 1844. The father, Raphael Sr., made these surname changes in order to perpetuate the proud maternal Sephardic, or Spanish Jews, heritage that goes back to the golden era of the Spanish Inquisition only to be driven away, killed, and converted to Catholicism. Indeed, the strong adherence to his Judaic birth rite and heritage were important influences in Raphael Jacob Moses' life.

The middle son of Raphael and Eliza Moses, Albert Luria, whose death in the battle of Fair Oaks (Seven Pines) is recounted in Part II, was a very active, popular teenager. There were several Moses families and a Moise family living in the Columbus area, some related by marriage, some by blood, some both ways. These large families, perhaps because of their Judaic heritage, tended to socialize and visit. The eldest son of Raphael and Eliza Moses, Israel Moses Nunez, called "Major", married a cousin (Eliza's niece), Anna Marie Moses in 1859. Albert became acquainted at an early age with a much younger cousin (niece), Anna's sister, Eliza, referred to as Lize. Raphael and Eliza did not encourage the relationship between Albert and Lize, considering their very young ages, he was sixteen, she not yet fourteen; and, there already had been a marriage between first cousins, Israel and Anna (Moses) Nunez. The unstable political clouds of the time did not seem a proper setting for a "long engagement or pledging."

Remarkably, a short military journal kept by Albert has been preserved, along with extracts of a diary by Eliza, and of several letters to Albert. To circumvent restrictions placed upon Albert about encouraging the heart of the young teenage "Lize," the letters were addressed to cousin Julia Lazarus, who understood the matters of the heart of the young lovers.

The youngest son, and namesake, Raphael J. Moses, Jr., was to enter the United States Naval Academy at Annapolis, Maryland, in September 1860, and he resigned in January 1861 when Georgia seceded from the Union. His five years of adventure cannot help but move the imagination. It was during this Confederate Naval service, while on duty in England, that he met the teenaged Georgina Samuel, who was to become his wife in 1866.

Raphael and Eliza's daughter, Penina Septima Moses, married William Moultrie Moses of Columbus, Georgia, a Confederate Army veteran who served in the 2nd Georgia Infantry, part of Longstreet's Corps, the Army of Northern Virginia.

Daughter Isabelle Adeline Moses married Lionel C. Levy of New Orleans. He was a Confederate Army veteran who enlisted in the Louisiana Infantry at the age of 15, transferred to the famous "Fenner's Artillery Battery," and served throughout the war in battles in Mississippi, Alabama, and Georgia.

The Moses family drew together after the end of the hostilities. The surviving Confederate soldiers returned home and attempted to resume their lives. Raphael and Eliza, though their hearts were heavy with the loss of their son, Albert, were thankful for the return of young Raphael, of their son Israel to his wife and their home, and of their future sons-in-law, Confederate Army veterans Lionel C. Levy and William Moultrie Moses. Indeed, they now worked towards a reunited country and were highly thought of amongst their friends and neighbors. They had fought for the "Lost Cause," and now would give their energies and prayers for the future. This unfolds for the next 28 years of Raphael and Eliza's lives, and that of their children and their descendants and their heritage.

Part I

The Ante-Bellum Years

1812 - 1861

Chapter 1

1812: Dear Marie
I Was Born January 20, 1812
[Date of Letter: About 1890]

Dear Marie:

You want me to write my autobiography. You have sent me a book to write it in and a pen to write it with, so that I am fully equipped with everything but a subject of interest, while [since] I have always considered myself "a pious fraud" in impressing the public with a reputation for talents which I did not possess.

I think I have always had one element of wisdom which is said to be uncommon; I have always known myself. My conception was quick, my language good, my business education a great advantage in my profession as a lawyer, and because I understood bookkeeping and business methods, and could always understand a merchant's case, and because I evinced a familiarity with their business pursuits, I soon earned the reputation of being a first-class "commercial lawyer," irrespective of how much of little I might know of the commercial law contained in the books. While I had (not altogether undeserved) considerable reputation of being a first-class orator, there was one thing that I could never do: make something out of nothing, and that is what I am required to do now. My temperament was sympathetic, and I had language and manner enough to make others feel what I felt, but unless I feel the subject myself, I could never have made others feel. So that, boiled down, my legal reputation could be largely attributed to my business education and my oratorical standing [which] spring[s] chiefly from my strong, sympathetic nature. My knowledge was more the result of observation than reading; my taste for books was limited, my memory was never good, and getting ideas from books was with me like pouring water through a sieve; the fluid passed quickly away but the sediment remained. And so with my reading: the language passed away, but some of the ideas remained, and particularly in law, the principles remained, but the book, page, case, etc., soon passed out of my mind.

As I said before, my perception was always quick and my judgement good. I seldom had a case presented to me that I did not at once form an opinion upon it, what lawyers call "first impression," and afterwards, in searching the books, I usually found authority to sustain my views.1 I was never a technical lawyer, nor what is familiarly known in the profession as "case lawyer." The two preceding pages ought to compose the begin[n]ing and end of my autobiography, but what you want, I suppose, is an anti[e]-mortem diary, a sort of retrospective glance at my life from the cradle to the grave, or sufficiently near the latter to leave it an easy matter for you or anyone else to fill out the few blank pages that may remain.

Well, then, to begin, I was born on the night of January 20th, 1812, in Beaufain St., Charleston, South Carolina. Like most babies, I suppose I entered upon life with a cry. I was born an ugly baby, remained an ugly boy, and lived an ugly man. My mother had two other children, both handsome, but they died in infancy. Death loves a shining mark; they shone, I didn't, and so I was left to become the pet of my mother and the pest of everybody else, a "spoiled child," and I went through an extraordinary share of spoiling, and nothing saved me from utter ruin except good luck or some undeveloped, innate virtue.

At two years old, I have heard, I knew my letters, and my dear mother thought she saw the germs of a concealed genius which has remained invisible ever since. She kept a school, and I was on of her scholars, cutting a figure in her classes when I should have been cutting my teeth!

My boyhood may be condensed into one word: I was the impersonation of mischief; my pranks were without limit and much to the annoyance of a maiden cousin, Bell Cohen, who had the charge of me in the occasional visits paid by my parents to Philadelphia and New York. At school I never took a very high stand as I was much more given to play than to study. I had the reputation at school of having excellent capacity, but lacking industry in my classes. I was seldom "head," and if I got there by accident, I seldom remained there more than a day or two at a time. When the examinations came on annually, I crammed for them, and as I could acquire very rapidly, I generally took a stand with the boys that were up with their lessons all year round.

Chapter 2

1817: The First School

The first school that I have any recollection of after leaving my mother's school was kept by a Mr. Southworth. He was an excellent teacher and a severe disciplinarian. I improved very much under him, but one day one of the boys who shall be nameless, but who belonged to the South Carolina aristocracy and was the bully of the school, undertook to whip a little boy, and I interfered, and tough I had never been much of a fighter, being neither active nor particularly strong, I found my adversary like many other bullies, not much of a hero when put to the test, and it was my good fortune to come off victor in the fight. But alas, as we fought in the school yard, which was against the rules, Mr. Southworth was even more victorious than I was for he whipped us both. I, of course, complained to father, and he went with me to the teacher, justified my course, denounced his inflexible rules, and withdrew me from the school. I was then between ten and eleven.

From there I went to Bishop England, a celebrated Catholic Divine. He had a very large school -- all the teachers were Priests. The Bishop did not teach but visited the school about once a week. There was no discipline at all. The boys "ruled the roost" and ruled it with a high hand. I remember on one occasion I loitered by the way having become much more interested in a game of marbles than in Heathen mythology which was the lesson for the afternoon; arriving late, Mr. Monk, the Priest and teacher gave my companions and myself a sharp lecture on our being tardy! At that time the fashion prevailing were Wellington boots and Wellington coats; in fact, everything was Wellington, and when the Priest asked me how some Heathen God's feet were covered, for want of a more historical answer I replied, "in Wellington boots"! Monk, already outraged at our late arrival lifted his rattan, a kind of cane, and was about to come down on me when I presented a pistol minus a cock, which deficiency being unknown to the Priests, his rattan remained suspended in mid air, and instead of the whipping I was ordered to leave the class and informed that I would be reported to the Bishop, which being done on the Bishops's next visit, I was summoned to his room for a confessional not to be absolved by payment of Peter's pence.

I trembled in my shoes for the consequences, and waited before the Bishop's steel gray eyes -- they were the grayest eyes I every saw in any human head.

I was of course very penitent, and I think the cockless pistol which I exhibited to show how utterly harmless it was and that there was therefore no malice pretence [pretense], that the action was the result of a sudden impulse and as the darkies "done unthoughtly," for all of which I was very sorry, the Bishop let me off with a well deserved lecture on the impropriety of my conduct and required that I should express my regrets to Mr. Monk before the class, which I did, resolved in my own mind henceforth and forever, or as long as boyhood lasted, to be a model boy.

I don't think, however, it was many moons before some of the boys -- one of which was your little reformer -- ripped up the flooring of one of the school rooms. Why or how he did it I do not remember. The big boys were the master minds in this escapade, and the perpetrators of the diabolical act were never discovered.

The next thing on the tapis was the examination. I remember it well, It was in the cathedral. At one end of it there was extemporized a platform about five feet high all around which there were benches, and the Priests seated thereon, their legs encased in knee britches and black silk stockings. The Bishop occupied a seat in the center of the platform. The cathedral was crowded. The recitation were made on the platform. I recited with eclat, beginning "Aurora Fair Daughter of the Dawn," but in the intervals we boys who were not in "tickling the public" for the time being, stationed ourselves around the platform and tickled with pins the underpinning not of the platform, but of the Priests, and when the signal was given "stick a pin there," Priest's legs were rubbed and lifted as if mosquitoes were gathering a harvest and none of us boys ever knew whether a Catholic Priest knew the difference between a point of a pin lightly inserted or the bill of a mosquito perserveringly presented. I remained at the Bishop's school about a year, and not being entirely without conscience nor unlike John Gilpin, who, although on pleasure bent had a frugal mind, I actually acknowledged to my parents that I was not learning anything but mischief at the Bishop's, in which, by the way, you will see that I was pretty well graduated, and requested them to send me to another school! Alas for the change!

They sent me to Isaac Harby, father of Octavia Moses, a splendid teacher who believed in "as the twig is bent the tree is inclined" and "spare the rod and spoil the child." He bent the twig but never spared the rod. I remember a mulberry tree that grew in the yard. I remember it denuded of many limbs; I remember further the uses they were put to and the further fact that the boys with whose backs they were to be made familiar, were with a quizzical look (I think I can see it now) ordered to go and cut a bunch and to be sure and get good ones too.

I think I would know a twig of that mulberry today if I met it in a wilderness of mulberrys. I was familiar with every twig of it from the bark to the pith and if I live to be as old as Methuselah is reputed to have been, I shall never forget the mulberry sensation that overcame me one day for having shown his son Julian how to work out a problem, the solution of which to my short vision reached not to the mulberry figures.

I continued with Mr. Harby until I was twelve and a half years of age. I was studying Latin and was just about to commence Greek when it suddenly occurred to me that I had absorbed through the skin as much knowledge as I cared to acquire in that way, and I proposed to my ever indulgent parents to consider my education finished and they so considered it. I then left school and entered on the business of life of which more anon.

I ought not to omit from my boyhood memories, as illustrative of my father's character, the mortal dread I always had of a butcher boy named Coagley. He was a sort of a John L. Sullivan among the boys. He looked to me as tough as a lightwood knot and was certainly as pugnacious as a bulldog. I have many a time gone a square out of my way to avoid meeting Coagley, I had a mortal dread of him, and my father, seeing me one day trying to shirk him, came out with a coach whip which in his hands was as formidable a weapon to me (he weighing over three hundred pounds) as was Sampson's historical jawbone to the Philistines. He said: "I see you are afraid of that boy. Now you have either got to whip him or I will whip you." The choice of two evils in this instance was full of difficulties, but when I looked at little Coagley, and my big father with his threatening whip and his flashing eyes supplemented by an oath or two indicating his determined purpose, I think if Goliath had stood before me I would have sailed in. By no means regardless of consequences, but wisely considering the blows of the butcher boy the lesser evil of the two, and with the consequences of the defeat present in my mind, I came out victorious, but so battered and bruised that it would have taken a very short argument to satisfy me that "ten such victories would be equal to a defeat." The boy never troubled me again, but I always thought his peaceful bearing was attributable more to his vision of the father of the boy who conquered him than to any apprehension he would have felt for your humble servant if he had no daddy; but the lesson was a good one, for it taught me, like the Irishman, that the best way "to avoid danger was to meet it plump in the face." So much for this digression. I also forgot to say that I can't remember the day that I didn't have a pony. He was an Indian pony or marsh tackey, and his name was Cherokee. He had a mind of his own, and when he said stop, stop it was. Many a time I started to go to Tivoli Garden, or the Four Mile House, but if Cherokee took a notion when I was half way, to go thus far and no farther, Cherokee had his way, especially after on one occasion, when I was imprudent enough to get down to cut a switch to face him onward, I found myself, with my first returning consciousness, emerging from a ditch, bespattered with mud from head to heel, and saw Cherokee looking on as totally unconcerned as if he hadn't done it, and did not know who did. From that day forward he had pretty much his own way, and when ever he indicated that he had gone far enough I invariably yielded to his better judgement.

    Another peculiarity of my youthful career was that I

never put on a new suit of clothes that I didn't get a whipping before the day was over, generally because I had not worn them with due care and circumspection. My good mother always had excuses for me, but unfortunately my father, in spite of them, stuck by his maxim not to "spare the rod and spoil the child." But I was spoiled nevertheless.

Chapter 3

1825: Soon After I Quit

Soon after I quit school I went to Philadelphia with my parents and stayed with my aunt, Mrs. Esther Hart, the grandmother of Louisa Lyons, nee Hart, who is the mother of Rachel Huestes. They left me in Philadelphia. I nominally stayed in Bacon and Hart's music store in the day time and attended law lectures at night given by Judge Hopkins, and I was very much interested in them. They were altogether of commercial law, but my mind was too much on pleasure bent.

I was not much more than thirteen. My companions were generally several years older than myself. I had the very free use of money and used it. I always though my father was wealthy. He was then in the auction business, kept horses and lived up to his means, if not beyond them, as I discovered in later years, and being an only child whose wishes were law, I was not very particular about what might or might not be his bank balances, so that my purse was not empty. It would fill a volume to detail all of my indiscretions, they were as thick as leaves of Valambrosia, but I had no vices or fixed habits, good or bad, but my pursuit of fun indefatigable that I enjoyed it, careless of what older heads thought about it. My impulses governed me, and fortunately they were not bad, but only mischievous; I had an old maid cousin, Anna Hart, who late in life married Mr. Bacon, of the firm of Bacon and Hart.

She was a typical old maid and a model housekeeper, always kept the rooms darkened to keep the sun and flies out, and I always opened them to let the sun and air in, irrespective of how many flies might come with them. Of course I was her horror.

Then I had another cousin, Louisa, a very cultivated and charitable woman and as ugly and outre in her style of dressing as she was intelligent and benevolent, and she found out that I had said or somebody said that I had said I would not walk with her on Chestnut Street because of her ill favored face and want of dressing. Of course with her my fat was in the fire and sizzled as badly as if I really had staid it, which, by the way, at this late day I am not prepared to deny. I soon quit attending law lectures at night much preferring the theater for which I had a passion.

Chapter 4

1826: The Next Year

The next year when father went North, as he did every summer, I returned with him and went to stay with Abraham Tobias, an auctioneer, and a particular friend of D.C. Levy. I received small compensation but after being with him a few months he raised my salary and paid me at the increased rate from the beginning. I think I stayed with him about a year and then another auctioneer, Calvin Baker, offered me better pay and I left Tobias and went to Baker. He was a very fair man but he had a son, Calvin Baker, who was as tyrannical and overbearing as he could be. There was another boy who stayed there with me. I forget his name, but we got into a way of not being able to repress our immoderate laughter on very trifling occasions, and one day a man came in and asked if we had any "boiled cider." Neither of us had every heard of boiled cider and the idea excited our risibility. We tried not to laugh and the more we tried not to laugh like two fools as we were, the louder we laughed. The customer looked on in amazement. About this time Calvin Baker, Jr., came in and I went behind the desk. He got into a passion and abused us for everything he could lay his tongue to, for we couldn't stop laughing, until he became so abusive that the pendulum swung to the other extreme, and I hurled first a ruler and then an inkstand at him and broke for the door, to return no more.

I went from there to father's auctions store.

These experiences make me say to young men always -- STICK. If I had stuck to law when I attended Judge Hopkin's lectures I would probably have entered life in the profession which I finally adopted. If I had stayed with Mr. Tobias instead of going to Baker's for an increase of salary, I might very likely, in time, have become a partner in the business, for he was very much pleased with me. Certainly I made nothing by the changes then made or afterwards, so that my motto now is: "STICK."

Chapter 5

1827: Again I Went to Philadelphia

Again I went to Philadelphia with father; I suppose I was about fifteen. We dined with Mr. Peixotto, a West Indian. He had been quite wealthy, but was less so because of the Emancipation of his slaves, but he was well off -- had no children, but had adopted two nephews and two nieces and a very sweet girl, Betsey Shaw. The latter was a Christian and although he was an orthodox Jew, he was scrupulously exact in her attendance of church. He was a very arbitrary man. His wife, who we all called "Gam," an abbreviation for grandma, was as kind as she could be.

Much to my surprise and satisfaction -- anything to stay North -- father arranged with Mr. Peixotto for me to stay in his office and be an inmate of his house. He did a large business in Kingston, Jamaica, and had a copy of his day book sent by vessel to Philadelphia. There the entries were journalized and posted, so that he always had before him the daily transactions of his West India business. The books were kept on L.S.D. and it was with him that I learned practical bookkeeping.

I think I must have stayed with him about two years. It was to me a very happy home: I was really one of the family, and very fond and admiring of Betsey Shaw, but never thought of engaging myself to her for I knew that Mr Peixotto would never consent to her intermarriage; besides we were both too young for serious love. Gam was like a mother to me; she was a warmhearted West Indian. Mr. Peixotto, as I have already indicated, was a very benevolent man but very dictatorial. I was then -- as much as it may contrast with my present habits -- very fond of dress and fashion. Chestnut Street was the fashionable street. I generally walked that way home, wore gloves and twirled a rattan. One day about dinner time he came into the office and said, "Ralph, I have bought a pair of turkeys, they are on Front Street and I must take them home. You come with me and I will take one and you will take the other." I was amazed. Our path home would be right down Chestnut Street. I respectfully declined the "hazardous adventure." Mr. Peixotto insisted. I resisted. At last he said, "When I hire a boy he must do what I tell him." I replied, "You employ me to keep your books. I am no hired boy." "Well sir," said he, "hired or employed, you will carry it," and quit I did. We always remained friendly but with him it was absolute obedience -- with me it was anything but toting a gobbler, and we split on the turkey.

What next?

From Mr. Peixotto's I went back to my aunts, and soon after, as I was very much troubled with dispessis. I got from Simpson Dreyfous (who boarded there and was an importer of Swiss watches) an assortment of Swiss watches and a travelers trunk, made to carry samples, and started for Easton, Pa., where my Mother had lived in her early life. I went by stage coach and stopped at Redding, Allentown and other small places between Philadelphia and Easton, exhibiting my watches at the different small towns and made more than enough to pay all my travelling expenses. Between Philadelphia and Allentown there was a very pleasant fellow traveller, a Dr. Myrick, who hailed from the neighborhood of

Easton. We got to be as thick as two thieves. He stopped over with me at Allentown and we took a walk together. In the course of our ramble he casually mentioned having lost his pocket book and gave that as his reason for stopping over, as he would have to write to Buck's county for money and await its receipt. He did not ask me to lend him any but as we were going the same way I volunteered to let him have what he wanted. It was only a small sum, about $10 or $15, I think. He accepted the loan with apparent reluctance, and we travelled together as far as Easton; Pottsville was then just being started. Coal had just been discovered there, and iron in close proximity. There was a perfect craze for town lots, and I remember there were so many people going to Pottsville that we had with many others to sleep on the floor of the hotel at Easton. The next morning Dr. Myrick bid me an affectionate farewell, expressed his great obligation and promised to send me the money as soon as he got home. But I suppose he forgot to do it; I never heard of him any more until I returned to Philadelphia, and then I found out that my interesting friend had just been discharged from the penitentiary where he had been imprisoned for some time for forgery. He was of good family and did live in Buck's county near Easton. The lesson I then learned was not to get too intimate with travelling acquaintances, and I have given travellers a wide birth ever since.

I stayed in Easton for some time and then went on to Mauch Chunk R.R. to the mines, and went into the mines and saw the miners at work. The railroad was propelled to the mines by horse power hauling the cars upgrade empty and they came back loaded down a gradual incline by their own momentum. Contrast that mule team with the great Pennsylvania R.R. I went to the Delaware Gap and other places of interest, was charmed with the beautiful scenery and returned to Philadelphia sound in health and purse.

I then clerked for Dreyfous and boarded for the time at Mrs. Reynolds, on Chestnut Street, and the way I happened to go to Mrs. Reynolds was this: I saw a very pretty girl on Chestnut Street and followed her home. She went in to the house just opposite the Mint. I took another opportunity to look at the door plate, and found Mrs. Reynolds, then ascertained that she kept a boarding house and to make the story short, I left my aunts and went there to board, made the acquaintance of pretty Kate, for such was her name, attended her wedding soon afterward and there became acquainted with a lot of good fellows, all seven or eight years older than myself, and all in business and able to spend freely. It was there that I became acquainted with Albert Hale, Daniel Day and his brother Jerry, with whom I made a lifetime friendship. Albert Hale after marrying was drowned at Cape May. Daniel and Jerry Day settled in Apalachicola. They afterwards moved to Savannah, while in the former town we again met and renewed our friendship. Mary Hale, Albert's daughter, married our particular friend, Tom Austin of Apalachicola. After moving to Savannah Austin died, and our friendship was again renewed with his widow in Atlanta, to which place she moved from Savannah. My son Albert was named after her father. Isn't it strange how people sometimes come together later in life who have known each other in youth, and in this instance, at a place far distant, at the time unknown to any of us, and as far as I am concerned the last place on earth that I ever dreamed of making my residence?

Of my acquaintances at Mrs. Reynolds, or rather my intimate acquaintances, there was only one other, Bill Kenyon. He was a rollicking, impecunious rover, no doubt long since gone to his Fathers. He was the senior of the set, at least ten years older than myself. It was while I was living at Mrs Reynolds that I walked one night down Chestnut Street with Hetty Pisoa and her cousin, Henry M. Phillips. When we were between Second and Third Streets, near an alley, someone from an upstairs window cried out that the house was on fire! I ran round the alley, got over the back fence and into the back door. The front room on fire was a cigar store. I rushed upstairs and at the second floor called aloud to the inmates but received no reply. By this time the fire was spreading rapidly. The stairs were burning. I came down as far as I could without going through the flames. I jumped the balance of the way over the banister into the back room behind the store. It was filled with smoke. I remember distinctly keeping my head near the floor to breathe and the singular thought that passed through my mind was this: I had written an article for the paper, I don't remember the subject, and I thought -- "When Mother reads it, I'll be dead," I remember getting up and feeling round the room for a place of egress and I came to what I supposed to be a window and tried to dash it through with my hand, when to my despair it proved to be a looking glass. I have not the least idea of how I escaped, but when I woke up I was lying in the yard bleeding. Someone came to my assistance and I asked to be carried to my aunts. I was taken there and had something like pneumonia; I remained in a sick chamber several weeks, was severely cupped, my wrist was badly cut (I have the mark yet) and just missed severing the artery. The doctor determined that my only safety was to return South, and once more I was home again. There were two or three persons killed at the fire, inmates of the house, by attempting to jump from the third story on to a kitchen roof in the rear. I remember another time I was nearly drowned in the Delaware River; the boat that I rowed got under the bow of a steamer and I was caught up by one of the sailors. She was just coming into the wharf.

These two escapes confirmed my detractors that the old adage was true; that a man or boy born to be hung could die only by the rope; but I have disappointed them in this for I am nearly seventy-nine and still unhung.

Chapter 6

1829: My Trips To and From

My trips to and from the North were so frequent that I am a little confused in dates, but I think this is a trip that I made by stage, via Washington and Richmond. At the latter place Abraham Cohen lived. He was quite a talented man and was Rabbi (then called Hazan). For a number of years his father, my grandfather for whom I was named, was minister for about thirty years in Philadelphia, and my Mother inherited all of their Orthodox ideas so that all the influences of birth and education were with me on the religious side, but I never became indoctrinated with their views. I always doubted the interviews that the Bible asserts were so frequently held by the Lord with his Chosen People, but I never doubted that a supreme intelligence controlled the world, and I have always felt (long before the advent of the Fox sisters and the rappings) that there was no death and that the dissolution of the body was but the transition of the soul or mind or whatever you may choose to term the element that lifts man above the beasts of the field (and which predominates so unequally in different men) continued to exist after we ceased to occupy this mortal casement, and I have always felt further that those that loved us and guarded us on earth, continued to love us and care for us after they have passed away. So fixed has this impression always been in my mind that I can truly say that I have never undertaken an important matter or become involved in serious trouble that I did not involuntarily seek or pray for the interposition of the spirit of my Mother for direction in the beginning or extrication when difficulties surrounded me, and I have generally felt that my appeals were heard and answered. This by some will be called superstition, by some it will be called sentiment and by the majority of persons it will be called weakness; but call it what you please, though it may have no foundation in facts, it has been my strength and support in many a trying hour.

I did not intend this digression, but I am writing down now whatever impressions occur to me at the moment, assured as I am that my children, at whose request I have somewhat reluctantly consented to write this sketch of myself, will not criticism my style so long as they have a reflex of myself in which my faults, as they will see, are not extenuated nor my virtues ostentatiously exaggerated. The former will mark the causes of my failures, by them to be avoided and not imitated, and the latter may serve to animate them to improve upon my feeble efforts to retrieve the errors, resulting in a great measure from over-indulgence. My escape from utter and hopeless ruin may be attributed to the fact that I inherited no vices from either parent; had I done so it is easy to see what would have been the end of an impulsive boy, under no earthly restraint from the time he was twelve years old with a Mother to find excuses for all his faults, having the free use of money, living most of his time in Philadelphia and New York away from parental influence and respecting no authority that relatives might vainly have attempted to exercise.

The extent of my over-indulgence cannot be better emphasized than in the fact that I was an only child. My parents were of course devoted to me and they would have asked for no greater happiness than my companionship at home. And yet, with no view of any advantages that offered, but merely to gratify my pleasure, I was allowed to spend most of my youth away, the parental heart accepting the sacrifices of domestic desolation that their idol might seek pleasure at more congenial shrines. I tremble when I look back at the temptations that surrounded me. While I revolt at the selfishness that could reconcile me to the unnecessary separation, it certainly was not from want of filial affection, for I loved both my parents and my feeling for my Mother was one of devotion. But they showed me the gates of youthful pleasure and gave me the Silver Key to turn them on their hinges that I might tread the labyrinth of what seemed to youth more gorgeous than Tallmadge's Gold Street and pearly gates of Heaven. There were but few of pleasure's path over which I did not ramble, but as I had the good fortune to escape the evils of excessive indulgence I found safety in surfeit, and after a few more lessons which I will go on to recite, I began life in earnest at an age when many men first embrace its follies.

What changes have taken place since the time of which I write, not only in myself, from youth to age -- old age -- but in this world of ours; no telegraphs, no railroads, no steam, no electricity, unless it was Benjamin Franklin's experiment with his kite and the lightning, not even a match to catch a light wood knot, no gas, no kerosene, no Heralds or Worlds or Tribunes with 30 page Sunday editions, no Wall Street, with its robbers, and last, but not least, no millionaires. I might almost say no New York, certainly none compared with the present. When I remember it, Canal Street was high up town and Harry Kostar, who kept Bachelors Hall on Canal Street, was a very Croesus, his wealth being *estimated at $150,000 to $200,000.*

I will not take time to state the changes, you who will read this know them all. But I state a proposition the truth of which you may doubt, but it is true nevertheless.

People were happier then, with their tallow candles run through a mould than you are now, with your electric lights. There was not the same unrest, the same envy of those whose heart burnings are concealed beneath the diamonds that we hopelessly covet. All were not at the top of the ladder, but its topmost pinnacle seemed to be a possibility to the humblest. I must stop for today -- I see no other way to escape from the moralizing mood; tomorrow I will go on with the incidents that grew out of my youthful follies.

I suppose I might as well state here that my uncle Abraham Cohen fell in love with a Christian girl. She went through the usual probation of converts so as to ascertain whether she was influenced by any other motive than a conviction of the truth of Judaism. She passed through the ordeal without the smell of fire upon her garments, became a Jewess, was married to my uncle and I remember visiting her at her house in New York, in my boyhood when she was scrupulously particular in adhering to all Jewish forms, dieting and others, and she so remained until sometime after her elder daughter Rebecca married a cousin of the distinguished Rabbi Isaac Leeser, and was herself the mother of a child. Mrs. Cohen, who had always lived happily with her husband who was then minister of the Richmond congregation, lost her youngest son and afterwards became herself seriously ill. During her sickness in a nervous condition she imagined (this I suppose was the effect of early education) that her son appeared to her and urged her re-conversion to Christianity, which she then re-embraced and joined the Episcopal Church, which was the church of her childhood. She then had three single daughters, Ellen, Henrietta, and Esther. My uncle, then a minister, separated from her, but they lived in the same place, Richmond, and he continued to support her. Two of her daughters, Ellen and Esther, joined the Episcopal Church. Henrietta in religion was a free lance, but she also married a Christian, a Dr. Long of Mississippi. Ellen married a Mr. Walters of Norfolk, and Esther married a Mr. Peters of Baltimore. Esther Peters, the mother of Tom Peters, and Ellen Walters are the only survivors of four daughters. Rebecca Ansel's daughter also married a Christian, a Mr. Whitley of New York. Rebecca herself died a Jewess! I still keep up a correspondence with Esther, who is very grateful for some services that I rendered to her family in obtaining political positions for them at Washington when they were in great pecuniary distress; with the rest of the family I have not had any direct communication for some years, though I believe they all remember me affectionately and I still feel a friendly interest in them.

I mention this incident in my uncle's life to show the strong impression made upon the human mind by early religious education. Mrs. Cohen was a strict Jewess for forty or fifty years, and died a believing Christian in about her eightieth year. She lived a Christian until her marriage when she was about seventeen, so that about half her life she was a devotee to Christianity and about half equally devoted to Judaism.

Chapter 7

1830: I Think It Took About Eight Days

I think it took about eight days, night and day travel, to reach Charleston by way of Washington, Richmond, Columbia, etc., the travel was of course slow and rough, but it was much more sociable than railroad travel today. In less than twenty-four hours every one tried to contribute to the amusement of every one else in the stage. Those who could sing, sang; those who could tell good stories, told them; the audience was appreciative, and as I was a good mimic and a good Racounteur, if good for nothing else, this made me good company, and while I told all the jokes that I knew and they were many, it was in stage coaches that I learned some of my best with which I would afterward set the table in a roar. These experiences made me a "jolly good fellow" but did little else to improve my business education or fit me for the great battle of life which sooner or later all men are compelled to fight and often discover when too late that only earnest work makes success possible.

When I reached home I went to my father's auction store. I think Mr. Isaiah Moses had some interest in the business. At all events, L.I. Moses, the father of Moses Bros., of Montgomery, was bookkeeper and in imitating his signature I obtained my present sign man'l. In order to equip me better for business (I suppose) my father purchased for me a horse and gig, a two wheeled concern. Four wheeled buggies were then unknown. My Mother gave me a library. I did not use the library much but I never failed to use the horse if the weather was fine. An afternoon drive to the Tivoli Gardens or the Four Mile House, where you men congregated to roll ten pins, play billiards and drink brandy smashes, mint juleps and other inspiring drinks, was my regular routine. In the mornings I stayed in the store, in the evenings I drove out and at night I helped to regulate the town. I have outlived all my friends, for I was by many years the junior of all my companions; I will only mention one who must have then been about thirty-five. He was a leader among the young men in everything. He was aide to the Governor, a high officer in the Jockey Club, and then Charleston was famous for its fine horses. He was a fine boxer, an exceptionally good horseman, an incomparable mimic, the terror of all men who had the misfortune to have a peculiarity that would make them ridiculous if closely imitated. He labored as a teller in a bank and found the chief pleasure in life in being a practical joker, his name was Abraham Miller, and no man was more popular or better known in Charleston than was this unconquerable joker in his day and generation. I could fill this book recounting his pranks, but I will only mention one or two when I was an eye witness and participated in the sport.

There was an Italian trumpeter in Charleston named Salvo, whose wife was a famous fortune teller. The 4th of July was a great day for military parade, and Salvo's trumpet was in great demand of course. The weather was always hot and as a consequence Salvo always perspired freely. Being very careful of his uniform, he was accustomed to hanging it out of his window as my wife does after a hard day's work. Miller knew this to be his habit, so in the small hours of the night, when sound sleep was endeavoring to restore Salvo's tired nature, Miller would happen to pass by, and with raps loud and long, and strong enough to arouse the dead, he would hang away on Salvo's door and when he would at last be raised from his slumber, open the door and exclaim, "what for you breaky down my house?" "Excuse me sir, but I was passing and saw your coat hanging out of the window and I thought I would let you know as you had no doubt forgotten it!" "No sir, I not forget! I hang him out to dry!" "I am sorry that I disturbed you, good night!" In about half an hour, when Salvo would again be asleep, Miller would return and with a broad Irish brogue repeat the same conversation, and again Salvo would say, "I hang him out to dry!" He returned after awhile with as genuine a Dutch accent as if he had just come from the Fatherland, and go through the same uncalled for information, when salvo exclaimed in broken English, "American, Irish, Dutch are all d-d fools, I parade today, I sweat much, my coat he is wet, I hang him out to dry but I will take him in; he will have to stay wet or I have no rest and tomorrow me have to work all day."

Another of his victims was Dr. Fabre, a highly respectable citizen and a member of the German Friendly Society. So was Miller (being of German descent). The society had a night meeting to celebrate one of their anniversaries. Miller slipped off and went to Fabre's house. Now Fabre was celebrated for his fancy poultry of which he had all the new varieties of fowl, ducks, geese and turkeys; Miller knocked at the door and called out imitating Fabre, "I hurried home from the society to let you know that I am going to bring several members home to supper and I want you to have everything nice."

"My heavens, Dr. Fabre, how can I prepare a supper this time of the night?" "Why not, you have plenty of servants

and plenty of poultry!" "But Dr. Fabre, your poultry is all expensive." "Never mind the expense; kill anything, light up the dining room, and be ready. I must go back to the society. I just slipped out to give you time to prepare." When he did come home he was surprised to find his house lighted up and when he entered he was still more surprised to see preparations for a feast. "Mine Got, Elizabeth, vot is all this?" "Why Mr. Fabre, you came here and told me to prepare for company; you were going to bring some friends from the society, and when I told you it was impossible you ordered me to kill your fine poultry, or anything, not minding the expense but to have everything nice, and I woke up the servants and have worked myself nearly to death to do as you wanted." The doctor assured her that he had not been near the house and as he had on several occasions been the victim of Miller's mimicry, a light flashed upon him and he exclaimed, "Betsey, it is not me but that rascal of Abraham Miller has been at his tricks again."

Another of his victims was a dyer named LeBleux. Miller woke him up one night and asked him if his name was (imitating an Irishman) LeBlux and if his business was to dye clothes.

LeBleux told him his profession was a dyer but his name was LeBlue, not LeBlux. Miller apologized for his erroneous pronunciation and informed LeBleux that he wanted to know if he could dye him a black coat white." "No sair, c'est impossible, I can dye a white coat black but no man alive or who ever was alive can dye a black coat white -- it is not possible!" To which sad information Miller expressed his regrets and told Mr. LeBleux good night.

I mentioned this joke to an old Frenchman that I knew very well, named David Brandon. He was a mattress maker and lived on Meeting St., next door to a mulatto barber named Ingliss.

He said to me, "I wish Monsieur Miller would come to me vis his joke, I would tell him my name is not LeBleux but Shower Bath and I would wet him all over; what for a man is zis Miller vis his tom foolery?"

I told Miller about this and he said, "In a day or two I shall let you know and we will go and see this Monsieur Brandon." And we did.

Miller, imitating inimitably an Irishman in distress, knocked at Brandon's door and when he put his head out of the window said, "Sure and are you Ingliss the barber?"

Shaking his white locks, Brandon said, "Have you ever seen a mulatto vis white hair like this?" "Faith and I don't know the color of his hair! But vot I want is Mr. Ingliss to come and shave me friend dats dead."

Brandon slammed down the window, exclaiming, "Ingliss the barber live next door; for me your friend can go to hell visout shave."

Exuent Miller for two days and on the night of the second day he reappeared and about midnight rapped Monsieur Brandon up. He appeared at the window and Miller said, "Pardonnez moi Monsieur mais I want to know if Monsa Brandon live here? He follow ze profession to make ze mattress?"

"Oui, I am Monsr. Brandon." "Ah! I am so happie, can you tell me vessier it is better to sleep on one mattress which is made of stroi (straw) or one which is made of moss?"

The reply was a bucket of dirty water, Brandon exclaiming, "Ah Monsr. Miller, zar is for you!" "I am very much obliged, but you missed the mark. How much do you charge? I don't want your shower bath gratis." Brandon uttered a volley of oaths and slammed down his window and we went off rejoicing. The next day I stopped in to see

Brandon, as I often did and he told me of Miller's visit and said he would go up to the bank and mash his head. I dissuaded him from this by stating truly Miller's physical powers and his experience as a boxer, when he shrugged his shoulders and exclaimed, "What shall I do?" I said, "Do nothing; I know Miller very well and will see him and tell him not to disturb you again, and I hardly think he will trouble you any more," which of course he did not, and old Brandon was grateful for my interference.

Such companionship, while it gratified my appetite for fun, did not materially improve my business habits. I always had a night key, came home late or early (generally late) as best suited my pleasure, and was never chatechised as to how or where I spent my time. While I stayed with father I made my first money outside my allowance for services by buying samole cotton and realized a profit of $30.00, which $30.00 I invested in a lottery ticket and had visions of untold wealth. But unfortunately my tickets drew blanks and my $30.00 and fortune vanished into thin air. I ran this schedule about nine months when one day father sent me to the Post Office and I for some reason demurred about going. He was very quick tempered and I was not very amiable, and we had some altercation about my going to the Post Office, when he took up a twenty-five pound weight and threw it at me, I suppose with no idea of hitting me, but rather to frighten me into obedience. But it didn't frighten me worth a cent! I went to the office but as I was going I called back to him that I wouldn't stay with him any longer, that I would go back to the North. I remember his reply, "You may go to hell if you want to after you go to the Post Office."

I went to the office and then home and told Mother that I couldn't stay with Father and that I would sell my horse and gig and that I was going to New York and from there out

West, and that I would not come back until I had made a fortune. She tried to persuade me not to go but finally contributed to my going by buying my library. This with the sale of my horse and gig gave me between $200.00 and $300.00, and I started for the far West via New York. I must then have been about nineteen and still believed my Father to be rich when in fact he was comparatively poor, but he always lived easily and looked rich, he was of very bright cheerful temperament, never fretted about anything, was remarkably handsome, weighed then about three hundred pounds (and before he died weighed 387 pounds), was fond of jewelry and fine clothes, always kept horses and was typical of what a youth would suppose a rich man would look like, when in fact, a lean and hungry Cassius would better represent the unrest, care and anxiety with which avarice paints a genuine "Gold Bug."

Chapter 8

1831: My Preparations

My preparations being made, I started for New York with my mother's blessings in the sailing ship "President," Capt., Halsey. We had a splendid run to New York bar and were expecting to take a pilot when we were blown off in a dreadful storm that lasted three or four days. During the height of the gale the bowsprit was blown away and the sailors were ordered to take in the debris; one of the men was slow, and if I live to be 790 instead of 79, I shall never forget this oath that Capt. Halsey hurled at him, "You d-d wishy washy Molly, put the kettle on; you need never be afraid of going to hell for you haven't got soul enough to be d-d." This seemed to me to embrace all the epithets known to the vocabulary of oaths.

We weathered the gale and arrived safely in New York; I went to a hotel somewhere near Wall Street, on Broadway, I forget the name of it but in a day or two several of my friends found me out and we had a royal time. I was about as far West as I ever got. New York was good enough for me. I paid about $75.00 for a circular cloth coat lined with velvet facings, they were called Spanish cloaks, one end was drawn over the chest and thrown over the left shoulder hildago fashion. I gave a champagne and broke a looking glass. This absorbed about $60.00 more; after a few days *with $20.00 left I went to Philadelphia, boarded at a tailor boarding house (not being on terms with my aunt's family) at $2.00 a week, swapped my Spanish cloak off in cold December weather for a season ticket to the theater and soon got to where I could count my dollars on the fingers of either hand, when I again got a place with Simon Dreyfous, the watch importer.*

It was at this time in the history of the young Republic, the United States of America had only a few years earlier celebrated its 50th year of independence, that events were beginning to manifest themselves, which thirty years hence, would greatly effect the country and the life and family of Raphael J. Moses. Moses, at this time, 1831, was but 19 years old.

In the North there was the beginning of the Industrial Revolution; the first railroads were in operation, albeit for only short distances; steamboats traveled the major waterways, connecting the States to the West along the Mississippi River, and beyond into the vast undeveloped Territories. It was a period when the authority of the Federal government was openly questioned and faced with threat of secession. In 1828 and again in 1832, Congress passed Protective Tariff Acts, which mainly benefitted the New England and Mid-Atlantic States at the expense of the agrarian South. South Carolina, led by its fiery John C. Calhoun, denounced these acts as detrimental to his State and to the South. He argued, with support of others, that a State had the right to nullify or abolish such "Laws" within its own borders. However, tempers were quelled, and a compromise Tariff Act of 1833 defused-temporarily-the issue of States Rights.

Chapter 9

1832: I Stayed With Him

I stayed with him until about the year 1832 when South Carolina proposed to nullify the tariff law. I then returned to Charleston, joined the Heavy Artillery of which John Lyde Wilson (the famous duelist and author of the Code) was captain and my Father was lieutenant. At one of the meetings I made some statement about tactics which I had read and Wilson said, as I thought, that what I said was not true. I gave him the lie and he challenged me. E.W. Moise acted as my second. I accepted the challenge. but to my satisfaction the matter was referred to a board of honor when it turned out that Wilson had said that what I read was not true, and as that impugned the veracity of the author of the tactics and left mine untouched, of course I retracted and the matter was peaceably settled to the honor of all parties, no one being more gratified than the writer of this. Wilson's moderation, I afterwards understood, was in deference to my Father's conduct, who allowed things to take their course without any interference on his part. This third escape made it still more probable that my way out of this world was predestined to happen, but some men disappoint all reasonable expectations, and I seem to be one of that class.

I think that I went once more to the North, but I am not sure, but I do know that about this time I realized that my

Father was a poor man. My Mother owned the house that we lived in which was also in Beaufain Street next to the one that I was born in -- she bought it with money earned from her school, and I inherited it when she died.

As soon as I realized that my Father was poor and that I had been a drain upon him, I determined to go to work in earnest with no capital but about $600.00 indebtedness, principally for tailors' bills in Philadelphia, and I stepped down from my platform of fun and fashion to the earnest work of life by opening a very small "Cheap Cash Store," retail, of course. Father helped me some and M.C. Mordecai helped me some, but it was not much help that I required. The auction stores seldom credit, making weekly collections on account, and I sold only for cash and soon began to drive a right smart trade. I quit folly and went into calico, and as I knew most of the auctioneers from having been employed on what was then called vendue range, I soon found myself on my feet and my vision expanded until it embraced purchases in New York. But how to make them was the question; I resolved to try. I went to New York without money and without letters of credit, I walked through Pearl Street and Maiden Lane and William Street; these were then the principal jobbing streets. Whenever I would see boxes marked for any of the Charleston retail merchants I would stop in and price the goods and when I was ready to buy I would tell a plain story, that I had no capital and no expenses, that I lived with my parents, had done a small cash business and had succeeded very well, that I did not expect to buy much, or keep a large stock, and I do not remember ever having been refused a moderate credit. The jobbers would of course inquire of the retailers with whom they dealt and they would confirm my statements, for I told only the truth -- I had, too, become well acquainted with several of the principal retail *men, and had occasionally bought small bills from them and being a genial and pleasant companion I soon became popular with those with whom I cam in contact. But to cut the story short, I did not want to buy much and I found no difficulty in buying what I wanted to buy and having made a beginning and met my payments, it was not long before I had to be circumspect in my purchases lest I should overload myself. At that time it was the practice to go North in the Spring and Fall, to purchase when the principal stocks had to be laid in, and the credits were four to six months. The present facilities for daily replenishing did not then exist. Several interruptions accompanied by a disinclination to continue these reminiscences of past follies has caused this interregnum in my jottings.*

My business increased and my credit with it. I soon did a leading business in dry goods. About this time the Bank of Charleston was established and there was a severe contest for the Presidency and consequent buying up of shares by the candidates and their friends. My Mother sent me down town to collect $500.00 for a negro girl she had sold. At this time $10.00 per share was paid in on the stock and it commenced rising. I invested, without consulting her, the $500.00. The stock kept going up and I kept buying, using my original purchase as a margin. I operated for about two days and then having a profit of about $2000.00 in the stock and hearing that one of the candidates had secured a majority, I directed my broker to close me out that evening at whatever the market might be, and he did so. The next morning the demand flagged and the stock declined, but I had made for Mother about $2000.00 on $500.00 and she had no complaint to make. The next bank started was the Bank of Camden and the charter required all subscribers to the extent of five shares to be supplied before any larger subscriptions could be filled, *and a premium was offered on the stock before the books were opened. I saw the opportunity and paid one dollar each for names to subscribe for and proxies constituting me the agent to subscribe. The next thing was to get the money to pay up the first payment. I enlisted my landlord, John C. Ker, who was a rich man, and Dr. De La Motta, whose endorsement of my note would insure its discount in bank, for I was to allow them one half of the profits. I think I gathered up about three hundred names. The subscriptions in fives was so large, for I was not the only agent who had names, that, as well as I remember, the subscriptions for five shares only got a prorata of two shares to each name, but these shares were immediately worth a premium of five dollars to six dollars per share, so that my profits in this transaction were over $1,500.00, and besides I made the reputation for knowing how to turn a penny. Then I got on the right side of as mean a miser as the Lord ever made, one Jacob Barrett, who by degrees endorsed for me to the extent of $5000.00 and his endorsement was good for that amount as Vanderbilt's would be for fifty thousand dollars. He would never charge me any commissions because he always wanted to be a preferred creditor (as he was) in case of accident, but he never endorsed a note for me in his life that he didn't buy enough out of the store to amount to a 5% commission and he always forgot to pay for anything that he bought and as I understood his tactics of course I made no charges against him.*

I ought to say here that I never knew Father was poor and that I had been a drag on him until I opened the Cheap Cash Store, and as soon as I knew it I went to work with a will — on looking over these notes I see that I have already stated this fact.

Chapter 10

1833: At This Time

*About this time another piece of good luck befell me,
perhaps the best luck that had ever befallen me in all my life
before or in all my life since – I met your Mother, not having
seen her before since we were about 13 years old, she being
one of the girls that attended my Bar Mitzva party. She was
very ill with country fever when I returned to Charleston, and
the probabilities of her death was a constant subject of
discussion among our friends when I returned to the North.
My sympathies became enlisted for this Miss Eliza Moses,
whose life was hanging on a thread, and when I first met her,
a fresh, blooming, pretty, modest girl, my heart went out to
her and I am happy to say the feeling was reciprocated. We
were soon engaged with the understanding that I was not to
marry for two years. I tried courting her for six months and
found it very pleasant, but began to think marriage would be
more to my mind and so proposed to her Father to have the
marriage consummated. To this he was opposed, and I well
remember his coming to our house to convince Father of the
propriety of waiting two years, and I equally well remember
my Father's reply. It was this: "I don't know whether it would
be prudent for Raphael to marry now or not, but if you know
my son as well as I do, you would know that he never stuck to
anything two years in his life, and if you expect him to marry*

Eliza you had better let him marry her now. That is all I have to say about it." The argument, I suppose, was unanswerable, for on the 22nd day of January [1834] thereafter, about six months from the time of our engagement, we were married, and although we have lived together fifty-six years, we have never had occasion to regret our early wedding.

Marie suggests in a letter received last night that I be sure and tell about my courtship. Now as I have said very little about it there was very little to say, and have omitted to declare that I made as big a fool of myself as most young men do, and that Eliza seemed like most young women similarly situated, to be very well pleased with the folly, I make this declaration and say that all these facts existed:

There was nothing peculiar about my courtship. Very shortly after meeting Eliza at Mr. Nathan Hart's where I was dining, at which time I fell in love with her, I commenced paying her marked attention. She went with her sister Caroline, Mrs. A. Moise, to spend a part of the summer on Sullivan's Island. I used to go down to see her and walk on the beach. One day after having walked with her the evening before, I called to see her at Mrs. Moise's, while her son Charles, a boy about two years old, came into the room and said to me, "I saw you kiss Aunt Eliza on the beach." No such thing had happened. Eliza caught the unfortunate child in her arms and rushed out of the room with him. They say she put him to bed and he never woke for twenty-four hours. There has always rested a suspicion on Eliza for having given the child an overdose of catnip tea or some strong narcotic! How the child ever got the idea into his head no one ever knew. It was surmised that on Eliza's part "the wish was Father to the thought." Charles slept with her and it is supposed that she kissed the boy in his dream and called him Raphael and that he was awakened by it, got the thing mixed in his mind, and when he saw me he had a confused notion that he saw me kiss his Aunt on the beach. But certainly there was no truth in the statement.

While I was paying court to Eliza it was reported that the parents on both sides were trying to make a match with her and a cousin of hers, Marx Cohen, who afterwards married Armida Harby, the Mother of Lee C. Harby, now of New York; it was further reported that the young people took kindly to the arrangement.

This was to me a source of considerable anxiety, and one Sunday evening at Mr. Lopez, E.M. Moise and Theodore, his brother, who were my very intimate friends and confidents in this love affair, they and I had a conference on the chances of my success. The result of the caucus was that they thought there might be some understanding between Eliza and her cousin, and advised me not to precipitate things; they thought that if I would give myself a year (whatever E's present feelings might be) I could succeed in my suit. And after due deliberation and consideration of all the surrounding circumstances it was unanimously resolved that I should wade in and keep wading for a year and then try my chances sink or swim, and they through I'd swim with their assistance.

That night a proposition was made that we with the Misses Lopez would go over to Mr. Moses and then all go to walk on the Battery. Have you ever been on the Battery?

'Tis a beautiful promenade with the sea washing its base, and on a moonlit night, bright as it was that night, its surroundings are all provocative of love. Well, it so happened that Eliza and I were paired and in watching the billows and the moon we somehow got separated or fell behind the party; I made myself as agreeable as I could, sounded her to the very depths on the Marx Cohen situation, and found her "fancy free" but resolved if I could help it she would not long

remain so, and about the time we were nearing her home, I proposed. She wept, whether for sorrow or joy I never knew, but guessed. She never either then or since has given me any answer. But she did not object, only cried a little more when I told her that I would ask her Father's consent. I suppose I did, and he must have consented for it was soon reported that we were engaged and the unanimous opinion of our friends was, that Eliza Moses was a brave girl to risk her reputation with Raphael Moses, but she was in for taking risks and she took them. While we were engaged she went to Edisto Island to visit her brother Charles. The steamer plied between Edisto and Charleston weekly. I kept a kind of diary which I used to send her by the steamer. Sometimes they contained thirty pages. what was in them I don't remember, but I am happy to say they were all burnt in one of the fires that pursued me and that they can no longer be brought up in judgement against me.

When Eliza was in Charleston I went to see her every night and stayed until some sign was given that the house was about to be locked up. Along about January it began to be cold and disagreeable going out of a warm room into the wintry air, and I proposed to stop that foolishness that we might begin the voyage of life together. We started out as I have already said January 22, 1834, and we have had an exceptionally happy life.

I read the foregoing to Eliza and she says that it is not true that which I relate regarding Marx Cohen' that there was no such understanding, etc. I never stated that there was an understanding. I only said that there was a report to that effect which gave me some uneasiness, but as she wished the truth of history to be recorded and is unwilling that this statement be handed down to posterity, I now say to posterity that the report was without foundation.

My business grew with my happiness. I carried a large stock and did a large business, and it occurred to me one day (very fortunately) that if there ever was a large fire on Kings Street, the chances were that the Charleston offices would fail and be unable to pay their policies, and even if this did not happen it was safer to insure in foreign offices. And carrying out those views I placed most of my insurance in Augusta offices and kept them there. In a year or two the most disastrous fire that had ever been known in Charleston broke out on King Street, and the losses were so heavy that every insurance office in Charleston had to compound with the assured. My policies being principally in Augusta, they were good. I bought a pair of horses and a dray the night of the fire and saved about fifteen hundred or two thousand dollars of my stock after moving it two or three times.

Chapter 11

1834: My Business Grew

I made an assignment to M.C. Mordecai and had no trouble in getting a discharge. I had a customer, a Dutchman, to whom I was in the habit of jobbing goods which he sold in Tallahassee and other points in Florida, and he persuaded me to buy the remnant of goods saved at the assignee sale and take them to Tallahassee. I arranged with Mr. Mordecai to do so, and my recollection is that I had to ship the goods by wagon from Augusta to Tallahassee. When I got them there a Mr. Maynu was selling out a retail stock of goods, and I volunteered to help him sell out (without salary) so that I could learn the prices and know what to ask for my goods. In this way I familiarized myself with Florida values and got rid of my goods at fair prices and paid for them after I sold them in Florida.

Raphael Moses, but 22 years of age and newly married, was proficient enough in business to set out to new territories. In the United States most persons set out for the territories west of the Mississippi River. However, some few chose to seek opportunities in Florida. The territory of Florida was acquired by the United States in 1821 and did not become a state until 1845. Thus, Raphael Jacob Moses was quick to recognize the opportunities available for those who would leave the comfort of friends and community and seek a future in the northern part of the new region. The areas off to the central and south part were still under threat of Indian uprisings, RE: the Seminole Indian Wars of the mid and late 1830's and ending in 1842.

Chapter 12

1838: While at Tallahassee

While at Tallahassee, the new town of St. Joseph had been started, and lots had sold for immense prices. It was started in opposition to Apalachicola, which was owned by the Apalachicola Land Co., which held the lots in Apalachicola at exorbitant prices. St. Joseph had a fine climate and a bay said to be as beautiful as the bay of Naples. Its approach was easy while Apalachicola had a very expensive lighterage and was not regarded as healthy. A syndicate from Columbus bought out the land on St. Joseph's bay and connected it to the river by railroad. I went over to St. Joseph with a party of gentlemen having no idea of locating there, but when I got there the town was "on the boom." Lots 80x100 were worth $5,000. It was but a few months old and shipped 30,000 bales of cotton. Butran, the secretary of the railroad, died while I was on a visit there and, strange as it may sound, I got the situation of Secretary to the Lake Wimico & St. Joseph railroad at a salary of $2,000 a year. So much for being a pleasant fellow, knowing how to tell a good story and telling them on all occasions, and with all being a good bookkeeper, the very thing the railroad company wanted. I think that was along in 1838.

I tried to hire a house and offered $600.00 a year for one that I couldn't get. I then hired a temporary place and *had a house put together in Charleston by David Lopez at a cost of about $600.00 and shipped to St. Joseph, but carpenters wages were so high that this house in the course of three or four years with improvements and additions cost me over $4,000. I soon got to know everybody in St. Joseph and everybody knew me. I made friends there that lasted all my life -- the Hardins, Jenkins, Mrs. Hardin's sister-in-law and sister of Mrs. Tom Barrett of Augusta, Ga., Hawkins, the Woods, Joe Croskey, afterwards Consul to Liverpool, Loring, afterwards General Loring, the Duvals, D. Price and Mrs. Price, a daughter of Governor Duval. I spent about five as happy years in St. Joseph as I ever spend anywhere. It was a delightful climate, a lovely situation and had as generous and wholehearted a population as is to be found anywhere. But about the year 1843, the yellow fever broke out in St. Joseph and was very fatal. I myself had a very narrow escape from death, as did my wife. I forgot to say that after I had been in St. Joseph about a year Dr. Price, the agent of the Union Bank of Florida, wanted to go to Kentucky to spend the summer and to my surprise asked me, a comparative stranger, to take charge of the bank during his absence. As this added to my income and no bond was required of me, I accepted and attended to the bank and the railroad books! When the cash was turned over to me in packages I took the precaution to receipt for the loose bills and so many sealed packages, not opened or counted.*

After a while my deposits began to fall short and I found I would have to open the packages or have money sent to me from Tallahassee. I therefore wrote to Col. Parkhill of the Union Bank at Tallahassee either to send me over money or to come over and see the packages opened, as I would not break the seals except in the presence of some other fellow officer of the bank. He came over -- we opened the packages *and one package was $13,000 short, and had Prices Memo in it for that amount, which accounted for his willingness to trust me with the bank, for nothing would have suited him better than to have me turn out dishonest, run away with the funds including his Memo and they cover his default, but the course pursued by me uncovered his default, caused his removal and the appointment of Parkhill's relative, a Mr. Hixon, as agent. Price moved to Texas.*

During my residence at St. Joseph my Father and Mother followed their wayward son and built a house next to mine. My Mother died there and my Father died about six months after in Apalachicola; he never recovered from the blow caused by my Mother's death, had her body buried in the yard near the house and used to pray at her grave daily, though he was never before religiously inclined. My Mother was a very religious woman, a strict conformist to all Jewish customs, and the day before, though in apparent health, she seemed to have a premonition of her death. I tried to rouse her and made her go to walk with me. On the way we met an old Irish woman, on whom she had been accustomed to bestow charity. She took her aside and talked with her and the Irish woman told me she gave her $1.00 and told her to take that and remember her by it. The next day as Nina's birthday and she promised me if she was well she would throw off her depression and give her a party, but she felt that a calamity was impending over us. We parted that night and she told Eliza to be sure to take care of Father. This I did not then know.

The next morning I went over as usual to see her but she had not been out of her room and Father said he supposed she was washing. I knocked at the door and receiving no answer made our boy Joe go in at the window, and alas! Mother was on the bed -- dead. Her shrouds were on the bureau and a slip of paper written, "where the tree falls let it lay," intimating, I suppose, that she did not wish her remains carried to Charleston to be laid in the Jewish cemetery. She had her best linen sheets on the bed and every indication that she expected her room to be visited by strangers! Knowing how scrupulous she was about Jewish rites, Eliza with her usual self sacrifice performed all the duties of preparing her for burial and thus at 72 passed from earth as pure a spirit as ever dwelt in human form. God bless her memory -- I know that she has gone to her reward and feel that she still lives and loves us.

I must now go back a little to my own life. The town went down, the railroad company failed, and I bought for $37.50 the house and lot that a few years before I had offered $600.00 a year rental for.

With the failure of the railroad and the town, I was in a bad way. No money and no business; the only thing that I could do that required no other capital than self reliance, of which I had a goodly share, was law. I decided to study law. I studied six weeks, knew just as much law as I did when I began to study -- examinations were private then and I managed to get my friends Hawkins and others appointed on the committee; they reported me qualified and I appeared thereafter not a briefless lawyer for I had already won my spurs by what was considered a very shrewd trick in humbugging a court of three magistrates, of which trick I was innocent as a babe unborn, but I had sense enough to keep the world in ignorance of my simplicity.

It happened thus -- a young man from St. Andrew's Bay about 30 miles from St. Joseph's, came in with about 10 head of cattle no doubt had been stolen from a farm on St. Andrew's Bay and belonged to a very respectable citizen of St. Joseph, named Blackwell. He demanded the cattle. The young man and the butcher refused to give them up. Blackwell, by advice of his son-in-law Chandler Younge, a lawyer of some eminence, sued out a warrant against the young man and had him arrested for larceny. Some of the neighboring Circuit Courts were about being held and Younge and all the attorneys were obliged to be absent on the day set for the trial. But Younge very properly told Blackwell all he had to do was to prove the cattle his property by marks and brands and then it would devolve on the accused to show how he honestly came in possession, and failing to do this, he would be bound over to the Supreme Court for larceny.

All the lawyers being absent, Schuyler gave me a conditional fee of $20.00 to defend the young man. He said the cattle was his Father's and I really believed him, really believed him.

The court met, three Justices, one I well remember, presided in his shirt sleeves.

Blackwell took the stand, was sworn, and would have proved property in the cattle, but I objected on the ground of his interest and made a conscientious argument on this line, that the young man was a stranger in the community, and if Blackwell was allowed to testify the result of his evidence would be to transfer this man's property to himself and what was vastly more important its effects as a thief a poor youth whose good character was his only capital. I pressed this as a man would press it who believed it true. The accused mouth was closed, he was away from home, and without witnesses and I appealed very feelingly to the Court not to be instrumental in the commission of such an act of injustice. Consequence -- Blackwell had to come down and remain dumb as an oyster, my client was discharged and I received my first fee of $20.00.

When the lawyers returned they twitted me with having

humbugged the Court, and my character for shrewdness was established. They little knew that I was for the first time learning that I had humbugged the Court, when I really thought that I had made a fair law argument, but I made no sign of it and it was a long time before I "let the cat out of the bag."

I sued some promissory notes of an estate of which I was administrator and did some other small business, but within the year I made one fee of $2,500.00. It happened this way, or rather the half of it:

The railroad had judgement against it for $180,000.00, and it had about $50,000.00 in bonds which were deemed of no value but each bond said on its face "the property of the Company mortgaged to pay this bond." I examined the mortgage and found that it anti-dated all of the judgements, and it occurred to me at once, that every bond holder was an equitable mortgagee. I went to work and got control of the bonds on a contract of 5%. With more experience I should have charged 25%, which would have been freely paid, on the amount of the recovery. Now my trouble was that if I was right on the law, I didn't know what legal steps to take to asserts the rights of the bond holders, so I went over to Tallahassee, consulted Leslie Thompson, afterwards Judge of the Supreme Court of Florida; he said I was right and that we would have to file a bill. I associated him with me, and to be brief we got a decree subjecting the property.

I then got a new charter passed under a different name from the old ones, went first to Columbus, and got several stockholders in the old stock company to agree to buy the property for the amount of the old bonds if I could get a new Charter so that they could reorganize and start St. Joseph free from the old judgement.

I did all this, sold the property to the old company, collected the bonds and my fee, and they spent several thousand dollars refitting the railroad and wharves, and then it was that St. Joseph was visited by yellow fever and the whole thing went to smash.

I then commenced practicing in Apalachicola, twenty-four miles from St. Joseph. Used to get up early enough to ride the twenty-four miles before breakfast. My family remained in St. Joseph. I came home every Friday and returned to Apalachicola on Monday.

I remember the first case I tried in Apalachicola was before Judge Carmack of a question of where administration attached on a particular estate. I took a great deal of pains with my brief. Brockenbrough, a very talented lawyer, was on the other side. When I commenced my argument he was reading a newspaper; he continued reading it all through my argument, and when I concluded, he merely read a few lines from the Code; the Judge sustained him in his objection to the States having any jurisdiction over the administration and I was nonsuited. My client said that if he hadn't had a jack legged lawyer for his case he would have won it. I was terribly mortified and crest fallen at the idea that when I had supposed that I had an impregnable brief, it was not even considered worth an argument in reply. I went to my office, took up the Code, read the statute that Brockenbrough had read, wept over my obtuseness, pitched my book away and resolved to quit a profession that I as so obviously unfit for.

That night I dropped in at Brockenbrough's office. I was intimate with him, and told him I was going to quit law. He asked me why. I told him very frankly that I had studied the question very closely, made my argument, that he read the newspaper all the time and that my argument did not even elicit a reply! He laughed and said, "Moses, the only reason

I didn't reply to your argument was that it was unanswerable. Unless the statute controlled the question there was no getting over your argument." And he advised me to stick to law.

This made me feel much better and I thought I would go round and see Judge Carmack. Maybe he might say something about my brief. I hadn't been in the room long when he said, "Moses, I have been thinking about my decision today and I think I was wrong. If you will move to reinstate the case and Brockenbrough does not cite some authority to change my views, I will make an order reinstating it." I told him what Ned Wood, my client, had said about a jack legged lawyer and that I would have nothing more to do with the case, and that I had pretty nearly made up my mind to quit practicing! Judge Carmack said, "Quit practicing! Why it will not be long before the best man at this bar will be more than your equal." When I left Carmack's room I was on stilts. But I never moved in that case again and I told Wood why I didn't move.

I cannot remember now whether I realized my $1,250 fee before or after I commenced practicing in Apalachicola, but I either collected it long enough before I went to Apalachicola to absorb it all in expenses, or else I collected it after I opened an office there, for I distinctly remember that my office was on the third floor of a brick building. The lower story was a ship chandler store and the second store was a carpenter shop, and many times when I though I hear the step of a client on the stairs it would stop at the carpenter shop. Either one of the mechanics, or some one having more use for a carpenter than for a Tyro at the Bar, and I further remember that I slept on a cot without a mattress, made my own coffee and lived on crackers and cheese and cold ham, and I am very sure that I would not have done this if I had

had $1,250 or any considerable part of it. I got on rapidly in Apalachicola and was on employed in all the principal cases. I made a very large fee, I think it was $2,500 foreclosing a mortgage on the St. Joseph railroad, a mortgage made by the new Company in favor of John D. & Wm. Gray. They bought it at the sale, took up the iron and carried it to Georgia to complete a contract they had for the building of the Monroe railroad.

St. Joseph went all to pieces, every brick chimney were taken down during the war to make salt vats for evaporating the salt water, the grave yard is the only land mark left of the former city. It is again as it was before St. Joseph was founded -- a wilderness of pines where the bear and deer roamed unmolested. It is so utterly deserted except by the beasts of the forest that after the War I had what was left of my Father, Mother and Uncle exhumed and they now lie in the grave yard at the Esquiline.

I remained in Apalachicola until 1849. My family moved over after awhile, but not until I was burnt out once in an office that I had removed to. We moved into a house that I had won in a litigation. We lived there in the winter and at St. Joseph in the Summer, next to where my Father and Mother lived, until she died, and then my Father moved over and lived with us a short time when he died from a surgical operation at the age of 62. He commenced sinking soon after Mother's death, a blow from which he never recovered.

One summer while we were at Apalachicola a carpenter walked over from St. Joseph to inform me that my house was burned down from a fire originating in the neighborhood, and he wanted to secure a contract to re-build. I didn't re-build but collected my insurance, about $900.00. It was a small house.

About the time I settled in Apalachicola there was a

great deal of litigation growing out of mortgages to the Union bank. The Union Bank was founded somewhat on the Sub-Treasury plan. It was a kind of Farmers scheme, but instead of advancing on cotton it advanced 3/4 the value of negroes and land. These advances caused money to be abundant, and as negroes and land were the favored securities, they rose, and rapidly, in value. This left a margin between the original 3/4 value and the 3/4 caused by inflated value. For this excess the Farmers would make a second mortgage. When I first went to Tallahassee the Union Bank was in full blast, the planters all had money, the Bank had mortgages on all the planters' possessions -- times were flush. Four in hands were as common as pairs are now, parties were given in the most expensive style, and Tallahassee was one round of fashion, frolic, and fun. But alas! What a change came over the people: about the time I commenced to practice law in Apalachicola the mortgages began to mature, the interest was in default, foreclosures were being pressed, negroes had legs, and the debtors commenced to run them off, principally to Texas. Apalachicola was a good shipping point. There the debtors came with their negroes in the night, and the bank following up with the mortgages, attachments and foreclosures. This made a legal harvest and I gathered in the fees.

Some of these mortgages had been transferred by the Bank, I remember one was assigned to a Frenchman. I was employed in the defence. He came to see me and I said, "Mons. (I forget his name), it is a very plain case. My clients' rights are so and so," and I went into a long explanation. The Frenchman kept getting more and more excited, pacing up and down the room, shrugging his shoulders at every half turn; at last he turned round to me and said, "Monsieur Moise, you cal zis a plain case, oh! I like you to show me one

which is complicated. "
My business prospered so much that I was after awhile able to refuse a fee of $1,000.00 from one, A.T. Bennett who was robbing with a high hand Parish Carter of Georgia. He had mortgages on negroes, that were being run off and followed them to Apalachicola. Bennett bought them with knowledge of the facts and attempted to defy Carter, his attorneys and the Sheriff with shotguns and a lot of roughs. It was therefore that I refused to be employe, but I lost nothing by it, for when Brockenbrough, Carter's lawyer, died about a year later, Carter employed me. The litigation lasted till sometime after I went to Columbus. I argued and gained one branch of it in Tallahassee before the Supreme Court and another branch of it at Jacksonville before the United States Court. Jacksonville was then a village, without sidewalks and the sand ankle deep. It is now a magnificent resort with fashionable hotels. I suppose first and last I made several thousand dollars out of the Carter Bennett case. It not only involved $20,000 or $40,000 but an immense amount of feeling.

Chapter 13

1844: About the Year 1844

About the year 1844 my wife and children went to Charleston where my son Albert was born. That summer we went North. Eliza, Isabel her sister, Isaac, Hannah, Major, Albert and a white nurse. I had about $2,500. The money went so fast in New York I could hardly realize it, and we all started for Stamford, Conn., where my wife's Father soon after our marriage was killed by being thrown from a buggy and his wife was so much injured that she died about six months after in Charleston. We went to visit the grave of her Father, Mr. Isaac C. Moses, and stayed with the Beach family, at whose house he died. It was on this trip that I insisted that I was made cross eyed by watching the children and the baggage at the same time. I had some business in Portland, Maine, and left the family at Beaches about ten days or two weeks. They were a plain Connecticut family, lived very comfortably, had an apple orchard, the delight of the children, and it was on this farm that I caught Isaac turning the handle and Major literally with his nose to a grindstone where it has been metaphorically ever since. He was then proposing to have his nose rounded off so as to be as nearly like mine as possible. Eliza had made a nice lot of preserves with the assistance of Mrs. Beach and her grand-daughter. They kept no servants. The children milked the *cows and cleaned the shoes, and everything was neat and clean. When I asked for my bill, Mrs. Beach hesitatingly inquired if I thought $10.00 would be too much. I emphasized my opinion by handing her $20.00 and considered that I got off cheap. They lived on a farm about a mile from Stamford, which was a village of 1/2 dozen houses. Now it is quite a city, penetrated by railroads and fine hotels and board $2.50 and $3.00 per day, and everything is so changed that in 1887 or 1888, when we were in New York, my wife wished to visit her Father's grave but the oldest inhabitants remembered nothing of the incident and the sextons of the grave yard had no record of his burial, so that in less than half a century when his body was turned to dust from whence it sprung, all trace of him was lost! Except to our immediate families, such is the fate of man! and even in our own families after two or three generations our descendants have a very confused idea of who their ancestors might have been.*

After my trip to Stamford above referred to, we returned to New York, and my funds were being reduced so rapidly that I took the precaution to buy a draft on Apalachicola for $250.00 so as to be sure to have a little cash on my return. And it is very well that I did so, for after paying our passage home (by sailing vessel, of course) I had just $5.00 left and with that I purchased "Stephens on Pleading" to read on the passage, and as we were three to four weeks at sea, I had time enough to study it thoroughly and found it one of the most useful and interesting law books that I have ever read.

I forgot to say in the proper place that when I finally left St. Joseph to move to Apalachicola, I sold my house that cost about $4000 and my Father's house that cost about $1500. The house that I offered $600.00 a year rent for, and afterwards purchased lot and all for $37.50, all of which was *well sold at $75.00 and bought by someone who carried it by seas to Apalachicola and utilized the windows, doors and some of the other lumber in building some other houses. I remained in Apalachicola until 1849. During my stay there its shipments had dwindled from 130,000 bales to about one half that amount. The railroads were carrying the cotton direct from Columbus and other points to New York. I saw that the end was coming and determined to seek another location. I went to Texas at the suggestion of Judge Duval, stayed in Galveston about a week, found a strong bar there and found further that there was more land than cash in fees. I finally determined to settle at Columbus, where I had a good business acquaintance, as many of my clients that I had in Apalachicola were residents of Columbus. When I went from Apalachicola the citizens gave me a very handsome farewell banquet, and I left there with many friends and not an enemy that I knew of, Bennett and Caro had moved to New Orleans. I have already stated who Bennett was and will now develop Caro. He was a Spaniard who kept a store in Apalachicola and I had some suits against him. He prepared for his failure and had nothing that I could levy my judgements on, but in examining into his affairs I found that a steamboat stood in his name which really belonged to his brother-in-law who was then running her as Captain, on the Apalachicola river. His brother-in-law became embarrassed a year or two before and Caro, then being in good credit, the steamer was registered in Caro's name, and I suppose they forgot to change the register when Caro failed. I levied my judgement on the steamboat and this made Caro furious.*

The morning after the levy as I was going to my office with my mail in my hand he overtook me in a side street and commenced to have an altercation with me. He finally called me a liar and I drew back to strike him, and Spaniard-like he had a sharp knife concealed in his sleeve and in an instant I was cut across the throat. Being unarmed I stopped to pick up a brick, but he ran off and it was all I could do from loss of blood to get back on Bay Street and sit down until Dr. Gorrie could be sent for. All that saved my life was my whiskers that I wore very heavy on my throat. He cut me right over the carotid artery. Dr. Gorrie sewed it up. I went home with my head in bandages. Your Mother had a fright of course! The knife was so sharp and the cuts so smooth that it healed by the first intention, as the doctors say, and I suffered very little pain. I was confined to the house for some time. Never saw Caro any more. He considered New Orleans a safer place and went there; this was the only serious trouble I had while in Apalachicola.

Chapter 14

1848: I Lived in Apalachicola

I lived in Apalachicola five or six years; it was then a gay place, it had a fine set of merchants and so its principal business was cotton and as cotton buyers either made a great deal or the reclamations for losses are so large that they can't begin to pay them, economy in expenditures had no place in their programme. Water was scarcer than champagne, and jolly good fellows were plentiful as blackberries.

Apalachicola, like St. Joseph, went down, down, down, until it ceased to ship a single bale of cotton. Of late years it has done a considerable trade in lumber, sponges and oysters, but before I was forty two cities once flourishing were afterwards ruins, "all of which I saw and part of which I was."

In 1849 I came to Columbus; I came to meet the strongest bar in Georgia, but I had among my Florida clientage living in Columbus, Daniel McDougald, the brainiest merchant I have ever been intimate with, John G. Winter, then President of the St. Mary's Bank and an acknowledged power in Columbus, Hamp Smith, a kind of cotton king. I knew all the Howards from having been associated with Thacker B. Howard as President of the St. Joseph Railroad Company, I being the Secretary. I knew Seaborn Jones intimately, he having been interested in the St.

Joseph where he made frequent visits. I was the same with Benj. Fontaine, another leading merchant. So I did not come to Columbus a stranger and the fact of my having done business satisfactorily with all these men while practicing law in Florida was the main reason why I selected it as my future home. Still the Bar was a formidable one and it took a man with a large development of hope to confront it and hope for success.

Chapter 15

1849: I Came to Columbus/Reminiscence

The leading members of the Bar were: Wm. Dougherty, Walker T. Colquitt, James Johnson, Marshall P. Wellborn, Mines Holt, Seaborn Jones, Henry B. Benning, Alexander McDougal and Josephus Echols, all of whom except Judge James Johnson, now nearly 81, and myself, nearly 79, have passed over the river, and we are listening for the call of the ferry man to row us to the other side.

I had about $4000 when I came to Columbus; I bought a house for $1,000 and spent about $500.00 improving it. I bought a carriage or landau and a fine pair of horses. Believing that the best way to procure business was to seem independent of it, I determined to place myself in a position that where a client came to me I would know that he came because it was his interest to come and that he did not come to help me, or to get cheap work because of my necessities. I had been in Columbus a very short time when John C. Winter, for whom I had done business in Florida, employed me as counsel for the St. Mary's Bank of which he was President. He gave me an office in the Bank building, and $200.00 for a year. The salary was small but Winter had the leading business in Columbus, and of course threw into my hands all the business that he controlled and as at that

*time collections was an important part of the business, this
situation paid me more than my salary, and besides, it was a
good send off for a man new to the place. The very fact that
Winter, who was a power in Columbus, had confidence
enough in me to give me his general business was in itself a
valuable endorsement. At the end of the year I resigned the
position. In the meantime I had been retained to defend the
stockholders of the broken Banks against suits brought by
Dougherty on the bills in circulation under the personal
liability clause of their charters. Nearly every citizen of
prominence of Columbus was a defendant to one or more
suits, and this employment threw me into close relationship
with every leading lawyer and every prominent citizen. The
year after I left Winter's employ he was sued as a subscriber
of the Southeastern Road for $10,000. I defended him, on the
ground that the terminus of the road had been substantially
changed and that the road built was a different road from the
one that he had subscribed to; the case went to the Supreme
Court, and Winter was relived from his obligation; I received
$1,000 fees, being 10% on the amount involved. Then Echols
and Clayton informed against him, for issuing shin plasters
or change bills, the penalties on the several issues amounting
to about $50,000. In preparing for the defence I found a case
on the Fugitive Slave Law decided by the Supreme Court of
the United States on which this principle was involved, that
an informer had no vested right in the penalty until after
judgement and the repeal of the statute fixing the penalty
after information lodged and before judgement defeated the
informers claim and was constitutional because no judgement
having been obtained before the repeal. There was no vested
right. To render this decision available in Winter's case I
drew up a statute more stringent than the existing one, but
wholly different, and in this new statute repled the old one.*

Winter took charge of it and through third parties lobbied it through the Legislature. When his case came on for trial I pled the repeal of the Statute. Plaintiff claimed that the repeal could only effect the States interest that the half coming to them was a vested right and to defeat it was unconstitutional.

I cited my U.S. Decision but Judge Iverson overruled me and Plaintiffs recovered about $25,000. I carried the case to the Supreme Court, reversed Iverson, and Winter was free. In this of course, I got a large fee, but I don't remember the amount.

Another important case that he had was an ejectment for a part of the Esquiline, then the property of Winter; the plaintiff in ejectment had the States Grant, but I resisted. I resisted on the grounds that Winter's grantor had paid all four notes given to the State for the land, that he had the equitable title, that the State was his trustee, and that the mere omission to pay $3.00 for the grant did not authorize the State to issue a Grant to a third party.

This was about the defense, and I was sustained by the Supreme Court and in one of these cases about 9th or 19th Georgia, Lumpkin, Chief Justice, in delivering his opinion paid me a very high compliment. My practice grew steadily until I finally had the most lucrative practice of any member of the Bar.

Now to go back to more recent dates, my life in Columbus. I had a fine practice, my family consisted of Isaac, Nina, Albert, Lea [Raphael, Jr.], and Hannah. The latter was quite delicate and could not stand the summers in Columbus. On account of her health I had to go to Warm and Chalybeate Springs in summer. My son Isaac was also very delicate, and I sent him with a friend to the Hot Springs in Arkansas. When he reached there the physician said that he had rheumatism of the heart and it would be fatal for him to use the waters, and that I must meet him in New Orleans, at his Aunt Septima's, Mrs. Solomon Levy. I went there for him and was terribly shocked to find him swollen with dropsy. I brought him home, he lingered a few months and died; this was the second death among my children. The first was my daughter Sarah, whose apron was drawn into the grate when she was standing near it and burned her chiefly around the neck down to the carotid artery. The burning was a sad misfortune to us, she was our first child, but I never wished for her recovery after I learned from the doctor that if she recovered her neck would always be drawn down to one side from the contraction of the muscles, and it would have been pure selfishness to wish a girl to live deformed and a constant mortification to herself. Life may be worth living to a boy despite a deformity but I doubt it, for my opinion is the life is only worth living under the very best conditions. Isabel was born a few months before Isaac died. In the fall of 1850, on account of Hannah's health and my love of suburban life, I purchased from John G. Winter my present home, then called by Winter, "Bunker Hill," but when I purchased it my friend John Forsyth, then editing the Columbus Times, compared me (jocularly) to Macenas who delighted (in his leisure) in horticulture on the Esquiline, one of the seven hills of Rome, hence the name by which it has ever been known, one that I much prefer to any New England production.

After removing to Columbus I took an active part in politics and was decidedly in favor of seceding when the admission of California destroyed the balance of power as provided for in the Constitution. The issues of 1850 were very exciting, in fact they were the same that culminated in the War of 1861; but individuals changed their positions. Toombs, who was at the head of the Revolution in 1861, was a prominent Unionest in 1850; Stephens and Cobb were also for the Union; McDonald, Colquitt and others were for secession; McDonald and Cobb opposed each other for Governor on these issues. Excitement ran very high. It was in one of Toombs' Union speeches at Columbus that he said, "he had carried the first white shirt into the Democratic party that ever entered it, and now these fellows with Calhoun at their heads talk about overturning the government." "Why," said he, "they have not strength enough to overthrow a smoke house 8x10." He was otherwise very abusive of Calhoun and South Carolina.

There we made our first acquaintance. I pressed my way up to the front of the stage, and pointing my finger at him, hissed him, and announced that I would reply to him at the same place that night, which I did. I invited Toombs to be present, but he didn't come. The meeting was the stormiest political meeting that I ever spoke to. I don't remember exactly when Toombs and I met again, but I think it was long after, in a consultation on the Bank cases, when all the counsel for the various defendants (of whom Toombs was one and I another) met for conference. After a time we became excellent friends and when the issue was made in 1861, we were both on the same side and became very close friends.

ALBERT MOSES LURIA
(@ age 16)

(Either)
RAPHAEL JACOB MOSES, JR.
(@ age 14)
or
WILLIAM MOULTRIE MOSES
(@ age 16)

@ 1859

Chapter 16

1860: Esquiline and the Family

Shortly after we moved to the Esquiline, Hannah married Mr. Isaac I. Moses. We had a very large wedding, I think about three or four hundred guests, and about thirty slept here that night. Hannah had two children, a boy, Isaiah who died in infancy and is buried in our cemetery, and a daughter Rebecca Hannah. Her Mother [Hannah] was attending a Miss Jonas in Montgomery, warming some water for her, when her clothes accidentally caught fire and burnt her dreadfully. She suffered terribly, lingered some months and died just across the river in Alabama. She is buried in our cemetery. Her daughter [Rebecca] Hannah survived her, married Jacob I. Moses, has two children (boys) and lives in New York. This was our second child burnt to death.

Nina (Penina) Moses, writing of her life, sets forth the carefree, free-spirited activities in June of 1859, shortly after the wedding of her brother, Israel Moses Nunez to Anna Marie Moses. She went on a visit with her mother to Charleston, Savannah and Philadelphia:

My first party

Philip Cohen, Camillus Moise and several other boys were added to my list of acquaintances; Camillus' mother was Cousin Louisa, and I was made supremely happy by having Camillus give a party for me-the first time in my life. I had formed quite a number of acquaintances by then and remember having thought Mother unnecessarily proper because she was not willing to let me go to walk on the Battery (the public walk of Charleston) with more than two boys at a time.

The boys draw straws as to who shall dance with me.

I was an unsophisticated country girl, not quite 13-the night of the party, when several wanted to dance with me, at once, I let them draw straws, and danced with the boy who drew the longest. I cannot remember many incidents of that time in Charleston, but Miss Penina's stories and the party for me stando out in my mind, Harby Moses, Philip Cohen, Edwin and Camillus Moise made favorable impressions.

I forget how long Brother Maj. [Israel] and his bride remained, or exactly when we left-we could hardly have been there more than a week or ten days-Mother and I went from there to Savannah, and were the guests of Mother's cousin, Mr. Octavus Cohen-his son Octavus had his Cousin Gratz (brother of Belle and Mamie Cohen) were my special attendants-Gratz went with Mother an me to Philadelphia, where he was to visit his aunt, Miss [Rebecca] Gratz (who inspired Sir Walter Scott, when in a visit to this country with his ideal of Rebecca of Ivanhoe) and I wnt to my aunt-Mrs. David C. Levy, Amanda and Septima were 16 and 18 years of age, Sol was three days older than I and yet I scarcely remember his being there, Lucien and Willie were beaux for Amanda and me.

I meet Dr. Isaac Leeser-

I met socially, and heard in Synagogue, in Philadelphia at that time the famous Jewish Divine, Isaace Leeser-I was expecting my Brother Lea when Rabbi Leeser called-I rushed to the door and finding my mistake was much embarrassed and said "Oh! I thought you were Lea, sir" to which he laughingly replied "It is Lee-ser."

The preceding paragraphs, reminiscences of a woman about her young teenage, happy experiences and that of her relatives, could not, in 1859, realize the dark foreboding of the tragic drama-No-Holocaust!-of the American Civil War. Nina's brother, Albert, would give his life for the "Lost Cause" at the battle of Fair Oaks, VA, May 31, 1862. Septima Marie Levy would soon marry Charles Collis, who became a much promoted, highly decorated Union officer; but had to face the harsh realities of a Southern family and mourn the death of her older brother, Lt. David Cardoza Levy, who would give his life for the "Cause" at the Battle of Stones River, Murphreesboro, TN, December 31, 1862. Young Gratz Cohen was killed in action at the Battle of Bentonville, NC, March 19, 1865, in the final weeks of "The Lost Cause." Harby Moses served with the 6th SC Cavalry, his brother, Lt. Joshua L. Moses was killed in action defending Fort Blakely, Alabama, April 9, 1865, the day Lee surrendered to Grant. The Moise's served with the Palmetto (SC) Guards from 1861 to the end of the war; and Philip Cohen enlisted in 1861 in the Washington (SC) Artillery.

Rebecca Gratz would mourn the death of her nephew,

Captain Carey Gratz, son of Benjamin, who was killed August 10, 1861 at the Battle of Wilson Creek, Missouri, while leading his command, Company E, 1st Missouri Infantry, Union Army. At the end of hostilities, Isaac Leeser would be sent by the Board of Israelites to tour the ravaged South to seek out the remnants of the small, once thriving Jewish communities. Of particular note was his short visit to Chattanooga, Tennessee, in December 1866. He reported:

> At the end of last December (1866), we spent a few hours in this town, to become acquainted with the resident Israelites, who received us exceedingly cordially, to such a degree that we regretted that an engagement in Atlanta prohibited our staying longer with them. They had just purchased a large plot of ground on an elevated position for a cemetery, and we now learn that, under the management of a Society of which Mr. Morris Bradt is president, they have resolved to disinter the bodies of Israelite soldiers, who fell during the fearful struggles around that place on both sides of the late deplorable civil war. Political prejudices, we are glad to observe, are entirely ignored, and those who were not personal enemies, but merely driven to slaughter each other by the folly and madness of rulers, will sleep side by side in undisturbed rest, awaiting the resurrection.

Despite announcements, the Jewish Civil War Cemetery was not a reality. Those who lost loved ones wanted to let them "rest in peace" in their graves; in many instances, unknown and unmarked.

Raphael Moses, Jr., writing in 1906, describing the members of the family in the years before the Civil War, wrote about several of his brothers and sisters.

... Father had five children in Florida. My eldest sister Sarah was burned when she was about three years old. Son Isaac, who lived until he was about 12, died of rheumatism of the heart. From the inscription of his tombstone, I judge he had always been delicate and one of those gentle natures who never knew how to rebel. My only recollection of him is of sitting under the shade of a tree with bow and arrows, while I would play a deer and run by to see if he could shoot me. The third son was Israel, who was always known as "Major." When we moved to Columbus in 1849, Israel had on his first pair of boots and he was so proud of them and strutted so up and down the deck showing them off that all the passengers nicknamed him the "Major," a name which has curiously held on to him the balance of his life. Next to "Major" was born another girl, Hannah, whom we always called "Sister." She was a particularly lovely nature and between her and me there was a recognized special affinity and attachment. When she was seventeen in Columbus, Ga., she married a Mr. Isaac I. Moses, nearly 30 years old and had by him two children, one Rebecca H., and a boy, Isaac, who died when he was three years old. My sister Hannah was burned in March 1860 and I nursed her for four months in Montgomery, Ala., and we moved her back to Columbus where she died July 1860.

Thus, the Moses family suffered the agony of the deaths of children and young adults: daughter Sarah, burned and died at age 3 in 1838; son Isaac's death of a birth defect at age 12 in 1850; Hannah, age 20, of burns in 1860; grandson Isaiah at age 3 in 1862; and son Albert, mortally wounded at age 19, in 1862.

The ante-bellum lifestyle at Esquiline Hill was that of a warm and generous family. Friends and relatives visited from far and near. The adjacent plantation, one mile away, Torch Hill, was owned by Dr. Frances O. Ticknor, a Columbus dentist and poet of regional recognition. He was a very close family friend. Dr. Ticknor had three daughters die at early ages, and the daughters of Raphael and Eliza became particular favorites. Penina was born in 1846 and called "Nina." Isabelle Adeline was born in 1850. At Esquilline, they were outgoing, attractive young girls. "Belle," as she was called, had a small area surrounded by cherry laurels which was a particular place to these young children where they played. Dr. Ticknor took a special delight in "Belle," whom he called "Brownie," and in "Nina." He wrote poems which he dedicated to them:

To "Nina" he wrote this poem:

Nina - Her Eyes.

I know the Summers that can speak
For all the olive of thy cheek;
I know the gentle lineage rare
That crowns thy head with midnight hair;
But whence - don't send me to the skies! -
The splendor, Nina, of your eyes?

Now, Nina, there's your needle! knit!

Your lashes droop, a little bit;
I'm writing "letters" and afraid
Of brilliant cross lights;
Lend me shade.
Nay! there's a dimple at your lips,
And there - you dazzle, past eclipse!

Was it of much or little "grace"
To mock these clouds of commonplace
With a while Summer Sun set's dyes,
Because you must lift up your eyes?
Sending my missives all amiss,
Turning my "letter" into this!

You couldn't help it! once amid
A temple's twilight, it betid
The soft glow of a vestal's light
Slept on the crosslet of a Knight,
And wrought - nor, Nina, might it less
Of loyalty and tenderness -
That matchless radiance that lies
Deep in the splendor of your eyes!

To "Belle" he wrote this poem:.

Brownie Belle of the Esquilline

Where the almond blossoms first
Where the nectarines are nursed
Grew with cedar and with pine
Grew with violet and wine
   With her eyes of calm,
And her eyes devine,

With her breath of balm,
Brownie Belle, of the Esquiline
Grew in grace
  Like the blue glycine;
Grew in grace
  Like a jasmine;
In stateliness
  Like a Norfolk pine;
With tender gloom
  In her eyes devine,
And her olive bloom
  Through her blush like wine,
Grew in grace,-
  And I knew her well,
From the honey-dew
  To the nectar-cell;
From the morning mist,
  Till the manna fell
On the tents, the lips
  of Israel.

In stateliness, like the star of trees
With silver lace, from the Indian Seas
  Where the silver mist
    And the stars are met
    On her coronet;
On the stately crest of the stateliest
    Star-lit Tree-star
    Bright Beodar.
    Sweet the air of the Esquiline,
From morning paper till nuts and wine;
Where the discerning gods of days divine
Might dance on gods embordered fine

With the richest tints of the ripest wine
Of every land where the sun doth shine

We'll gamer all
  Of the bright and sweet;
We'll lay them all at Brownie's feet.
We'll gather all for garland feast.
When the stars recall our star from the East
  When she comes, she comes
With balm and bloom; and the tender gloom
  Of her eyes shall shine
To crown the lights of the Esquiline.

Resuming Moses' journal:

  I don't think of any other incident worth recording that happened before the war, unless it may be that the Esquiline had a fine orchard and that I shipped as an experiment the first peaches etc., sent from the South. This was in 1851, before there was any through connection by railroad. The two champagne baskets, one of peaches, one of plums, went by stage to Macon, then by railroad to Savannah, and from Savannah to New York by steamer. I received for them $30.00 per basket. I then extended my orchard and when the railroad commenced, shipped largely to New York, getting very remunerative prices. I started a fruit and flower nursery with a Mr. John Lee, an Irishman as superintendent. This failed. Mr. Lee and my son, Major, had a quarrel about a cow getting into the nursery. I was out riding, when I came home Mr. Lee had left and the nursery went "where the woodbine twineth."
  I continued extending my orchard and the year the War broke out my sales had reached $71,500 per annum. I

then had 100 acres in fruit, twenty thousand trees young and old, a vineyard of eighteen acres under the management of a Frenchman, Joseph Dantell, who drew none of his salary but during the four years made enough outside to pay his current expenses. When I returned from the War, to my amazement, his salary of $2,400.00 was all due him and he demanded it all in gold. I refused to pay it. He moved to Tennessee, sued me in the U.S. Court and I finally had to pay about $3,200. After that the vineyards were ploughed up, they being principally Catawba grapes, which rotted easily.

I started a canning factory which was also a failure, as the War broke out about the time I was ready to operate it. I built a fruit drying house, and this burnt up with all the fruit in it owing to a defective flue. My time was wholly taken with a large law practice and I could give these matters but little personal supervision.

Moral, undertake nothing that you can't give sufficient personal supervision to reasonably insure success.

When the War broke out I had forty-seven slaves ... .

Part II

The War Years

1861 - 1865

Chapter 1

January-June, 1861:
Albert's Journal, Sgt., C.S.A.
Albert's Letters

Milledgeville,Geo.
Jan. 17, 1861.

Dear Lize:

We arrived all safe last night and found the place very much crowded, we could get no accommodation at either of the Hotels, but afterwards succeeded in getting quarters at a private house. Col. Stratton, Mr. Wm. Mitchell, Father and myself were in one room. There are a good many persons here from Columbus. I have not seen Loudie, except for a moment in the Hall of Representatives. The convention now (12 M.) has recess. Immediately upon the reorganization the commissioners from Alabama and So. Ca. will speak. I do not expect I will be able to hear them for every corner and crevice in the hall is literally packed.

I was very sorry to hear that you were sick and would have stopped to see you, but for Cousin E's desire that I should not come there, for fear of the scarlet fever. Dispatches just received from Congress say the Clark resolutions (proposing to use the power of the government to coerce) have been carried. I have not seen father since breakfast. I will probably be home tomorrow or next day.

Love to all, from Y'r devoted Coz

A.M. Luria.

Jan. 25, 1861.

Dear Lize,

Day before yesterday I wrote you a long note in reply to yours of Sunday, but have since decided not to trouble you with it. Suffice it to say, if it be essential to your happiness, I accept your proposition and remain

Y'r Coz. and Bro.
A.M. Luria.

[Undated]

Your note has just been handed me and in reply I have only this to say. I will not promise to regard you only as I would a sister, because I think that affection of such a nature and temperament as my own can only be overcome by time and circumstances and even then, the accomplishment of the object in view is uncertain. For this reason I am unwilling to promise, unconditionally, to receive your love as that of a Sister, but this I will say -- I will make an earnest endeavor to overcome the feelings I now entertain, for the next three years. At the end of that time, if I have succeeded in changing them, I will offer them as a Brother; on the contrary, if I do not succeed in changing them, I will offer them as they are now, and await y'r decision, to receive or reject.

Believing that "there is a divinity that shapes our ends" I will wait patiently and in the meantime I am

Yrs affectionately,
A.M. Luria.

ALBERT MOSES LURIA
@ age 17
at Military School in N.C.

ELIZA "LIZE" MOSES
@ age 14

Columbus, Ga.
March 18, 1861.

My dear Lize:

I am very sorry that our conversation this morning was interrupted, as it has, I fear, cut me off from a verbal explanation of several affairs upon which I desired to speak with you, and not knowing when I may get an opportunity or when I may be called off by military duty, which admits of no delay, I will write you an explanation. But before entering into a detail of these matters I will state that the only manner in which I can prove to you the truth of what I say is by your having a firm and unshaken confidence in my honor and my word. This I believe you have, and further that I do not make these explanations in order that a knowledge of them may prevent a change in yr feelings, but so that an ignorance of them may not induce a change, and as what I consider due myself.

Just before I went to Milledgeville I learned from a party (whose name I am not authorized to use) that it was generally believed that I had centered my affections upon Loudie Lyons, and this belief was sustained by a letter from me to Loudie, which letter Sister [Hannah] had shown to Father and Mother and a part of which she had read to you. Immediately I made an explanation of that letter to Father and yr Bro., as to how it came to be written, etc.

The circumstances connected with it were these: When I left Columbia I did not correspond with Loudie. In July I sent her an invitation to our Ball, (also one to Nine and Loudie's sister). Possibly Albert's visit to Columbia had been prearranged, with a purpose. Nina says in her journal that she was sent to Columbia to visit the Lyons and later discovered that it was arranged in the hope of breaking her attachment for W.M.M.) "She acknowledged receipt of the invitation by a letter commencing, "Mr. A.M. Luria" and continuing in a very formal style, but concluded by asking me to reply, which I did in a very ordinary manner, only remarking that I thought her letter rather formal. Her next letter she commenced, "Dear Ally (I should say "Dearest") and continued her letter in a strain corresponding to the beginning. (Remember, Lize, I do not desire to cast any reflection on Loudie, but only to state the facts, as I deem it highly necessary to prevent yr receiving a wrong impression, and I think it cowardice for a Gentleman to seek revenge for an injury received at a Lady's hand). I replied to her letter very much in the same strain, never dreaming of being in earnest nor supposing for a moment that she was.

Her next letter was in terms rather more extravagantly affectionate, and my reply in keeping wither her letter, I supposing all the time that it was merely a joke without any meaning in the world. Well, suffice it to say, that from one point to another the style of our letters was carried until it reached the one you saw. Thus I wrote her the letter in an extravagantly affectionate style only to respond in the tone of a letter received from her. You now see, my dear Lize, how I came to write Loudie in a manner so affectionate.

I will now tell you how that letter came to contain what it did, relative to yourself.

In Loudie's letter (to which the one Sister showed you was a reply) she asked me if I had given up the idea of marrying you and if I had entirely overcome the feelings, (Her information on that matter she did not get from me). Allow me to digress a little: When I was at Hillsboro, (because I then deemed it essential to the happiness of my parents) I determined that I would never marry a first cousin. In reply to Loudie's question, (more with a view to closing the subject than anything else, for she was not a person in whom I would like to confide), I wrote her that I had determined never to marry you under any circumstances. -- I have now, Lize, explained, and satisfactorily, I hope, the letter, but as I know there are those who will use every means which petty trifles can afford, to persuade you that my affection for you is not firm, I will anticipate them and here explain a circumstance connected with my Daguerre I sent Loudie, as it may come to your knowledge, and without any explanation you would be at a loss to account for it. When Loudie sent me her Daguerre, (without my asking her to do so) she enclosed in the back a piece of her hair and a slip of paper on which were written these words, "Forget me not" and she wrote me a letter asking for a piece of mine. When I sent her the Daguerre I enclosed her a piece and wrote in the back, "I have found out the secret of yr Daguerre and return the compliment. 'Thine and only Thine'". Altho I did that merely (so to speak) to be even with her, yet I know that some persons will use their endeavors to construe this little matter a very serious affair.

But, remember, my Beloved.

[April 26, 1861]

Well, Cousin Julia, I have at last found an opportunity to hold a little conversation with you.

... Have you noticed _____ [Luria left the name blank] since I left. I hope she attends our separation well -- I trust in God that all things may turn out for the best. I shall so conduct myself that if I live Envy can point to no spot on my reputation, and if I fall, I have the extreme satisfaction of knowing that altho' I died in defence [sic] of my country people, there was one among them far dearer to me than the life I have sacrificed. I feel confident that whatever course _____ [left blank] may pursue, the course will be dictated by a sense of duty, or no, I do not mean whatever course, but I mean that if she takes a course I would not like her to, it will be a triumph of a sense of duty over her feelings, but she should allow herself to take the opposite course and bring about a consummation of my heart's dearest wishes. I shall feel that it is a triumph of true lover over every obstacle, but, Cousin Julia, I have made up my mind to await the issue, leaving it with her to decide my destiny; feeling fully confident of the purity of her heart and the depth of her affections, I know she will do nothing wantonly and I am decided that when the time arrives for that issue, I will demand it and abide by it, let it be what it may. My feelings are too irrevocably fixed ever to center on anyone else, but if it is necessary I will endeavor to so control them that they shall never cause _____ [left blank] any unhappiness. ...

Naval Hospital (Portsmouth, Va.)
May 9th, 1861.

Dear Cousin Julia:

If, as you say, never, when a little girl, did you experience so much pleasure from the receipt of a letter as when you received mine, I may say almost the same thing, when I tell you that seldom, when a young man, have I experienced so much pleasure from the perusal of a letter, as was afforded me by yr's of the 2nd inst. I assure you that I felt happier after reading your very affectionate favor than I have done. I wish, my beloved Coz, I could find some metaphor or some language by which to express the feeling my heart cherishes for you. I would not say Love, Friendship, Esteem or Admiration -- for neither would satisfactorily define my feeling -- but something expressing a combination of all these would be nearer what I desire. But how excellent was the work of our Creator when, anticipating some such feeling, he has inaugurated a something, which communicates to two sympathetic souls what language cannot express. ...

Yesterday was my eighteenth birthday, and today I commence my nineteenth year with new resolutions and hopes for the future. ...

I am very glad indeed to see you mention that Lize allots a part of every morning to reading. I mentioned to her before I left home that I thought it would be well for her to do so, and not tax her physical strength too much. Lize is just about the age when she will appreciate fully anything she reads. No doubt, my dear Cousin, she would be glad to have you assist her in a selection of books to read. I assure you I miss the library at home very much. ...

Love to Cousin Esther, Aunt C., yr Mother, Lize and Addy. Remember me to Uncle Abram, Cliff and Cousin Edwin. With the earnest prayer that the rays of happiness may ever light yr way thro' life, I remain,

Yr Sincerely attached Coz.
A.M. Luria.

Sewell's Point, May 27, 1861.

My dear Cousin Julia:

After having completed three pages of a letter to you I had the good fortune to have a cup of water spilt over it, compelling me to abandon that issue and commence anew. The incident suggested to me the very good idea of leaving the camp and retiring to the woods near the beach. Yield all self-control and allow Imagination to lead you a willing captive to Sewell's Point. It will point out to you a youth of 18 in his shirt sleeves, collar off and shirt thrown open at the neck, a "Washington" in his mouth, from which clouds of blue smoke are constantly emitted, seated on a rail fence beneath the foliage of a gigantic oak and commanding a magnificent view of the Hampton Roads, and a portfolio open on his right knee. This you will recognize to be yr humble correspondent.

From over the water a splendid breeze is wafted -- cooling the atmosphere, which has hitherto been oppressively warm. As I sit here and admire the supreme beauty of all nature as it surrounds me I cannot but wish that you were here to enjoy it.

Nor can I thank you, dear Cousin Julia, enough for yr kindness in endeavoring to make my darling Lize take more care of her health. Yr remarks relative to her and myself, lead me to make a candid confession and relieve yr mind of any uneasiness by giving you a just account to the effect that young ladies have on my heart. I do not restrict in the slightest degree, my intercourse with them. I mingle freely, endeavor to render myself as agreeable as possible -- make many pleasant and interesting acquaintances sometimes, and often very warm friends, but I never entertain any young lady a feeling of the same nature as that I cherish in my heart's inmost recesses for Lize. I love some who are related to me but it is a love as different form that as day is from night. For instance -- I love Minnie, Alice, Addy, yrself and others -- love you all very much, but yet I do not entertain for you a love whose nature is the same as that which I feel for the being highest in my estimation. No, Cousin Julia, she is the first and the only one I have ever loved in that way. The heart I gave her more than three years ago is hers now and shall be hers until life has passed away and I shall be no more. Further, I shall always believe that she cherishes for me feelings as unaltered now as the were immaculate years ago. A mistaken sense of duty may ultimately induce her to pursue a course that will wreck my happiness for life, but I assure you I will never appreciate her the less for it -- only the more -- for I shall feel conscious that she has, after long battling, achieved a triumph of what she considers her duty, over her feelings -- as true and tender as ever were nourished in the heart of a woman.

I often think that I love her too much and that God will punish me for attaching so much value to anything earthly.

Last Sunday, (the day the Monticello bombarded Sewell's Point), when Dr. Taliafero called for someone to go outside the battery with him, believing death inevitable, I thought of the pain she would experience at my fall, but quick as thought, I said to myself, she will be proud of me when she hears where and how I died -- these things ran thro' my mind in 1/20 the time it takes to read them, and knowing that she would be gratified to know that I died in the discharge of my duty in advance of my comrades, I commended my soul to its Maker and sprang thro' the embrasure. The rest you know already. ...

I will merely ask you, dearest Cousin, to do all in your power for her happiness and even though I should never return to thank you in person, rest assured that my heart is ever welling up with gratitude and my last breath shall invoke the blessing of Almighty God on you for your kindness.

From Albert's journal:

One Saturday morning, the 20th of April, 1861, I was sitting with the rest of the family around the breakfast table -- we had finished but were then only talking of one little matter and another -- some standing, some sitting -- when suddenly Old Simmons (Cousin Edwin's boy) appeared with a note from E.W.M. saying that our company was to leave for Norfolk Va. that afternoon at 4 o'clock -- it was then near 8 in the morning & the note stated that our company would have a called meeting at 10 A.M. so I had to hurry up and pack my trunk and say good bye and get to town, 5 miles in about two hours. I was very glad that my departure from home occurred under such circumstances -- for I always dreaded parting scenes. I went in to Columbus that morning and on my way stopped at Cousin Edwin's to bid adieu to his household. I saw them all and bade them an affectionate farewell, having seen them, as I thought then, for the last time, but after getting in town I made all my preparations and joined my company City Light Guards -- Captain Colquitt P.H. at the armory from which we marched to the Depot where we were met by an immense concourse of citizens -- assembled to bid us "God Speed." Among them were all the girls from home and Cousin Edwin's except Alice -- come to bid me adieu. I did not anticipate seeing them for as it was Saturday I knew they could not ride [sic: observant Jews do not ride on their Sabbath] & hardly expected they would pay me the compliment of walking in. As I bad adieu to Eliza -- her whole soul (ed) pressure of my hand was all that I could bear. I kissed her & whispering a God Bless you turned off leaving home with a happy heart, for I felt then and feel now that time cannot abate the nature of her affection, & I felt fully that her feelings would undergo no change. No apprehension on that score has ever crossed my mind -- however I got on the train and was soon hurrying off to Va. -- where I was to figure among mounted men and dashing youths.

We arrived in Portsmouth on the morning of the 23rd and were quartered at the Old U.S.N. Hospital where we remained for two weeks. Then we were removed to Fort Norfolk and stayed there just a week -- when we left there for Tanner's Cross Roads. At this place we arrived on Wednesday morning together with the rest of our Battalion, 2nd Ind Bat. res vol. We remained at the Cross Roads until Sunday. While we were seated under the spreading branches of an immense oak listening to a very poor sermon a courier rode up, bringing an order to Major Hardeman, who was in command of our Battalion -- to detail one company to march in 10 minutes to Sewell's Point -- where they would prevent a landing by the enemy.

Our Capt being the oldest -- by commission -- we were ordered to get ready for the march -- about 5 miles -- and started off -- all of us "eager for the fray." We arrived at Sewell's Point about 12 1/2 -- having left the Cross Roads at 10 1/2. When we arrived we were divided into two platoons on the left and right of the sand hill just in front of the Monticello (a Federal gunboat) which was then anchored about 3/4 of a mile from the Beach respectively (?). We lay on our faces so as to conceal ourselves from the enemy and in this position we remained until about 2 o'clock, when an order came from Genl Gwynn (who was then about 1/4 of a mile from the Battery), that we should repair to the Battery and mount the Guns, which were there preparatory to firing on the Enemy the next morning at 7 o'clock. We went to work with an energy that (only) the isolation of our position -- together with our keen desire for a fight could give, and we did not have to wait very long, for soon the booming of cannon told us that the Battle had commenced and further that we have no inexperienced gunners to deal with for their very first shot tore down the Blanket which hung before our Port Holes, their second buried itself deep in the Fortification -- their third flew high over our heads, cutting Branches off the trees down and fairly making the blood creep through our veins as it whistled over us -- but in the mean time our brave boys were not idle -- we were ready -- & as the enemy threw down the Gauntlet we fairly sprang to pick it up.

No sooner had their first shot whistled thro' our

embrasures than we replied in a language that was unmistakable, for two hours the cannonading was kept up with unabated fury -- when at last as night closed on the scene the Monticello was towed off to Fortress Monroe by two little stem Tugs which had come down to her assistance, when she sent up a signal of distress. Throughout the engagement our men displayed great coolness and bravery. Capt. Colquitt was perfectly cool, and kept continually calling out to us, not to get so excited -- to 'keep cool' -- 'aim lower' &c. ... This was the first engagement that took place in Va. -- the victory was won by the City Light Guards of Columbus Ga. assisted by 30 Virginians who had come from several companies. [Then came speeches, heavy rain and picket duty] after marching 6 miles of a hot, dusty day -- and working and fighting until night without a mouthful to eat. ...

I was Sergeant of the Guard that night. Our men had no tents. In the hurry of our departure we could bring nothing except a little uncooked provisions and our Blankets; but in spite of the rain we laid down -- those who were not on guard -- wrapped up in blankets and slept soundly until the next morning -- when we were reinforced by an Artillery corps who took command of the Batter -- and we pitched our tents after a day or so -- about 3 or 400 yards father off from the Beach. From this position we removed about 1/2 of a mile -- still further from the Beach. Sewell's Point is about 12 miles from Norfolk, the road leading to it is a fine level one -- sometimes the branches of the oaks almost meet over it & form a perfect kind of an arbor -- the road is certainly the most beautiful I ever travelled over.

I remained with my company at Sewell's Point until the 17th of June, but I have not mentioned that my friend Mr. John Lee (an Esquiline overseer) arrived as a new member of the company, just before we left Tanner's Cross Roads. He

was in the battle and behaved very well indeed. He was with
the company when I left and every one was perfectly devoted
to him. He was the life of the camp -- kept everybody amused.
He is a warm-hearted, generous man -- a warm and true friend
-- and who fully merits all the esteem he has so generously
received.

-----

*The History of the Twenty-Third Regiment, North Carolina
Troops, 1861-1865:*

On April 20, 1861, Albert Moses Luria was called to
arms with the Columbus City Light Guards, Wright's Brigade,
Army of Northern Virginia. He served with this unit until June
17, 1861, when he was appointed a 2nd Lieutenant of
Company "A," 23rd North Carolina, serving with college
friends form the Hillsboro Military Academy of North
Carolina. The above named source pays no higher tribute to
Albert Moses Luria than with these elegant words:

> ... Luria was a gallant young fellow. It was
> at Sewell's Point (Virginia) that he did a heroic act,
> which, had he been a British soldier, would have
> brought him the Victoria Cross and caused the
> world to ring his name. While there early in 1861
> as a visitor or as a member of Colquitt's Command
> before joining the Twenty-third, a shell from the
> Federal gunboats dropped among the
> Confederates. With rare presence of mind and
> devotion, he seized the shell and threw it over the
> works before it could explode. At our
> reorganization, he refused promotion, saying he
> wished nothing unless was on the battlefield. ...

The following newspaper item appeared:

COLUMBUS LEDGER-ENQUIRER
LOCAL NEWS ITEMS
THURSDAY MORNING, JUNE 5, 1862

The Guns at Sewell's Point.-- A participant in the first engagement at Sewell's Point informed us that the apparent discrepancy between the statement copied from the Atlanta Confederacy and our subsequent notice of it, in reference to the soldier who dug away the earth before the mouth of a cannon of our battery, under the fire of the enemy arises from the fact that there were two of our cannon thus obstructed and that they were cleared away for service by different men.

We are informed that at the commencement of the attack by the Monticello upon our incomplete battery, we had two small field pieces and three short thirty-two pounders in position; that two of these last were disabled because of embankments of sand lying at their mouths; that one of these obstructed guns was assigned by Capt. Colquitt to the command of Dr. W.H. Taliaferro, and that the Doctor, seeing the condition of the gun, called for a volunteer to assist him in the hazardous work of removing the sand with the spade; that the noble, brave and lamented A.M. Luria (who has recently fallen near Richmond) seized a spade and dashing through the embrasure over the cannon, cried out, "Come on, Doctor," and that he and Dr. Taliaferro worked together at the embankment until a clear space was opened between the gun and the enemy. This gun, it is believed, did good execution, as the Monticello and two tug boats, each having guns, were driven crippled from the battery, and the city of Norfolk probably saved from a visit by them at that time.

Another of the three thirty-two guns was disabled in the same way, and Privates Zack Mayo and Albert Porter undertook the hazardous work of removing the embankment.

This gun, no doubt, was also served with good effect.

All the parties above named deserve the highest encomiums for their conduct on the occasion, for they voluntarily undertook acts involving them in great danger, and performed them coolly and successfully. Our Informant speaks with especial admiration of the cool and determined manner and the smiling face of the brave Luria. A braver and nobler man, he says, never shouldered a musket.

The action referred to in the preceding newspaper article is reported in "The Official Records of the Union and Confederate Navies in the War of Rebellion" --[OR-N-I-5(646-8)].

In a report dated May 20, 1861, "Headquarters Forces of Virginia Around Virginia," and written by Major General [Robert E. Lee, Commanding Officer of the Virginia Military Forces before his commission as a General in the Confederate Army, gave a detailed report of the action at Sewell's Point on the 19th. The report pays high tribute to Captain Colquit's command and refers specially to an accompanying report of Captain Colquit. That report, dated "Sewell's Point, VA, May 19, 1861, further describes the engagement between the Confederate forces and the Union ships , particularly the Union steamer "Monticello." The report concludes, "P.S.-Two members of the City Light Guards (Georgia) dug away the sand in front of one of the port holes during the hottest part of the fight."

One of these men was Dr. Taliaferro, the other Sgt. Albert Moses Luria. It was also in this engagement which Lt. Luria performed another act of bravery which is described and commemorated. That being the picking up of the shell with a burning fuse thus saving the lives of his comrades. It was this incident that was written, "...had he been in the British Army, he would have won the Victoria Cross."

Thus our hero, Albert Moses Luria, was recognized twice for his bravery. Once for climbing to the seaward side of the parapet to remove the sand; and then again, when he picked up a "shell with a burning fuse."

June 11, 1861

Cousin Julia, I hardly think you fully realize how much I do love you.

That increasing interest that you have exhibited, not only in me, but in that young being so much dearer to me than myself, has riveted you to my heart and makes me think of you, almost every time that I think of the Darling girl. Last night, Sgt White wanted to go to town and I volunteered to act in his place, as I had to be up every two hours to post sentinels. I slept but little thro' the night. For hours at a time I sat and thought of dear Lize. I always feel so much happier after I have communed in my heart with her pure spirit, and, as I think of her, my confidence will not let me ask myself does she think of me? But I thank God, as I say to myself, I know that she often travels over the long distances between us and that her thoughts are continually with me. Sometimes I cannot help thinking how poor must be the love that is continually involved in doubt -- the one questioning the constancy of the other. ...

There is only one thing that I particularly desire and that is that circumstances were such as to permit you and her to enjoy that mutual confident which I have so long enjoyed. I suppose that it cannot be, and yet I wish it could. I love her so much, Cousin Julia, and she reciprocates so warmly, that to me it is a source of great regret that you cannot open yr hearts to each other.

May God in his infinite mercy watch over and bless you both and guide all things for the best; [bid] adieu to this. I say adieu, and yet I hardly feel as tho' I could turn to any other subject.

You have all, I suppose, learned from Lea [Raphael J. Moses, Jr.] of the disbandment of the Geo. Navy, and his determination to join the C.L.G. I am glad he is coming, for he is certainly a gallant fellow and I will be proud to go shoulder to shoulder thro' this war with him, living with, or dying for, our country's rights. [Lea did not join the City Light Guards, but he went into the Confederate Navy, where he served with distinction.]

What a splendid time to write to you, dearest Cousin, seated in a good tent, well pinned down -- by myself, and the rain driving in torrents; in fact the hardest rain, I think, I ever saw; it reminds me of the bullets in battle -- the rain driving hard against the thick canvas much resembles the incessant and rapidly succeeding whistling of balls. Yesterday, while I was out directing my company, I saw Father riding up and so I turned over the company to Capt. Amis and met Father who gave me a couple of letters, one from you and one from my friend, Mr. Lee. ...

Today I walked over to Col. Williams' tent to see Father. He is very well and is staying with Col Charley Williams until Genl Toombs arrives. He has a splendid little bay horse, about the size and build of Ria, a very nice saddle horse, perfectly gentle, but fully spirited, does not regard in the least the music or guns, and in fact she suite me so well, that I concluded I would borrow her tomorrow, which I succeeded in doing. ...

Father has named his horse Lala, after Cousin Rachel
Lyons. (By the way, I received a note from Loudie the other
day.)

Chapter 2

May-July, 1861:
Eliza's Diary

May 1st, 1861.

I begin tonight what I long wished to begin, but something which I have never thought myself competent to do. Nor do I feel competent to do so now, but have at least common sense enough to write simple facts and such things in general as I feel like writing.

I will not pledge myself to write any state time or any length, but have made up my mind to write when and how I feel inclined, as I am not going to let any, or at least very few persons, see this nonsense: for such it must be if I write it.

I often wonder if any one can have as mean an opinion of me as I have of myself; mercy knows they cant have any worse.

I can't see how anyone can blind themselves to my faults, for such they must do to like me at all and I think several persons do like me and some few actually love me.

Oh would that I could see into the inmost depths of some persons' souls to find if they do love me. What extreme felicity it would give me to know that some persons in this world do truly love me. I suppose id there was anything lovable about me they would do so, but who can love me?

I say 'who': I think there is one; but a doubt sometimes crosses my mind, even about that. But then I think it is because so many try to convince me that such is the case.

But then comes the question; why should one who has seen so much of the world fix his affections on me if it were not from mere choice.

But then, why should he choose me? What merits have I above so many that he has seen? I cant but believe what he says. I dont think he would merely say so; he is not one that would say anything but what he means. He says so: it must be so: but I hope for his good he will find himself mistaken. If God should permit him to return from that dangerous expedition he is now on at Portsmouth, I hope that his mind may be changed, that his affections are fixed upon some one more worthy of them than I ever can be.

But if such should not be the case; it is evident that he still loves me, I trust that we will be able to clear up all difficulties and objections on both sides for I would give up the love of all others for him. The just God in heaven knows this assertion to be true. May He pardon me for breaking my promise to my dearest and only Brother and may He change my Brother's views on this subject: that is, if the person to whom I allude returns home with the same feelings towards me that he had before he left.

May God aid me in judging of his feelings, and if they are changed may He enable me to conceal mine, for it is all I can do. I know they will never lessen, but if they are not reciprocated it would certainly be best to conceal them; and may He enable me to do so.

But enough of this subject, on which I ought not to have written so much. But how can I help it! My thoughts are continually on it, although I know they ought not to be: but I cant help it.

Nina and Aunt Julia both got letters from him. Oh, would that I could enjoy that pleasure, but for his sake I deprive myself of it, and also had to refuse a request of his.

But I don't want to do anything to influence his feelings in the slightest. But in case his feelings are not changed I will conduct myself in accordance with what I know to be his wishes and try every day to become more and more worthy of that love which I feel confident I possess.

I read two hours and write one; that is, I try to do so; but I dont do it every day. But I have made up my mind to do so at one time or another in the course of the twenty-four hours. If not in the day, I shall do so at night. I have done precious little today at anything, I have felt so badly. Nina spent the day here. Would that I were near as attractive as she is. She is his sister and when he sees me like this how can he like me? What powers of attraction have I?

I read only an hour to-day, so must put this aside and read an hour more before retiring, in some light book, as I have not borrowed the book I intended reading. Besides the United States history by Lossing which I am now reading, "The Woman in White" because someone advised me to read it and I am always more than willing to do whatever he advises. He always gives such good advice to every one. They cant help but do right if they follow it. But no more of this tonight.

I will write as soon as possible again.

I may go to the Farm tomorrow, but as Mother is now sick, though only a headache, I fear she will not be well enough for me to leave her.

And then again, I am not at all certain that I am welcomed out there. I hope I am mistaken though, as I often have some pleasant as well as sad recollections of the past.

May 2nd.

I don't feel very much like writing to-day, or, rather,

tonight; as it is almost eleven o'clock and I have just finished making up bread for breakfast. I have had quite a pleasant day, as my Aunt Julia spent the day here. I do love her; and why should not I? Every one who knows here, even ever so slightly, knows that she is lovable and cant help doing so. She seems to like me. What can a woman with such fine qualities of character herself find in such an insignificant being as I am to even like? But I think I may go so far as to say I think she loves me. We took a walk in the garden and had a little chat together. She seems to take such an interest in me. She wants me to hoe an half hour in the garden every morning before breakfast.

I made no promise but will try to do so, if for nothing else than to please her. She also informed me I was getting freckled and begged me to wear a bonnet whenever I went in the sun. I did not promise that either, but will try to perform it, as I dont think I can afford to increase my ugliness in the slightest degree. She, that is, Aunt J., told me the contents of her letter: said she intended bringing it, but forgot to do so. I was very sorry, but did not tell her so, of course.

Oh, I do envy everyone who receives letters from him. Oh, would that I could be favored; but I should be thankful that I can hear of him so often. Sister got a paper from him last night. Cousin Esther got a letter from him tonight. He is still in Portsmouth; seems to be having a pleasant time, which I am glad to hear.

He has the prospect of being promoted one degree higher, which will make Orderly Sergeant. I am so glad of it. I hope he will continue to rise and soon attain the highest position. I know he will if it only depends on his abilities. Cousin E. wont believe he does not write me. Oh that I could feel that I was doing right in permitting him to write to me. I could and would then feel so much happier.

Mother and Aunt Carrie, who is now staying here, have both been indisposed to-day. I hope they will both be well tomorrow.

May 20th.
Well, I have come to you to confide in you again after an absence of 18 days.

Nina staid [sic] here, which I was very glad of, as I miss her much and have seen very little of her of late: spent the evening here and a very pleasant time we all had of it: that is, I did and hope the rest did.

Aunt J. took me out in the front porch and we had a little chat: she principally, though it was about my health. What a deep interest she does take in me. Would that I deserve it, but I shall always endeavor to show my appreciation of it.

She presented me with a hoe, which I intend to show my appreciation of by constant use of it as soon as I am able to do so. ...

Addy got a letter Friday from Fort Norfolk, where he has removed to. I am very sorry he had to give up his comfortable quarters in the hospital and live in tents.

They must be such uncomfortable quarters and then he, poor fellow, had such hard time while moving. I am glad he became acquainted with such a fine family as he describes his Cousin's, Mrs. Walter's, is.

[July 1861]
Well, well, two, yes two whole months have elapsed since I have been enabled to relieve my overflowing mind and heart in this pleasant and satisfactory way, because I lost my drawer key. But I have found it at last, and with it is this true

friend of mine in which I confide almost without any hesitancy, for I do not intend to let any eyes but mine ever even peep into this book. Oh how much I have to tell you after allowing all this time to elapse; but it has not been for want of inclination, for I have often longed for you. And when I tell you that it is now after twelve o'clock you may know that I am anxious to communicate to you many things when I begin this time of night to write, when I am going to get up so early in the morning too, to ride to the farm on horseback.

... Dear friend, will you excuse me from beginning this tonight as it is now past One o'clock and I am terribly sleepy.

My principal object in beginning this tonight was to be enabled to carry on my train of thought about that Dear, dear fellow; which I have been encouraging today by reading all of his delightful letters to Addy.

Oh how I did wish they were mine.

If they were I flatter myself they would have been more and longer.

I know he writes me as long and frequently as possible, and I think he thinks of me sometimes which helps (?) him in writing, and I know he writes as long as his time will allow; but he has his darling hands and mind so fully occupied he has not time for much letter writing to any particular person, for he has so many to write to.

But I feel so grateful for being able to see so many of his most interesting letters.

When he writes to Addy he writes so much about himself it keeps my mind tolerably at ease about him.

Oh how I did long to open my desk and read and re-read the few favors I have of his, and to gaze on that most handsome face. But my honor prevented.

I must now say good-night.

July 24th.

Well, I have let a whole three days pass and have not been able to gratify myself by writing anything. ... Aunt E. [Albert's mother] had a delightful time. She went direct to Suffolk where she hoped to meet her noble Son. Oh the dear fellow, how I wish it had been me.

But alas, for her disappointment, he had been there the day before, but was expected back the next week, so she waited there until he came; then went on with the dearest fellow to his particular friend Mr. Gregory. Oh what a kind fellow and how he does appreciate the dear fellow. But no one could do so more than he deserved. He offered him 1st Lieutenant in a company he had been elected in and was going to take a lower position himself, but of course that would not be heard of. But he got and accepted 2nd Lieutenant in the same company; so they were together some time, and are now. But at first, while the company was being organized, Mr. G. insisted upon his staying with him. So Aunt E. went there, where she staid [sic] some two weeks, helping to make their uniforms. She then went to [Weldon] with the dearest fellow. There Cousin Lea [welcomed her]. She wended her way homeward with him, stopping at different places. The darling had to camp at Weldon and expected to remain there until August; but there is no telling: hardly any moment where the dearest is, for now he expects to go to Manassas junction, where he has longed to be ever since he left it. Why? -- because it is the most dangerous place. He is now among all his friends that are left from that large battle which his company just did get too late to have a hand in the glorious victor. If his precious life could be insured I would be sorry that he had not an opportunity to distinguish himself again; but everything happens for the best. Oh what a glorious idea I have in mind! It is to go to Virginia and be nurse for the wounded, for in that way I could be of use to somebody. But alas, I have heard through the papers that nurses are not wanted.

I had to put this down in great haste the other night, as the light was in Mother's eyes, and woke her, and I fear such will be the case tonight. Oh would that I had a room to myself; I would spend half the night in this delightful manner. ...

Chapter 3

January-December, 1861:
Raphael's Memoirs, Major, C.S.A.

Active in politics and successful in business and profession, Raphael Jacob Moses was decidedly in favor of secession of the Southern "Slave" States as the balance of power in Congress began to favor the "Free" States as the new states were admitted into the Union. When the War broke out in April 1861, Moses was in Virginia on business. Almost 50 years old at the time, he sought out his friend, Brigadier General Robert Toombs, a former United States Senator and a powerful and influential Georgia politician. Initially refusing the position of Commissary Officer of Toombs' Brigade, Moses was prevailed upon by another friend and powerful Georgia politician, Howell Cobb, the former Secretary of the Treasury in the administration of President Buchanan and a Brigadier General in the Confederate Army, who persuaded him to accept the position. Moses, in his memoirs, recorded that Howell Cobb stated:

It was a matter of public duty. He [Cobb] said it was a place hard to fill, with a competent man, and he was sure that I could do more good in that position than any other.

Thus began four years of military service in the Confederate Army, four years of arduous field service, especially for a man in his fifties, which saw him in contact with most of the most recognized and prominent soldiers of the Confederacy. Initially serving as Commissary Officer of Toombs' Brigade, he was soon advanced to Commissary Officer of General D.R. Jones' Division. Subsequently, he was promoted to Chief Commissary Officer of General James Longstreet's Corps in July 1862.

From Moses' memoirs:

My position at headquarters threw me in contact with all the principal officers of the army – Hood, Wilcox, Pickett, [Stuart], Walker, etc. I never saw much of Beauregard. He was always hedged in by orderlies, guards, red tape, etc. I remember once he sent an order to Gen. Walker at Fairfax Court House, to reconnoitre the enemy and make "An ostentatious display." Walker, who was very profane, after a volley of oaths said "Ostentatious display." I suppose he wants me to wear a red felt, stand on my head in the saddle and open my legs like an inverted compass. Wouldn't that be an ostentatious display? Walker was a Georgian, killed near Atlanta, and proverbial for his reckless bravery. Pickett was a very dashing officer, and led the celebrated and fatal charge at Gettysburg. He was very foppish in his dress and wore his hair in long ringlets. He was what would be called a dapper little fellow but brave as they every make men.

Hood as Brigadier of the Texas Brigade won a great deal of distinction. He was one of the best Brigadiers and poorest commanders in the army.

Jeb [Stuart] was a splendid Calvary Officer, but oh, how frivolous! He carried a banjo player with him wherever he went, and his favorite pastime when not dancing with the girls was to have his banjo player thrum and sing, "Come, jine the Cavalry." He entered Winchester once with his staff and his band playing "See the conquering hero comes." He was as vain and frivolous as he was brave and dashing, a splendid horseman and "a jolly good fellow." How different he was to General Lee. The latter was a plain, splendid looking, courteous gentleman, with such wonderful self control that no one ever knew when he was overwhelmed with anxiety, in victory and defeat the same, unruffled exterior, kind to his men and kind to animals. ...

In my army intercourse, I saw General Lee almost daily, while in Virginia, for his headquarters were very near General Longstreet's always. I think he relied very much on Longstreet, who was a great soldier, a very determined and fearless fighter. He, Longstreet, had a high opinion of [Toombs], and I heard him say that if [Toombs] had been educated at West Point, where he would have learned self-control, he would have been as distinguished as a soldier as he was as a civilian, but his insubordination ruined him as an officer. Longstreet once ordered [Toombs], after a hard day's march, to send a detail of several men to guard a bridge. [Toombs] replied his men were tired and worn out, and that they could guard the bridge with an old woman and a broomstick. He didn't send the guard, and Longstreet arrested him and kept him under arrest for about six weeks. They were always friendly afterwards, and [Toombs] knew better than to disobey Longstreet after that. ...

Among others on General Longstreet's staff were Gen. Sorrel of Savannah; Osman LaTrobe, of Baltimore, a son of Mayor LaTrobe. He was also a very gallant man and ardent Confederate; Col. Fairfax, of the old Virginia Fairfaxes. Fond of his bottle, his Bible and his baths, always in front when danger pressed, very much given to show, a fine looking fellow, and nothing pleased him better when the army arrived at a new place than to be mistaken for General Longstreet, and this happened on more than one occasion. He carried all through the campaign a bath tub in the shape of a tin hat, and a chest supplied with all sorts of liquors. He took a bath and five or six nips (drinks) before breakfast. He always had changing in his tent a linen housewife or sack with two pockets, in one he kept his bottle, in the other his Bible.

Sunday was his maudlin day. He would lay down with his bottle and his Bible beside him. One Sunday when Tam O'Shanta like he was "o'er all the ills of life victorious," I wrote on two sheets of paper: On one --

This in a moment brings me to an end, on another: While this informs me I shall never die.

I fixed the first to the bottle and put the second between the scriptural Leaves. When Fairfax awoke he read them and said, "Moses, by the Lord!"

On another occasion in East Tennessee we stopped at Greenville, and I had my headquarters in the Capitol law library of Andrew Johnson, afterwards President of the United States, within sight of his office which, by the way, was in one of the side rooms of the Tavern. We were in sight of the little shop, still standing where Andy, as the Tennesseans called him, had his tailor shop.

After leaving Greenville we went to Morristown, about fifteen miles, and while there I happened to mention a heavy box in Johnson's library, which was nailed up. Fairfax immediately "snuffed, not tyranny but whisky, in the tainted air," and exclaimed, "By George! Moses, why didn't you tell me before we left? Old Andy was very fond of his 'nips," and I'll bet that box was full of good old rye whisky, and I mean to have it." He immediately got a detail of soldiers and a wagon, and had the box brought to camp. When it arrived, Fairfax's eyes glistened with anxious expectation, soon followed by despondency, as on opening the box it contained, instead of old liquor, nothing but Andy Johnson's old letters and private papers. ...

Chapter 4

January-December, 1861: R.J. Moses, Midshipman, C.S.N.

Raphael J. Moses, Jr., the youngest son of Major Moses, entered the United States Naval Academy, with fellow new midshipmen in September 1860, with the Class of 1864. At the time, young Moses was 15 years, 9 months. Most of his fellow classmates were also mere teenagers. The records from the Naval Academy reveal the outgoing personality of this young acting Midshipman which was to be the hallmark of his Naval career for almost five more years.

The records of the United States Naval Academy indicate appointment from the 3rd Georgia Congressional Districts. His classmates came from all the States and the Territories.

ROLL OF CONDUCT
(DEMERIT LIST)
R.J. MOSES

1860
Oct 16 - Throwing Spitballs	4 Demerits
Nov 14 - Laughing at Exercise	2 Demerits
Nov 27 - Disorderly at Drill	4 Demerits
Dec 17 - Skylarking [Frolicking] at Mess	2 Demerits
Dec 21 - Remaining in Study Room	
After Drum for Dinner	2 Demerits

<u>1861</u>

Jan 16 - Musket Out of Order 2 Demerits

Jan 23 - Noisy in Study Room 4 Demerits

Resigned When Georgia Seceded from the Union.

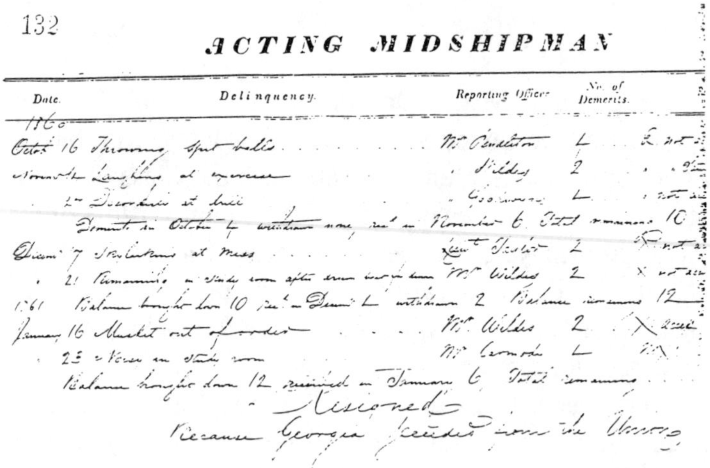

132

ACTING MIDSHIPMAN

Date.	Delinquency.	Reporting Officer	No. of Demerits.
1860			
Octr 16	Throwing spit balls	Mr Pendleton	4
Novemr	Laughing at exercise	" Wilder	2
" 2	Disorderly at drill	"	4
	Demerits in October 4 withdrawn none, recd in November 6. Total remaining 10		
Decemr 7	Skylarking at mess	Lieut Taylor	2
" 21	Remaining in study room after	Mr Wilder	2
1861	Balance brought down 10 recd in Decemr 4 withdrawn 2 Balance remaining 12		
January 16	Musket out of order	Mr Wilder	2
" 23	Noisy in study room	Mr	4
	Balance brought down 12 received in January 6 Total remaining		

Resigned

Because Georgia seceded from the Union

Records of the United States Naval Academy

Admitted: September 27, 1860-Class of 1864

Age: 15 years, 9 months

Departed: January 23, 1861

Resigned because Georgia seceded from the Union

On July 8, 1861, Raphael was appointed Acting Midshipman, Confederate States Navy. The adventures of this teenager would excite anyone, starting with the preceding at the United States Naval Academy. More was to happen. The Official Records of the Civil War (Navy), Flag Officer Tattnal, CSN, in his official report of a Naval battle aboard the CSS Savannah (Nov. 1861), stated: "Several excellent shots were made by Midshipman R.J. Moses, commanding the after-gun." Raphael Moses, Jr., rose to the rank of Master, In Line of Promotion, in the Confederate States Navy.

Moses' naval service record reveals: "On board the CSS "Savannah," including the Battle of Port Royal, S.C., November 7, 1861; CSS "Arctic," Wilmington, North Carolina, 1862." Extracted from a letter Raphael Moses, Jr., wrote in 1906:

...In Georgia I was in the Battle of Port Royal under Commodore Tattnel and then went to Wilmington, N.Car., where the Yellow Fever broke out and I was left the Senior Naval Officer. I had the good fortune to spy a ship on Frying Pan Shoals just below the mouth of the Cape Fear River. She was loaded with sale and deserted [by] all her crew but one having been drowned in attempting to land. We saved the survivor and brought the ship safely to Port, after having to jettison a very little of her cargo. To my surprise, I shortly afterwards received form the prize court $3000.00 in gold and my share of the prize money...

Chapter 5

July-August, 1861:
Albert's Journal and Letters, Lt., C.S.A.

[Albert's journal:]
My friend Nat Gregory wrote me offering me a second Lieutenancy in a company then being gathered up in his county -- and to which I am now attached. I accepted his offer -- & having been duly elected, I left Sewell's Point intending to stop over one train in Suffolk, but when I arrived at Suffolk I found Father and Mother there -- much to my surprise. ...

[From Albert's letter to Julia:]
You need not entertain [any fears] on the effects of the temptations of Camp life on me, for my love for that darling girl is a strict guardian over me and I never think of being led astray by any of the temptations that surround me. I feel that it is a duty that I owe to her as well as to myself that I should preserve a spotless moral character and distinguish myself as much as possible.

[From his journal:]
On the morning of July 23rd we left Richmond for Manassas Junction -- but when we left Richmond we had no idea that the day was so 'big with the fate of' the Southern

Confederacy. Our first intelligence of the fight [the Battle at
Bull Run] was at Gordonsville where a dispatch was received
saying 'We are sending them to Hell by Squads.' ...

Our men -- many of whom had double quicked for 6
to 12 miles to the battle field -- were completely exhausted
and lying down, where they stood after they made their first
halt from the little field slept until early morning when they
woke to behold -- the Day after the Battle.

What pen can describe, what inexperienced
imagination can picture the scenes that then met they eye.
Amid the booming of cannon, the sharp, shrill whistling of
bullets, the dead and Dying and the thousand excitements that
one finds on the field of action we do not feel all the attendant
Horror, but the "Day after the battle' when the mind is cool &
under the effect of that inevitable reaction -- which will always
follow a sever excitement -- then it is that the mind becomes
shocked with the horrors of war. At and near the Head
Quarters you see hundreds of wounded men -- men wounded
in all places -- some in the head -- some in the feet and in fact
there is no part of the body where someone was not wounded
-- the dead lying in one place and another -- Car after Car full
of wounded men passed by along the RR and to add to the
horror of the scene, it was pouring rain. Men who had
marched some distance and compelled to leave everything
except arms and ammunition were compelled to lay out and
walk about in the rain and without a tent to shelter them.

Visiting the Hospital I saw piles of arms and legs --
laying about -- just as you have seen rags and papers laying
about a floor where a little child has been playing.

I saw men who had died & no one knew that they
were dead. On one side you would see a dying man, on the
other side one almost in as bad a state between those two a
man who had breathed out his last -- without a kind hand or

a pitying heart to sympathize with him. I do not mean to attach blame to the nurses, for they certainly did all they could -- but there were more than they could attend to. On the Battle field hundreds of dead and unburied bodies lay in every direction. Guns, Knapsacks, Cap boxes, Cartridge boxes, crackers -- & in short every thing that a soldier carried lay scattered all over the field for a week after the most awful stench prevailed for 6 or 7 miles around the battle field. Not infrequently men -- hundreds of them -- were found in the woods where they had been borne away -- wounded -- in the thickest of the fight -- then in these bushes -- without a hand or heart near them, these men have died. ...

As will be seen I am relating what occurred in July -- these records are not made entirely from memory but from notes.

[August 24th]

Our Brigade, under Genl J.A. Early, is now in the right wing of the army. ...

[September]

The eating was certainly pleasant -- in fact it is almost curious to notice, how glad done is to meet with an old friend in times like these. ...

Mason's hill is a beautiful place, it is call Mason's hill because it is owned by Capt. Mason, Bro. of Senator Mason, formerly the place was unknown except as a family residence, but since the war commenced, the place was occupied by Federal pickets -- subsequently there were driven out by the Confederates, who now hold the position. The hill is about 500 feet above the level of the sea and commands a

magnificent view of about the most lovely country I have ever
seen for miles around -- as far as the eye can reach the country
is broken -- large hills & here and there.

Chapter 6

August-September, 1861:
Eliza's Diary

August 23rd [1861]

Oh my, what time has elapsed since you have been opened by me; for various reason: and to see this blot! It got here by my shutting my book in great haste for fear of some one's finding me out. And now I am writing while Mother sleeps and ma making Addy keep watch for me; so must enter all that I have to say in the smallest place possible. My hopes with regards going to Virginia were raised to the highest pitch. Mrs. Carrs, to comply with Brother M's request, consented to take Min. and myself with her. Mother partly consented to our going. She expected to go soon, so we made our clothes in a great hurry; when, lo, a letter from Aunt Anna, in reply to Mother's asking about our coming there; (she is in Richmond), she urged her so strongly not to let us come that Mother has positively refused to let us do so.

But I still have some shadow of hope, for Mrs. Carrs has not gone yet and there is no knowing what may turn up in our favor.

Oh what would I give to be at Culpepper hospital now, for the dear fellow is there by now: for in a letter from Uncle R.[Raphael J. Moses], who is now a Major, and is at Manassas, says he left for Culpepper; where he, and the dear fellow also, thinks we are. How I wish we could be; and, were it not for the pride of some people, we would be. But I live in hope if I dye [sic] in despair.

The dearest one on earth to me was well and enjoying himself when he last wrote.

A valise of things were sent to him last Monday. I know the fine fellow will be glad to get it. How I did want to put something, anything, in it, but I dared not do it. But he has so many that love him, that can send him things, that I dont think he will miss my attentions much. But what pleasure it would afford me to be able to do so!

I hope by this time the dear fellow is relieved from his double duty, by Mr. Gregory's return; for he has been sick: consequently his duties devolve on the dear fellow.

Aug. 27th.

I had to close this in haste again and this blot is the result, so I will give up trying to have a neat book.

But before going further, I must correct a mistake I made about the dear fellow: I said he expected to go to Culpepper; but I made a mistake; it is Fairfax Court House. But Cousin Esther got a letter from him yesterday in which he says he does not know whether he will go next. He is still near Manassas: within seven miles, I believe.

Brother M, Aunt E. and Aunt Julia, all three got letters from him yesterday.

Brother M. read part of his to us; but most of it was about business. What he did read was about pecuniary affairs. I wish he had not read it aloud; but glad I heard it.

I do feel so sorry for him; to think of such a kind-hearted, generous fellow as he is; not being able to benefit himself or anyone else for the want of money, unless going in debt; as he has not received a cent of pay since he has been away: and it has been a long, very long four months to me.

But he, I am glad to hear, does not think so. But he changes about so much that I think that is the principal reason his time slips away so fast. But I am truly glad it does, for then he must be enjoying himself.

I hope he does not think of me; that is, if it is best he should not; but I never can help thinking of him all day and dreaming of him at night. Oh that some of my dreams about the dear fellow could come true! I do long to see him so much. Would that these dreadful times could cease; for I can only hear of the poor fellows suffering, but be of no benefit to any of them: for Mother has positively refused to let us go to any hospital. I heard the dear fellow said he was sorry that Mother would not let us come.

Is it because he had the same hope that I had? Oh that I could tell. If such is the case, the disappointment could not have been greater to him than to me. Would that I could look into the inmost depths of his heart just about now; for if they are the same, now, they are very apt to remain so: for I am sure I have not done the slightest trifle to continue his love for me. I want to try if absence can lessen it; but I hardly think it can. But if it does not there will be so much more happiness for me and, I hope, for him.

Chapter 7

September, 1861-January, 1862: Albert's Journal

From here a view of the Potomac -- and of the city of Washington -- from the summit of the hill you can have an elegant view of the whole country on every side, sometimes the eye rests on a tremendous hill -- at others on empty fields, but the whole country is hill and dale.

The Capitol in Washington is very easily seen and very plainly with the naked eye -- with an opera glass one can see the windows in the capitol and in a steeple in Alexandria -- at one point the Potomac is seen -- appearing to be about 2 miles wide -- this seeming as it does to lie between two mountains looks very beautiful.

Sept. 15th.

Interruptions are I think almost too numerous in this kind of life -- for a person to hope to make a journal of this sort very complete -- many scenes which fascinate the heart and mind in actual life -- we cannot portray with the pen on account of many interruptions -- and everything been convenient I think I might have recorded some pleasant events -- for I enjoyed my trip to Mason's Hill exceedingly. ...

[September 17th]

It is certainly strange to think how much a good hard rain adds to one's inclination to write, especially if he is -- like myself -- situated so that he can have no access to the charming society of women -- shut up in a 10 foot square tent, with nobody but a fellow Lt -- the rain falling in heavy drops upon the canvas -- acts as a sentinel by the door, & the sound seems to say what a splendid time for writing. If the rain continues, I feel like continuing my writing, but as soon as it ceases, I feel like following its example. There is yet another thought which never fails to arise in my mind when a rainy afternoon sets in. It is the thought of Home "sweet home." The image of loved ones will arise. A beloved Mother and sister sitting around a genial fire sewing some clothes of some member of the family -- or a Bro in my room, both of us smoking a "Cuba Six" sitting by a bright lightwood fire -- wrapt in revery or puffing away cutting out a horse blanket -- making [illegible] of martingales -- or some other [illegible] for our saddle horses or perhaps discussing the merits of some trotting horse -- or Saddle horse -- comparing them to his "Ria" or my "Topsy" or "Madge." Or Father driving up with old Kate in his buggy, drenched. These are scenes which I once enjoyed -- & now often rise before my mind's eye. And often I long to enjoy them again but when shall it be. Echo answers, then.

How I would like now to be seated in Cousin Julia's room, having a good nice little chat with her. She is certainly one of the finest ladies I ever knew and her intelligence is far greater than I have ever had the pleasure of enjoying in a lady's company. She has a very considerable knowledge of human nature, is quite fond of the profound and deep. Nothing delights her more than a study of Nature as developed in Nature's beings. She has an even temper, is remarkable for her amiability -- which is perhaps excelled only by the Generosity of her nature. She forms no friendships upon an hour's acquaintance -- but her affection or friendship is grounded on the true merit of the friend -- thus I would consider it a compliment to be considered by her as a friend -- her sympathies are great, and she well knows how to bestow them. Or I would like to be at Moise's with all those beloved cousins sitting in the parlor by the window playing backgammon with [illegible] or Addy -- or sitting on the sofa at home talking to Minnie. There is of course one pleasure that I would prefer to all these, but that one I will not mention here -- it is always in my heart's most anxious anticipations & need not be recorded -- thoughts like those I have written of this evening always arise -- either when all is quiet and I have just retired, or on a rainy afternoon like this, but on all such occasions the thought of that being so especially dear to me is most prominent & as I think of her I cannot help uttering to myself the constant wish of my heart 'God bless her.'

September 21, 1861.

Last night I was officer of the guard and the night was like this -- one of those lovely moonlight nights, when one is almost insensibly borne back to home and its tender recollections. How often on just such a night as this have I sat on the front porch at home either sitting on the steps laying my head in some of the girls laps or talking with Father and Major -- while we puffed away on some fine sigars [sic].

Again on such a night I have been seated on the front steps at Aunt Anna's with Lize -- Minnie & Addy enjoying myself very much. It is scenes like these that Recollections of dear Lize arise before me. ... For how many of the finest moments of my life am I indebted to this [illegible] young being. She little knows how much I prize them or how often in this stern life I [illegible] them.

Time but develops to be the more perfect [illegible] of her character. Some -- I know not what -- [illegible] I call it instinct -- taught me to single [illegible] from the group -- and love her more than the [illegible] -- when I was but 14 years of age -- four years [illegible] now elapsed & the interval has but strengthened my affection and made it of a more manly character -- from time to time my love for this [illegible] young being has been enhanced -- until now I feel that a reciprocation of that feeling is thoroughly indispensable to my happiness -- and I have learned to prize each day and regard it as [illegible] such a dimunition of the period that must elapse before my happiness is complete.

I have now set out in the world so to speak with my mind firmly set on as speedy a marriage as possible -- my desire to accomplish this as [illegible] after my maturity as possible makes me follow up every undertaking with redoubled zeal -- a pecuniary independence -- a spotless moral character -- and an unlimited regard for the views and feelings of Eliza are the prime objects ever present to my mind & I earnestly pray God that I may never in act or word forfeit my claim upon her affections. I regard it as most fortunate, that I have formed the attachment before leaving home, for situated as I am, with plenty of money in the Army and any number of temptations -- a warm and impetuous disposition -- I feel assured that I might have gone astray were it not for the moral restraint -- but now I never indulge in any immoralities because I feel it due to her to keep my character spotless.

I regret exceedingly that there is so much opposition on the part of my parents, but I trust to God that time may do away with this opposition and that when they see that I -- having arrived at maturity am determined on the marriage they will withhold all opposition.

October 5th.
Gregory and myself bought a very nice little horse that
we call Nic. He is a genuine camp horse & exactly one of the
kind that will stand this life admirably -- he is short-coupled --
heavy built -- and very easily kept. I gave $135 for the horse
and $10 for the saddle and bridle. I purchased the horse on
Sunday and on Wednesday night at 9 A.M. [September 25]
orders came for us to prepare 3 days rations -- to send our
sick and baggage back towards Manassas, while we would
move forward as far as Gangster's X Roads -- to meet the
enemy at 3 A.M. the next day.

... So whenever we were halted to rest -- each man
thought it was a final halt -- at one time I was walking along
with my thoughts somewhere else -- and of a sudden I found
myself alongside the company forth in front of my own -- so
I sat down to wait for it & then found out the real state of
fatigue under which the Regt. was laboring. Instead of being
in files 4 deep and marching 16 inches apart they were
scattered about marching in squads of 4 and 6 scattered from
30 to 40 inches apart -- many a one just marching along by
himself. Never wars dawning day hailed with more pleasure
than when it found us at Accotink.

... The whole place [Mrs. Fitzhugh's place, where the
Regiment, having missed the battle, was placed on picket
duty] was very beautiful & reminded me very much of home.
The place is on a high hill and has been under the highest
horticultural attention. Mr. Fitzhugh who married a sister of
Mrs. Gen'l Lee. He died in 1833 & left his widow -- without
issue -- leaving her 17000 acres of land and plenty of money,
but he liberated by his will in 1850, 400 salves. Many of them

I learned settled in Washington and a great many went to New York and Phila. Those who have been heard from have not fared so well as those who were slaves.

I had long intended, for future reference to write an ordinary comment upon the battle of July 21st [at Manassas] after the battle was over -- the details of which I have given elsewhere -- Genls Johnston, Beauregard & Davis met in counsil [sic] & I am fully satisfied that they -- composing probably as fine a military convention as could be assembled -- were fully competent to consider the facts that the past and the present had revealed & decide upon the best as well as the most prudent judicial & politic movement to be made. They decided to retain the old defensive position and not to advance on the enemy's intrenchments. All seemed at the time to be fully satisfied with the Decisions -- but naturally many persons grew dissatisfied & said that Beauregard ought to have followed up the success, even to Washington.

While these opinions were mostly advanced by Newspaper Genls. -- yet for the satisfaction of my own future meditations -- I will annex a few remarks on the matter.

Let us notice the matter in detail & see what would have been the result of such action -- the enemy numbered over 60,000 -- our own forces did not exceed 30,000 -- 15,000 only of them were engaged, the remaining 10,000 [sic] being for the most part inefficient as far as drill was concerned were held as a reserve. ...

Much blame has been attached by many parties to the person or persons who prevented an advance of our forces upon Washington immediately after the battle of Manassas July 21st. They say it was just the time to have struck a death blow to the cause of Yankeedom and to have reinspired our forces. While such is the opinion of a great many, yet it is far from being an universal one -- Altho' this sentiment is entertained yet the People know not upon whom to give vent to their wrath. Rumor at one time says that in Council Beauregard & Johnston were in favor of advancing on W. while the president -- Jeff Davis -- overruled them, and the plan was abandoned. Other Rumors say the Davis & Johnston both opposed the advance -- and Beauregard alone advocated it. And as Genl Beauregard's report has not yet appeared we know not who was in favor and who against the advance -- but the man is not the question of most importance.

The question is, would it have been proper or politic to have followed up our success at that time.

I think not -- And while I express my opinion I must give my reasons for entertaining it. In the first place we were naturally ignorant of the extent of the panic which had struck them. No one entertained the slightest idea of their retreating father than Alexandria, & all felt fully assured that they would stop in Washington.

Their force was vastly superior in numbers to ours. Their conveniences and facilities for travelling likewise. Had we then followed them up -- we would have found ourselves in front of the Enemy's intrenchments on Monday or Tuesday or more probably Wednesday, by which time a reaction would have taken place and with a force of 25,000 men at the very most. These men then, worn out with marching & fighting upon a piece of land with which they were entirely unacquainted would have had to face more than three times their number -- who would have been behind their intrenchments & defending their Capital -- and this the very thing which made our men fight so valiantly -- Defense of their homes -- would now actuate them, while we would be the aggressive force -- and owing to the small number of troops we would have had there we would have rendered ourselves liable to be cut off -- and thus hemmed in would necessarily have fallen victims to our Enemy's [sic] and by our own imprudence lost all the honors which but a few days previous we had gained.

Nov. 2nd.

Memory in its expanse over more than 18 years, does not carry me back to such a scene as I have witnessed since 4 o'clock yesterday afternoon. And the difficulty of describing it is fully commensurate with the greatness of the storm that has prevailed since yesterday afternoon without intermission.

About 4 o'clock I went over to Adjutant Young's tent and took a fine drink of whiskey. After that I went to Dress parade, and returned with the Adjutant who had quite an assemblage in his tent. Sgts -- Lts -- Capts -- Maj & Col. as well as Sgt Maj & Col's orderly.

We all proceeded to enjoy his hospitality by drinking his liquor & I in an unwary moment yielded to an invitation to try some fine domestic wine. I drank it off but not long afterwards I knew my fate was sealed & I was bound to be tight for I had mixed my liquor -- having taken whiskey first & then wine, which is something I cannot stand, and in a very short time I was a sight as I ever was in my life -- but it is the first time I have been really drunk since Nov. 1859.

I went to bed about 10 o'clock and woke up pretty sober, about midnight and as I lay in bed the wind was howling around & the tents fairly groaned under its strains. In fact one of the most severe storms that I have ever witnessed was then raging, the rain was fairly driven thro the tents, and it was all we could do by having our pins fairly secured to keep our tent from blowing over. However in this respect we

were more fortunate than many others. I think at least a
hundred tents must have been blown down in the Regt around
an [sic] in sight of us. The sight was really ridiculous. You
might look out and you would see a tent dashed to the ground
and the former inmates running across to some other tent,
maybe standing out with their oil-cloths over their heads. The
Adjutant's tent blew down, and one could not help laughing
heartily to look at the scene. On one side was the tent blown
down, on the other side was a bedstead, a box of papers, and
three mulets of liquor laying out in the rain. In another place
was a fine new cloth cap with gold lace on it, squashed in the
mud. The Col's tent was gone, and every thing of his was
laying exposed to the weather. As for my own part, I woke
early in the morning and soon saw that Home was the best
place for a man. ...

After breakfast I laid down and covering myself with
my overcoat, I remained thus, wrapt in thoughts of home and
loved ones until nearly 12 o'clock today when I resolved to get
up and write some in my journal.

The subject of my thoughts was the being who is ever
first in my mind.

The storm rages even now with unabated fury, and
while I listened to its ragings -- thoughts as to the fate of
Lincoln's fleet arise in my mind. I opine that they will suffer
much especially the blockading Squadrons which have no
ports but Southern ports to enter.

[Albert's letter to Lize, referring to Alice Moses:]
While she is rather peculiar -- or I may say eccentric
about some things -- yet when one knows her she has a
character that commands much admiration. No man could
have a higher complement paid to him as a man than to have

Alice's love -- for she will not, and in fact cannot love a man who has anything mean or unmanly about him. She is a woman of a very cold disposition. Although she may think highly of a person -- yet her demonstrations are very few and scarce. As a woman of very cold Disposition -- she gives a very striking illustration of one of the great peculiarities of Nature, namely -- when a man succeeds in gain the affection of a coldly disposed woman -- he has gained an affection, the Depth and strength of which is rarely equalled.

Now although Alice is remarkably cold in her nature, yet, a woman never loved a man with more warmth & fervor than she does her Bro. She is rather a good judge of human nature and a very appreciative nature. You cannot flatter her with words but you may by actions & delicate attentions.

If you will notice her favorite wants & see them attended to, modestly, and always so as to relieve her from any imminent obligation, you can make one step towards gaining her esteem. For instance she is passionately fond of horseback riding -- Well if you will take a horse to her school room & ask her to ride home with you, she will not only take pleasure in riding home with you, but will appreciate the attention -- although you may not even hear her mention it. Yet if you were to present her with a Side-Saddle or a horse or anything of that sort that placed her under obligation to you she would feel offended. And although she might endeavor from regard for your feelings to prevent saying anything about it, yet she would think you a fool and wish she hadn't ever know you.

... The longer you know her and the more minutely you notice her in all her bearings the more you find to Love & Admire. But if you want to gain her esteem, you must be ever on the "Qui Vive," and never be guilty of any unmanly act.

Really, I don't think that a man could undertake

anything which would require half so much care attention and particularity, as a Courtship with her. If it were not blasphemous, I would say that God had erred when he made her a woman -- I wish she were a man -- And I would give anything to see her well married. No ordinary man can marry her. But I think I have written quite enough on this subject.

[From Albert's journal:]
I have this afternoon while Discussing women and Courtship with Dr. Hicks -- who by the bye is a very Scientific man -- discovered a very grave mistake that I have made -- that is in mentioning Lize's name in connection with mine in my letters home to Cousin Julia & other parties. I know feel fully aware that if she could write to me she would request me not to do so, & I have determined to stop it forthwith, and I am resolved now that I won't mention her in any of my letters or remarks unless to send my love or something of that kind, for I know now it is wrong. While I acknowledge that I have erred in that respect up to this time, yet I think it due to myself to state that I think the circumstances under which I left home palliate in a degree the extent of the error, for every one then expressed the, or entertained the belief that I would soon forget her -- And I felt it Due to myself that I should by mentioning her keep them fully aware that I had not forgotten her. And now I close this subject in this book, unless some special event calls on me to recur to it & mention it again.

November the sixteenth is here -- and I am now in a little shanty -- Not exactly a cabin which we have recently had constructed. A strong oak wood fire burns healthily in the rock & log chimney and while the wind howls around the corners -- every now and then breaking out with fresh strength -- making a genuine howl.

The clear, calm light of a full moon sheds itself over everything -- and the feelings of us all make certain the auguries of the wild goose's flight to the South.

Yes, it is very cold outside -- the wind is biting but within things wear a different aspect the glowing fire -- by its reflections from the rock back of the chimney -- warms ever thing inside the shanty -- and thus it has been a pleasant night to us. ...

Major Christie & Adjt Young came around after we had finished a late supper and we all sat and chatted away until a late hour when Young went off to take a hand at Bluff with the Col & the Maj went over to bed. Carrington has gone to bed and Gregory is writing a letter.

While these things have taken place I sat and gazed in the apparently endless depths of the fire & my mind has been wandering off to scenes that are past and gone. ...

What propensities of thought bringing has a good, cheerful looking fire, for an hour past I have sat and looked into it & thoughts & remembrances of the past connect themselves as naturally as Does the ash follow the embers. ...

I had a long intended - for future reference to write an ordinary comment upon the battle [of Manassas]. ...

In a country where the Democratic form of government exists -- the country is governed --

'By the passions and prejudices of the great unwashed, played upon by political Demagogues for personal ends.' ...

[January 1862]

I had a very pleasant time Christmas having invited some 15 or 20 of he officers as well as Moultrie Moses from the 2nd Geo Reg to dine with me on that Day.

We had quite a soldierly dinner but as the Liquor was both plentiful and good -- anecdotes, songs and speeches -- as well as any number of songs and toasts, and any quantity of laughter prevailed, I don't know when I have enjoyed anything so much in a very long time. Some one or two of the fellows knocked under towards the last. Moultrie remained all night with me and as he was a warm friend and an old acquaintance it was very pleasant to have him to talk over old times with.

And how I wish I could spend the night of Christmas 1861, as I spent the same of 1860. Vividly dim my memory brings back that night and all its attendance happenings -- but I am happy to say that I have the good fortune -- unlike many other to be able to say that I was not more happy then than I am now, the same fountain of happiness which existed then, exists now, only the lapse of time, and its attendant revelations, have rendered it more dear -- if possible -- than it formerly was. It is certainly one of the greatest enjoyments of life to look back on these by gone times.

Dear Lize:

Having availed myself of your intimated permission to read your note to Minnie, I cannot deliver it without giving you in brief, my views upon the position she has assumed, and at least endeavoring to vindicate what I cannot but consider a wise move.

Whether Minnie will derive any material benefit from the change or not, -- I cannot say -- time must determine that. With regards to Yr Brother's desire to have the family together, I can only say this -- in the first place, a separation is necessary, as I will after a while show you, and "Necessity knows no Law." In the second place, there is a vast difference between the division of yr family as it now exists, and as it would have been had yr Brother accepted the proposition that was made for himself and Alice and yr Mother to board, and you 3 be divided between families.

Had that proposition been carried into effect, you would have been divided into 3 branches and your whole family would have been partitioned off (so to speak) thus destroying that harmony and unanimity that is so essential to yr happiness.

But how is it now? Yr family are all together except one, the separation of whom adds to, instead of detracting from, the harmony of yr family. That is a painful point for me to touch upon, dear Lize, but that candor which I have always possessed, demands it. I believe you know it to be a fact.

'Facts are stubborn things' and I will now endeavor to show you how and why it is necessary for yr family to be separated, how it is a fact that such separation adds to the harmony of yr family, and last but not least, the advantages that must accrue from it.

With regard to the independence which you seem to long for so, I can only refer you to the old adage, but true; 'Whatever is, is right.' A woman, my dear Lize, was never intended to be independent. An All-wise Creator has made her dependent upon man, has made man so that he feels a pride in having Woman dependent on him.

You should not, then, murmur against the decrees of Heaven. If God has made you dependent, he has made those [men] feel no higher or greater happiness than a knowledge of yr dependence upon them.

Hd. Qtrs. Co. I. 23rd N.C. Reg
Dec 18th 1861.

Dear Cousin Julia:

The fellows have just left here and as peace and quiet are, comparatively speaking, restored, in my humble domicile, let's have a little chat. Que dites vous?

We only got back from picket yesterday and today we have all appropriated to getting used to houses again. There is certainly a very varied monotony, or, to express myself more clearly, a monotonous variety in this kind of life. Tonight I am sitting by a good fire, in a comfortable log cabin, writing some friend a letter; tomorrow night at this time I have spread my blanket on the ground, and, lying down before the camp fire, which no covering but the Heavens, am musing of the Past, Present, and Future. ...

Our last trip was, however, to me a very pleasant one. Having taken 'Charley O'Malley' along to read, and in addition to that, I had the pleasure of making the acquaintance of a very interesting Yankee young lady, who lives about half a mile from our outpost.

I went over rather early in the morning, having learned from one of the cavalrymen who was with me that she was as lively as a cricket, I found her just clearing away breakfast table, and, having chatted away for a few moments, I requested that I should be allowed to ignore all ceremony and proceed at once to wash dishes for her. Would you believe it? Well, it is actually so, and there I was, washing dishes, with my sword hanging by my side, for a young lady, about 16 years old, beautiful, large blue eyes, Auburn hair, and a fair complexion, with an alacrity and gaiety about her every word and action, that completely baffles description, and, worst of all, I had never seen her more than five minutes. I could not help feeling a little amused, when I said to her, 'I wonder what

the folks at home would say if they knew what I was doing?'
And proceeded to make myself perfectly at home, related to
Miss Mollie many amusing incidents connected with the
campaign, and to make myself agreeable by petting her
favorite cat. ...

However, I passed a couple of hours very pleasantly,
and, promising to call again in the afternoon, when I took the
countersign around, I took my departure, but true to my
promise, I returned in the afternoon, and had not been there
very long, before it was announced that the cows had come,
and Miss Mollie giving me the stool to carry for her, went out
to milk them.

But I resolved to be useful in more respects than one,
so, telling Miss Mollie to give me the bucket, I told her that
altho' I had not milked a cow since I as quite a small chap, and
used to drive my Father's cows in the corner of the fence and
milked them in my wool hat, yet I would officiate on this
occasion and forthwith got to work. Now wouldn't you like to
have seen me milking, and then straining the milk and putting
it away for her? I tell you, 'Doosenberry' there is nothing like
being a soldier at last!

Albert's journal ends here. It would seem he probably
wrote in another pocket notebook which was lost at the time
of his death.

Luria continued to serve with the Twenty-third North
Carolina Infantry, which saw action at the Battle of Seven
Pines (Fair Oaks). It was on May 31, 1862, that Albert Moses
Luria, while leading the skirmishes of his regiments, received
his mortal wound.

So highly did Albert Moses Luria's comrades think of
him that members of that Command presented his mother with

this inscription on a monument. At his grave, in the Moses family cemetery in Esquiline Hill, Columbus, Georgia, is a weather-worn obelisk enclosing a shell. It reads, "This bomb, with burning fuse..."

His headstone reads: "He went into the field prepared to meet his God."

•••

On his death, an obituary written by an unknown friend and fellow soldier read...

He was engaged in the desperate battles of May 31st and June 1st, at Chickahominy and after leading his men over the works of the enemy in the brilliant charge of Hills Division, he fell mortally wounded, and was gone borne the field and died five hours later.

Chapter 8

December,1861-January, 1862:
Eliza's Diary

December 16th

[Eliza returned to her diary:]

O how sorry I am that such a length of time has elapsed since I have communicated with you: but I must confess that I have not missed you so much as usual, as I have been confiding in someone else. So before I go any further, I will tell you who he is; and then tell you, as near as possible, all he said to me, and all I have said to him.

He is a dear, handsome fellow: he is the elder brother of the darling of my heart: he is Brother Major [Israel Moses Nunez]; my brother-in-law.

But there never was a kinder, truer brother. No one would imagine, to see the love and kindness he bestows on all of us, that he was not our own Brother. There is not a kinder, nobler, more hospitable, amiable man than he is.

He is quite handsome, as I said before; but I dont think handsomeness adds much to a man: for handsome is as handsome does.

I never heard an unkind word spoken against him by anyone that thought of what they were saying. He never hesitates to do good for anyone, from the highest to the lowest.

How many kind things he has done for me: I fear I never will be able to repay him; but if love and thanks will do any good, I am sure I bestow any quantity of that on him.

But now to the point.

... While I lay on my bed of sickness [in Albert Luria's room at the Esquiline] how many times did I think of the time when that dear fellow was sick in the same room; and although I was suffering intensely, how much I did wish I could have all his sickness for him.

While I was sick, Nina and my little cousin Anna, who was staying there, left for Richmond: the former for school; the latter to go to her home.

When I got well, Brother M. and I had a long chat, on his bed on night; about the darling of my heart. It was what I had long wished for; so although it gave me much pain, and does now; it gave me pleasure at the same time.

He told me that he told a cousin of mine that I would not suit him for a wife if he lived in the city, but would if he lived in the country.

No, although it came from the best authority, I cannot bear to believe it until he tells me so. Or something else; that of his having been in love with Belle Cohen, and saying he would have asked if he thought he would have been accepted. Oh dear, how can I believe that either; for pretty much the same tale was told me about Loudie Lyons; which I afterwards found out to be false.

No; everyone is against us, and although I know my dear brother told me all these things with the best intentions, I cannot make up my mind to believe any of them until they are confirmed by him when he comes home; if it should please God to permit him to do so, as he expects to in July. But oh my, it will be whole fifteen months that he has been away.

I intend to ask him about these things, and one or two others; that is, if he has any private conversation with me. Of course, if he is cold and distant to me, I will be so to him; and will try to be so anyhow. But if it should please God and those that are most deeply interested in us to permit us to be intimae and friendly, if nothing more, I will, if I have an opportunity of doing so, ask him. For that was nearly his last request, in a note he wrote me just before he left: I mean, asking me not to believe anything I heard about him, as he knew a great many things would be exaggerated.

So I will most certainly comply with her request in this, as in all other things.

I thought once or twice of writing to him; but then I thought I would, in the first place, be breaking my promise to my Dear Brother if I wrote him without his consent; and if I told him my object in doing so, he certainly would not consent to my doing so. But if I wrote him anyhow, it might not do either party any good, and I would only have my conscience injured by doing something else which I promised not to do. I think with these things constantly in mind as they are and then sometimes doubt about them. They will help me to act in a manner that I should perhaps do to me, it is so long off; and then he says he is not going to stay but a month. And then to think of the many accidents that may happen to the darling of my heart. But I pray most fervently every night for his safe return to all who hold him so near and dear as I do. But I dont think there is any one that does so, quite as much as I do; and I know there never will be anyone who can do so more than I do.

Oh that I could know what he is doing this moment: -- would that I could fly on the wings of love to him.

I had a little chat on this subject with Brother M. Sunday; which has determined me to confide more in your, and trouble him less, and ask him less about the dear fellow; -- for although he always answers all my questions, I feel that I am doing wrong in asking him so many.

But I must now to my work -- I will try to write more frequently in this; but when we move I am going to make this a regular business; -- to put down the proceedings of each day; but until then I will just write by snatches such things as I wish to record in this.

Decr 23rd.

You see, my old friend, I have not neglected you so long this time; and have now come to you to tell you what joy the perusal of one of my darling's letters to Cousin Esther gave me.

Oh how I wish it could have been to me.

It was such a nice, long, cheerful letter. I am so glad to know he has such comfortable quarters; that is, comfortable compared to what he has had; for it is nothing more than a log cabin. I will not attempt to give his description of it, for I know I cannot do it justice. His letter was dated the 14th of this month. He spoke in his letter of his protoge [sic]; I wonder who he meant. I wonder if he will be as disappointed about not being able to spend Christmas night this year as he did last? I know I am; terribly. But I know it is perhaps for the best that he is not here; for I feel that if he were, and I had the opportunity of spending it as I did last year, I would break all promises and do so. I could not resist such a temptation.

He said in his letter that he was in hopes of being able to go to Richmond and thereabouts Christmas, but he feared he would not be able to obtain a furlough. But it was impossible to obtain one to come home, but that he hoped to do so in June or July.

But, oh me, what a long time off that is. But I have made up my mind to read and work hard and do everything I can to kill time as much as possible. But then, to think when he does come home I must shun his society in order to hide my feelings; for I know I cannot control them. But I have made up my mind to try very hard to do so, and hope and pray that God will aid me to do so.

He does think of me and love me, and I cant help seeing and thinking so: -- and to think of having to hide my feelings. But God's will be done. The darling fellow sent some crockery that he had got by stealth from the Yankee's house. And to think of my disappointment, that after he had sent me a cup and saucer it should have got broken, and then his mother thought is was not worth while to send it to me. But if she could imagine how much I prize anything that he sent me, she would have sent it. But when I go there again I am going to try and get a piece of it at any rate. He sent a piece to each member of his family.

January 1st, 1862.

You see, my dear friend, for such I insisted upon your being; I have, according to promise and inclination begun a regular journal and will endeavor to write every night, if it is only two lines, to tell you what has been my occupation during he day. That shall always be my first and all-important subject. hen I will tell you anything else that is of interest, or that I have the time or inclination of telling you. ...

I had the pleasure of hearing a letter read from the darling of my heart to his mother. His considerate Brother, knowing I was anxious to hear it and at the same time would not ask to do so, had Min. read it aloud.

I was delighted to have the pleasure of reading a letter of the dear fellow's to Brother M. which he, with his usual kindness and consideration, gave me to read: -- that he did not have to go on picket duty but half as often. I am delighted at that, for it is such a terribly venturesome duty. I am glad to hear, through his letter to his Mother, that he had some prospect of getting a furlough of 30 days by March, which would enable him to come home.

Oh how happy I will be if he does so.

What a birthday I will spend. Oh words cannot possibly describe my joy at the faint prosect of such being the case.

January 2nd.

... I got a letter from Cousin Lea, in which he mentions the prospect of the darling of my heart getting a higher position; I do hope he may. He also mentions his intention of coming him if possible for a short time while his Father is home, which he expects to be in about a week, if he succeeds in getting a furlough for a few days. ...

January 11th.

Oh, I forgot to give you the news we received yesterday of Uncle R's arrival, early in the morning. He has a furlough of 40 days. He is Major of the Commissary department of Genl Toomb's staff. He is the father of my darling. Oh that I could hear often of him, as I cannot hear from him; but I suppose I must content myself by thinking that no news is good news.

January 18th [following a visit to Esquiline Hill]:

One thing I was disappointed in: that was not hearing anything about the darling of my heart. I was very much in hopes of seeing some of his letters, or hearing something more direct form him. Uncle R., who I think is looking rather badly, did say he was as well and happy as possible and that was a great comfort to my anxious heart. But he says he is not going to stay in the army until he is thirty, as he spoke of doing, and I am sure I was delighted to hear it: for although that is quite an honorable position in life, yet it is so venturesome; when he can obtain a high position in any situation he chooses to place himself in. But, oh dear me, I fear I shall never be able to do the same. Oh how hard I must strive to hide my feelings when he returns, which I fear is deferred until April.

I do miss having the pleasure of reading Cousin Esther's letters that she used to indulge me in, and I would try to blind her by appearing to be indifferent about doing so; while all the time I was anxious to peruse the contents of those charming letters. She has received two recently, and I have been so anxious to peruse them: but yet I dare not ask for them. But I must not dwell longer on this all-engrossing subject of my mind.

Brother M. stopped here Monday and gave me a message which I was glad to receive. It was from the darling of my heart.

Oh how I do miss not being able to hear of him oftener. But never mind; Sister A. will be home soon, then I will hear of him. ...

It is better to toil for myself than have my Brother do so for me. I do hope he will never have to do so for me again. I am fully able to support myself and shall always endeavor to do so; but oh that I could work with an easier mind! My mind is so bothered all the time about the darling of my heart. Oh would that it could be kept comparativley easy by hearing from him, or even seeing some of the letters that are received from him. I merely hear by accident different things about the darling fellow: -- sometimes good and sometimes bad news; but I dare not question anybody, so am kept so anxious about the dear fellow.

I sometimes feel like telling Brother I can not stand it any longer and just show my feelings plainly and openly to the world. Oh that I could!

I must await time and circumstance to do so, if at all. I had not even seen a line from the dearest one of earth to me for more than two months; it seemed to me more than two years, -- until yesterday, when I did what I never did before in my life; I read all the letters that Sister A. had received from the dear fellow; but I did not think that she would care, and I was so anxious to see some of his letters I could not resist the temptation.

Chapter 9

January-July, 1862:
Raphael's Memoirs
(Battles of Peninsula, Fair Oaks, and Seven Days)
Albert's Death

Attached to Toombs' Brigade, Raphael Moses was soon to find himself in some of the earliest combat of the Civil War against the Union plan of action of the Commanding General of those forces, General George B. McClellan. The overall strategy of the Campaign was for the Union forces to move up the Peninsula of land located between the York River on the North and the James River on the South. The principal base of beginning the operation was the Federal stronghold of Fortress Monroe near the tip of the Peninsula. As the Union forces were advancing West-Northwest toward Richmond, another Union force under General McDowell was to move overland on the more direct route from the Washington area to link up with McClellan and capture Richmond. The combined Union forces exceeded 100,000 men, the Confederates at the beginning had but 17,000 men under General John B. Magruder, stretched in a thin defensive line across the Peninsula from Yorktown to the Warwick River which fed into the James River.

The South had providence on their side and there were unusually heavy rains in April 1862, which impeded the movement of men and material. This, combined with the overcautious General McClellan, who, through faulty intelligence, over-estimated the Confederate strength, delayed the attack. The Union Army laid siege, and when they finally took action on May 4, 1862, the Confederate Army had withdrawn back toward Richmond. The Army of the Potomac entered Yorktown, Virginia, on May 4th. On the following day, May 5th, the Battle of Williamsburg. This battle ended with casualties of killed, wounded and missing, for the Union about 2,400 men and for the Confederates about 1,700. General Johnston continued his phased withdrawal back to the outer defenses of Richmond. As the Union forces advanced, they were astraddle the Chickahomy River, usually a small river that offered fords and bridges, to keep communications open. The rains again came to the Confederate assistance; several important bridges were washed away, and fords became too deep and difficult to cross.

From Moses' memoirs:

He [Toombs] was decidedly given to boasting. I remember once on the Peninsular, in Virginia, at the battle of Dam No. 1, I was riding home with Charles Cleghorne. I had just bought a fish, which was hung on my saddle, having no idea of a battle. On our way the shells began to sing, and Cleghorne proposed that we should ride up to the line and see the fight. I consented, and we went up. It was getting pretty hot. When we got there the line opened for [Toombs] to pass nearer to the front. He was a very poor horseman. A shell whistled near him, and Alice Gary, his mare who had never before been under fire, pranced about a good deal more than [Toombs] bargained for. But after a little she went on, and our men made a most successful fight. It was afterwards favorably commented on. A Texas Commissary got his head shot off that day, and the army said it served him right -- what the devil right had a Commissary to be in the battle; he should have been with his wagons looking after the commissary stores. On this hint I did not speak, but said to myself if this is the way they talk about Commissaries with their heads shot off, I'll so conduct myself hereafter as to avoid similar comments, but let me go back to Gen. [Toombs].

The next day we went over to Gen. Cobb's headquarters. Cobb weighed about two hundred, and when he laughed all over, every particle of his avoirdupois shook like a jelly bag. [Toombs] commenced telling about the fight at Dam No. 1, his prowess, how his men fought, how he passed to the front, etc. And then, in describing the opening of the line to let him pass through he gave a glowing account of Alice Gray's antics. "Never saw a mare so frightened in his life. By God, Cobb, she trembled like an aspen leaf, and seemed to think that all the shells were aimed at her."

"Moses, you were there, did you ever see a mare as scared in your life, now say?" I replied that she was very much scared.

Taking advantage of the situation, General Johnston, now reinforced in strength, attacked the two Union Corps on the North side of the Chickahomy, near Fair Oaks, (Seven Pines), Virginia. The Confederate attack was only a moderate success, offering no real relief to the threat to Richmond. General Johnston was severely wounded and had to leave the field. General Smith took temporary Command, and the next day, President Jefferson Davis appointed General Robert E. Lee to succeed to the Command of the Army of Northern Virginia; a Command appointment which was to be one of the most important decisions of the Civil War. Of the opposing forces in this battle, the attacking Confederates suffered 6,100 casualties, the Union 5,000 men. Both sides had about 42,000 men engaged. General Lee organized his forces to defeat and drive the Union Army away from the immediate area of Richmond, and in late June 1862, fought the Seven Days Battle beginning on June 25; on June 26, the Battle of Mechanicsville (Beaver Dam Creek); on June 27, Gaines Mill (First Cold Harbor or the Chickahomy); on June 28, Federals abandoned their supply base at White House Landing and changed their base of operation to be from Harrison's Landing; on June 29, Battle of Savage Station; on June 30, Battle of Fraysers Farm (White Oak Swamp), and on July 1, the Battle of Malvern Hill.

The Army of the Potomac had an aggregate strength of 105,000 men and suffered almost 16,000 casualties. The Confederate forces aggregated 88,500 men and suffered 20,000 casualties, mostly wounded.

While serving with Toombs' Brigade, Magruder's Division and later with Anderson's Division, Raphael Moses was present at some of the heaviest fighting in the Civil War. These units were in the Battles of the Civil War opposing Union General McClellan from the Peninsula Campaign, March-August 1862, through the Battle of Seven Pines (Fair Oaks), May 31-June 1, 1862; through the Seven Days Battle, June 25-July 1, 1862, and then on September 17, 1862, the Battle of Antietam (Sharpsburg), Maryland.

In his memoirs, Moses, in his own words, writes of this period of the Civil War:

Near Richmond when I was Commissary for [Toombs'] Brigade, McClellan made a demonstration against Richmond. [Toombs] was at the front. I had charge of the Headquarters. You may say that I kept house in [Toombs'] absence. The situation of our Headquarters was deemed by General Lee the best location for him during the sudden changes that he had to make in the movements of his entire Army. He sent his cot down by a wagon and some other things and soon after followed with his staff. When he arrived he had on a light summer suit, (sack coat), brown thread gloves. His appearance was one of perfect repose. Soon after he arrived couriers came dashing in; Generals and other offices were dashing up ever and again for more last minute instructions. It was an important time. We were on the eve of a great battle. Corps, Brigades and Division had to change positions, and places so as to meet the contemplated attack. If [Toombs] had been in Lee's position, the vocabulary of oaths would have been exhausted. No one about the Headquarters would have known whether he was on his head or his heels, or how long it might be before the heels would have to be put in requisition to save his head. But how different it was with General Lee. He was as calm as a summer cloud, gave his orders with precision and courtesy, and anyone seeing him surrounded by a bevy of officers and not knowing the cause of their concentration, might just as well have supposed that they were specially invited to partake of hospitality of which he was the splendid and courteous host, as to believe that they were suddenly called to meet some important change in the grim visage of war.

This lasted the best part of two or three days, I don't remember which, but I do remember that one day when we were seated at dinner, I at one end of the table and General Lee at the other, with members of the staff on either side, an officer came to the door, saluted the General and said, "I am ordered by General Longstreet to inform you that General McClellan has retired"; General Lee bowed to the officer, and then said, "Well, Major, you see what trouble that young man has given me!" Only this and nothing more. We finished dinner and after dinner, General Lee ordered his traps

*packed up and returned to his own Headquarters. I think that
it was just after this that he made his great move into the
valley of Virginia, and fought the second Battle of Manassas,
etc.*

      The military operations of April through July 1, 1862,
the Peninsula Campaign, including the Battles of Fair Oaks
(Seven Pines), May 30-31, and the Seven Days Battle, June 25
through July 6, were very personal losses to Major Raphael
Jacob Moses. His 19-year-old son, Albert, was mortally
wounded at Fair Oaks; his young nephew, Perry Moses, was
killed in action in the Seven Days Battle.
      From his father's memoirs comes this heart-wrenching
story:

      *Albert (another son of mine) had an old friend in the
North Carolina Troops who had gone to college with him at
Chapel Hill, named Nat Gregory. At his insistence, he
(Albert) accepted a Lieutenancy in a North Carolina
Company and was killed at the Battle of Seven Pines near
Richmond in 1862. I was near the battlefield, and after the
battle tried to learn his fate. I saw several members of his
Company. They all knew him, of course, and the best
information that I could get was that he was slightly wounded
in the leg. This information I followed up and visited the
different hospitals to find out where he was, without success.
As I passed the Treasury Office in Richmond, Col. Clayton
called out to me that a young man by my name had been
carried by in an ambulance, and that he was shot in the head.
I never for a moment though of its being Albert, as his
(adopted) name was Luria, and as my wife's brother, Perry
Moses, had a son in the same battle, I naturally supposed that
it was his son, and I thought that I knew that Albert's wound*

was a slight one in the leg. But as I was interested in the fate of my nephew, I went to the hospital where Col. Clayton informed me the ambulance had carried young Moses, and inquired for the ward in which the wounded had been carried that day. The ward was pointed out to me and I passed among the wounded. I saw some ladies standing by a cot and heard one of them say: "What a handsome young man!" I crossed over to the cot, and my shock was beyond my power of expression when I saw my son Albert lying unconscious with a wound in his head. I removed him in an ambulance to Perry's house, where he remained unconscious, never recognizing me. He died that night from loss of blood when the surgeon tried to relieve the pressure of the brain, and it was in this manner passed away a bright, promising youth of nineteen.

Chapter 10

July-October, 1862:
Eliza's Diary

July 8th, 1862.

[After Albert's death:]

Oh what a length of time I have allowed to elapse before writing in this book, and what sad accounts I have to give it; for the darling of my heart is gone forever.

My principal object in writing this book has therefore been defeated. I will, however, continue it and record all the sad instances of the death of the one I loved and ever will love so dearly. And just at the time that my anticipation has been taken away. But God, who knows and does all things for the best, has seen fit to deprive me of my greatest treasure, so I must bow in submission to his will.

He has allowed me to enjoy his love for four years; for altho' it has always, ever since he knew me, been mine; he did not assure me of it until the 14th of April, four years since.

Although everyone has endeavored during all this time to try to make me believe that he did not love me, yet I never could but think that he did. It is true that I have at times puzzled my brain to know why he acted in certain ways if all his affections were mine; but yet I could never believe that he did not love me. And I have a great many instances to regret; -- the way I have acted toward him. And had I felt the slightest apprehension of his never returning I should have acted differently towards him during his absence; which was for thirteen months and eleven days.

Oh what hardships he had to endure during all that length of time. He went off from home as Sergeant in the City Light Guards; he remained with that company until the early part of June when he joined a North Carolina company and was 2nd Lieutenant. But before he left the City Lights he had one opportunity of displaying his Bravery, which he never failed to do on any occasion.

I have a paper in this book which gives a full account of it, so I will not take the time or space to do so. The shell is in his dear Mother's keeping. He was in a great many skirmishes before he was in this terrible battle of the Chickahominy, which ended so fatally for him, after being in it through almost all of the fighting. Oh what a soldier fell there. His equal never was, or ever will be. God knows he did his duty to his country, and he died as he said he wanted to die; -- on the field of battle.

Oh that I could have been with him when he was wounded. He did not live but four or five hours after the fatal blow was struck. He has been put in a vault, in a metallic coffin, in Richmond; where he will remain until his father can bring him to the lovely spot that he has at this place where I am now staying [at the Esquiline]. ...

I denied myself, and him, the pleasure of correspondence from the time he left, which was the 20th of April, until the 6th of February, when he wrote to request me to correspond with him: which I consented to do. As I deemed it best at first, I had refused to do so; but when he had been absent for nine or ten months and again requested me to do so, I could not refuse. So we enjoyed that pleasure for a short time. Oh how little did I dream such a pleasure would be stopped so soon. I shall never cease to regret not having done so from the beginning, for from one letter of his to Min. I see that he was very desirous of my doing so. But that was not requisite to make me think so, for I knew too well that my feelings were not to be able to imagine what his were.

But from all that people had told me, and what opposition I would have to contend with on both sides, I deemed it best for him not to do so.

He was fully prepared for death and wrote me and his Mother on the night of the 26th and his letters were sent to us after the terrible blow was struck. Oh what a precious letter it is, and always shall be; as well as a most excellent daguerre of him that he gave me last February a year ago; -- besides all the rest of his precious letters, and in fact everything connected with him, which has become, if possible, dearer to me than ever. I shall always prize them.

Aunt Julia has promised me her letters, and I am going to beg Min. for hers.

Every one has something in it about me. Oh would that I could have seen them when they were written.

Oct 13th, 1862.
My life is all a blank to me now. It makes but little difference to me now, where I am or what I do, so long as I am as near as possible to what remains of my lost treasure; and that I do what I feel and know would please him. ...

[Eliza moved to Texas, later married, and died in 1926.]

Chapter 11

July-December, 1862: Raphael's Memoirs and Military Records
(Battle of Antietam and Fredericksburg)

After the Seven Days Battle, both Armies were suffering from the heavy casualties sustained and from the need to resupply and reorganize. The preceding Campaign and Battles had established the need, particularly to the Confederate Army, that proper staff planning was necessary, and that there had to be a chain of Command. The Union Army was south of the James, further away from Washington, D.C., than the concentration of General Lee's Army. President Abraham Lincoln and his senior military advisors had foreseen this possibility and had the Army build strong fortifications to protect the nation's Capital and to maintain a large available manpower reserve to secure the Capital.

Dissatisfied with General McClellan's conduct of the operations, a new area of Command was established in Northern Virginia and the command given to General Pope. This bombastic officer had had some success in the West (in the region of the Tennessee and Mississippi rivers). General Pope began his reorganization of his Command and drew up a set of plans. The basic principal being to operate on a line of advance into Virginia toward Richmond, with his right flank secured by the Blue Ridge Mountains, and the Union forces across those mountains in the Shenandoah Valley containing the Confederate forces. What he did not consider was the

military genius of two Confederate Generals -- Robert E. Lee
and Jonathan Thomas "Stonewall" Jackson.

Lee took advantage of a few weeks' break in the
fighting to reorganize his forces, to recruit and re-equip, and
get the wounded of the previous battles back to their
Regiments. The overall reorganization was for two wing
commanders, General James Longstreet to Command the right
wing and General Stonewall Jackson to Command the left
wing. Adequate fortifications were constructed to defend
Richmond against future threats; Artillery units were given
more specific assignments, and the Cavalry consolidated into
a single command under General J.E.B. "Jeb" Stuart.

The organization of the Army of Northern Virginia
into two Corps took place in July 1862, General Longstreet
commanding the First Corps, General Jackson, the Second
Corps. The full staff assignments were completed in the
following months. Longstreet's staff included G. Moxley
Sorrel, A.A.G./Chief of Staff, and R.J. Moses, Chief
Commissary of Subsistence.

As the Union forces began their movements in late July
and early August 1862, Lee watched carefully, as McClellan
was still in force, south of the James River. When intelligence
sources informed Lee that those forces were slowly being sent
by water back to Northern Virginia, he decided to make use
of his interior lines of communication to consolidate his
separate wings so they would be in a position to be mutually
supportive. Jackson was able to contain the Union forces in
the Shenandoah Valley and began to move his command
through the few mountain gaps into the East side of the Blue
Ridge. In a stunning attack, he swept in behind General Pope's
Army, which had moved south, and was able, on August 27,
to destroy the Federal supply base at Manassas Junction.
General Pope went after Jackson with his entire force, which

considerably outnumbered Jackson. General Lee, using his interior lines of communication, in the last few days of August moved Longstreet's forces toward the battle in progress. The Second Battle of Bull Run (Manassas) was on August 29-30. General Jackson's forces held out on the 29th and were joined by Longstreet's forces on the 30th. With the two wings of Lee's Army united, the Federal attacks were repulsed and the Confederate forces counterattacked and drove the Federals from the field, and sent it retreating back to the protection of the Washington, D.C., fortifications. General Lee was just over 20 miles from Washington.

Lee's Army had engaged about 48,000 to 50,000 men and had losses in killed, wounded and missing of approximately 9,000. The Union Army at second Bull Run had 75,000 to 78,000 on the file and sustained approximately 16,000 causalities.

After the battle of Mannassas, the Union forces fell back to the vicinity of Washington, D.C., General Pope was relieve and General McClellan was restored to Command of the Army of the Potomac. General Lee's Confederate Army of Northern Virginia, with morale high and the sweet fruits of victory, was a tired Army; reduced by casualties, long marches, and months of Campaigning and hard-fought battles. The ranks were further depleted by stragglers, barefoot and ill-clad men who fell by the wayside. It numbered no more than 40,000 men of all branches of service.

General Lee decided to cross the Potomac and move into Maryland and possibly Pennsylvania. The concept was that the pro-Southern Marylanders would provide a source of new recruits and the untrampled farms would provide food and forage. Dividing his forces, he sent the greater part of his Command with General Stonewall Jackson toward Harpers Ferry, Virginia, to isolate or drive out the Union Divisions there. Lee, accompanying General Longstreet's Command, crossed the Potomac River at Leesburg, Virginia, and marched into Maryland, Enthusiastically greeted by the pro-Southerns as his ragged troops sang "Maryland, My Maryland," they were offered food and "milk and honey," but few recruits.

Both wings of the Army were in short supply of shoes, clothing, and forage. The Quartermaster and Commissary officers were under strict orders to pay for what they obtained (in Confederate money). The supply lines back to Virginia were being stretched to the limit, for want of fresh horses, mules, wagons, and other means of conveyance.

The Division of Lee's forces, outside of mutually supporting distance, was unknown to the Federals until one of those strange incidents of fate that do happen in wartime occurred. A copy of General Lee's Special Order #191 outlining his plan of maneuver was found in a former campsite, wrapped around three cigars. It was forwarded on September 13, 1862, to General McClellan, who realized the significance of the document. With over 90,000 men, well supplied and rested, McClellan moved toward Lee's forces.

From Moses' memoirs:

I remember once at Cromptons Gap in Virginia, a young cavalry man came dashing up to where General Lee was sitting surrounded by several officers. When he reached the spot he saluted the General, jerked his horse back on his haunches and delivered what he considered an important piece of news, and it was rather important. But this young Calvary man was out of his line of duty, or would never have known it. After he had delivered himself, he expected to be overwhelmed with thanks. General Lee said very quietly; "Young man don't chomp that bit so, you are worrying your horse. What command do you belong to?" The young man having answered, General Lee said, "You had better join your command." After the young man returned, Lee acted on his information, but the young man was improperly away from his command, and Lee's judgement was not encourage him to be off the line of duty. ...

In an effort to defeat Lee's segmented forces, battles were fought at Crampton's Gap and South Mountain. By September 16, the one wing of Confederate forces, General Lee, with Longstreet's Command, had advanced to Antietam Creek, at Sharpsburg, Maryland, while Jackson having invested Harpers Ferry. On September 15, Harpers Ferry fell to General Jackson, with 12,000 prisoners, leaving General A.P. Hill and his Division to work out the surrender and removal of the captured men and material, he moved to join Longstreet and Lee.

The battle began on the 16th, with Lee's forces spread thin, awaiting the arrival of Jackson. By early on the 17th, matters were serious, and the Confederates so reduced and stretched and outnumbered, that at one point Longstreet had his own staff working several of the artillery pieces of a half-wrecked artillery battery.

Jackson's arrival on the 16th, after a hard night's march, re-enforced Lee's "Thin Gray Line." Names of such parts of the Battle of Antietam, the Cornfield, Bloody Lane, and Dunker Church, ran red with blood of both Armies as McClellan committed his Divisions piecemeal into the battle. A.P. Hill's Division arrived on the 17th and was committed to the critical point of the line to stop the Federals who had forced a crossing of Antietam Creek on what is now known as Burnside's Bridge.

The Battle of Antietam ended on the night of September 17, 1862. Of the 75,000 Union troops engaged,

12,500 were killed, wounded, or missing; of the 40,000 Confederate troops at Antietam, 13,500 were listed as casualties. It was the bloodiest two days of battle in American history.

Both Armies remained in position during the day of the 18th; Lee withdrew back across the Potomac at Blackford's Ford on the night of the 18th, and during the day of the 19th, McClellan, despite having at least one fresh Corps, failed to pursue.

From Moses' memoirs:

Previously on this same campaign I went on a foraging excursion through the valleys of Virginia with a train of wagons buying bacon and flour and seizing cattle. While riding along I spied some cattle in a pasture and sent a detail down to drive them along with our herd and they were accordingly brought. When we had proceeded a half mile or so an old woman came up in great distress and said, "That's my 'pet heifer' you've driven away, and would you kill it?" She seemed almost broken hearted, at the loss and probable fate of her heart's darling, and my sympathies got the better of me, when I said, "Certainly not, take her back." I shall never forget the joy that illuminated the old woman's face and as she went back with her pet heifer it occurred to me that if she had a prodigal son who had strayed away and if on his return she killed for him a fatted calf, it would surely not be her "pet heifer." This is a small matter to note down but it impressed itself very much on me at the time, and it is one of my good deeds that comes back to memory and cheers me in my waning years.

My trip was a very fatiguing one. It lasted about two weeks, but as I returned to camp with a train well loaded with stores, for which the troops were in great need, I felt fully compensated for my labor and fatigue. I arrived in camp the morning before the battle of Sharpsburg, and that night we had to hurriedly retreat and leave the supplies. I let the soldiers take what they could in their knapsacks and on their bayonets, the adornment of a flitch of bacon being in no case objected to, and except for what was thus saved and the cattle which we could drive, my two weeks labor was lost. So much for the uncertainties of a boarding house keeper in the midst of War, and as I had, including teamsters and other non-combatants, a family of nearly 54,000 to provide for, this depletion of the larder was a very serious matter.

Just here an incident occurs to me in strategy which as it surprised me, I suppose I may as well relate. Lee had ordered Jackson's troops to join him. We were greatly outnumbered, and it was very important, as the fate of the day turned against us, that an impression should be made upon the enemy that re-inforcements had arrived. And General Lee effected this by having a considerable amount of brush cut and dragged by horses along the roads so as to cause an immense dust to arise, and make it appear to the enemy that it was caused by the arrival of fresh troops. I presume it had the desired effect, as we were not pursued and pursuit would have been very disastrous.

For the Commissary and Quartermaster officers of the Confederate Army, it was a very difficult order to resupply and replenish the various Commands. The captured material from Harpers Ferry provided some supply, but rations, forage and clothing, particularly shoes, had to be found for the men. The long lines of wounded were transported in any available conveyance, mostly rough, steel slate-springed wagons, subject to jarring at every move.

Through the remainder of September and October, the

Armies skirmished, Jeb Stuart's Cavalry raiding north into Maryland and Pennsylvania to keep the Federals close to Washington.

Most notably, on Monday, September 22, 1862, President Lincoln issued his Emancipation Proclamation which freed the slaves in those Confederate States not held by the Union.

Lincoln and the War cabinet staff urged General McClellan to begin offensive operations before winter set in. As President Lincoln's expression went, "His General had the slows." McClellan was too slow and too cautious, and on November 5, McClellan was replaced by General Ambrose Burnside.

In mid-November 1862, General Burnside, commanding the Federal Army of the Potomac, began the movement of his forces from encampments near Warrenton. The forces moved toward Fredericksburg on the Rappahannock River. They established positions and bases around Falmouth on the north side of the river. to cover this movement, General Longstreet moved his Corps and supporting troops from Culpepper, Virginia, to Marye's Heights, overlooking Fredericksburg, Rappahonnock River, and Falmouth. Lieutenant General Longstreet's Command was refereed to as the right wing of Corps and supporting troops. The left wing was at Winchester, Virginia. General Lee, watching the Federal movements, united his forces along the ridge line above Fredericksburg, being one to two miles' distance from the river, but commanding the plain below, stretching to the river and occupying the town of Fredericksburg with a strong skirmish line of Mississippi troops.

Major Raphael J. Moses' assignment in this soon to be fought Battle of Fredericksburg was referred to as "Chief

Commissary, Right Wing, Army of Northern Virginia."

(OR I-51(2)p. 641)

GENERAL ORDERS,   HEADQUARTER
RIGHT WING,
ARMY OF NORTHERN
VIRGINIA,

No. 45.   Near Culpepper Court-House,
November 4, 1862.

Maj. John H. Chichester, Commissary of Subsistence, at his own request, is relieved from duty as commissary of this Command and will report to Lieut. Col. R.G. Cole, Chief Commissary of Subsistence, Army of Northern Virginia. The duties of his office will be assumed by Maj. Thomas Walton, Commissary of Subsistence, who will report to Maj. R.J. Moses, Chief Commissary, Right Wing, Army of Northern Virginia.

By Command of Major-General Longstreet:

G.M. Sorrel,
Assistant Adjutant-General

Major Moses was very conscious of his duties and the ongoing efforts to sustain the Commissary subsistence. He could, however, be subject to admonishment when he made an independent, incorrect decision.

(OR I-51(2)p. 1046)

HEADQUARTERS
ARMY OF NORTHERN VIRGINIA,
December 4, 1862.
Lieutenant-Colonel Cole,
    Chief Commissary, Army of Northern Virginia:

COLONEL: The Commanding General wishes you to advise commissaries of Corps and Divisions that they will issue three days' rations, to be kept on hand for sudden moves, in addition to the supplies for daily consumption. Some misunderstanding existing upon this subject, Major Moses had declined issuing provisions, in accordance with General Lee's verbal order heretofore given on this subject.

I am, sir, respectfully, your obedient servant,
        R.H. CHILTON,
    Acting Adjutant and Inspector General.

Not withstanding the above, General Longstreet, in his after action report on the Confederate victory at the Battle of Fredericksburg, concluded his report with these words:

... My thanks are also due to Surgeon (J.S.D.) Cullen, Chief Surgeon; Major (S.P.) Mitchell, Chief Quartermaster; Major (R.J.) Moses, Chief of the Subsistence Department, and Captain (J.H.) Manning, Signal Officer, for the valuable services in their respective departments.

I have the honor to be, General, most respectively, your obedient servant,
        JAMES LONGSTREET,
    Lieutenant-General, Commanding.

Chapter 12

January-April, 1863:
Raphael's Memoirs
(The Suffolk Campaign)

On February 25, 1863, Major Raphael J. Moses was relieved of duty as Acting Commissary Officer of General McLaw's Division and ordered to report to General Longstreet at Petersburg, Virginia. (In February 1863 and through May 1863, General Longstreet was given the Independent Command in charge of the Department of Virginia and North Carolina, minus the Divisions of McLaws and Anderson, and was ordered to operate in the Southeast Virginia and coastal areas of the Carolinas.) These areas had been occupied by Union Forces early in the war. Citizens and scouts had reported that there was an excellent supply of food and forage in these occupied areas, behind Union lines and on to the Atlantic Coast. Major Moses' abilities as a procurer of badly needed supplies was well known and he was given the assignment to investigate the matter. The following exchange of correspondence between Generals Longstreet and Lee reveal the measure of confidence placed in Raphael Jacob Moses.

(OR 1-18-p. 942)

HEADQUARTERS,
March 24, 1863.

General R.E. Lee, Commanding, &C:

GENERAL: I have the honor to enclose a report of Major Moses on the subject of subsistence for our Armies. He has just returned from a tour through Virginia and North Carolina and from a visit to the Commissary-General. This report is the result of his observations. The particular counties referred to by him as containing abundant supplies for our Armies are now in the enemy's lines. We can occupy that country and draw the supplies out with another Division of my old Corps, but I do not think it would be prudent to attempt such a move with a less force. ...

I remain, very respectfully, your obedient servant,
JAMES LONGSTREET
Lieutenant-General, Commanding.

(OR 1-18-p.943)

HEADQUARTERS
Fredericksburg, Va.
March 27, 1963.

Gen. JAMES LONGSTREET, Commanding, &C.:
GENERAL: I received by the last mail your letter of the 24th instant accompanying the report of Major Moses on the subject of subsistence to be obtained in North Carolina. I do not know whether the supplies in that State are necessary for the subsistence of our Armies, but I consider it of the first importance to draw from the invaded districts every pound of provision and forage we can. It will lighten the draught from other sections and give relief to our citizens. As to the force necessary for this purpose I cannot so well decide. ... A sudden, vigorous attack on Suffolk would doubtless give you

that place. Of the propriety of this step you can best judge. ... Should you find it advisable to have a personal conference with me at any time I will be happy to see you here, or it may be that I could meet you in Richmond.

I am, with great esteem, very truly, yours,

R.E. LEE,

General.

There was limited military action; however, the Corps Commissary and Quartermaster Staffs were put to task to obtain the available supplies, most of which were behind Union lines. While this effort was going on, Longstreet's forces engaged and skirmished with the strong Union forces about Suffolk, Virginia.

There has been much written and "what if's" about General Longstreet and the importance of his Campaign around Suffolk. Had he been with Lee at Chancellorsville, would the Confederate victory have been even greater, perhaps destroying the Union Army? The significance and importance of Longstreet's mission in early 1863 and such "what if" commentary are referred to in Major Moses' memoirs:

Before leaving this part of my Journal I wish to correct an error that prevails as to the investment of Suffolk by Longstreet having been a failure, when the fact is that it accomplished all that had ever been contemplated. When Longstreet was at Petersburg, Virginia, the troops at Chancellorsville were in a terrible strait for rations, and we had no place to get them except on the coast of North Carolina, at Hertford and Edenton and other points, where some bacon and an immense quantity of fish in barrels could be obtained and I suggested to Longstreet that if he could prevent the Federals from coming out of Suffolk and raiding upon my trains that I could get a great many supplies. He smiled and said that that would require a movement of his whole Corps as he would have to invest Suffolk. I told him that I knew nothing about Army movements, but I did know that I could not do anything on the Coast of North Carolina if I was subjected to inroads from the Union troops, for they would not only gobble up all the supplies I could gather, but that my wagons, men and subordinate officers would all be taken and that I with the rest of them would be made prisoners.

After considering the matter, Longstreet invested Suffolk and I went to the coast of North Carolina with my men and trains, and we succeeded in getting a large amount of supplies, and forwarded them to the Army of North Virginia, then around Chancellorsville, and Suffolk remained invested until I got all accessible supplies, and as soon as I advised General Longstreet that the object of the investment had been fully accomplished the siege was raised, and if this investment had not been made the Army of Northern Virginia would not have subsisted.

Chapter 13

May-August, 1863:
Raphael's Memoirs and Military Records
(Battle of Gettysburg)

As spring set in and the weather improved, the Armies in Northern Virginia prepared for the certainty of a spring offensive by the recently appointed Commander of the Army of the Potomac, General "Fighting Joe" Hooker. President Davis in Richmond and General Lee from his headquarters with the Army of Northern Virginia urged General Longstreet to reunite his Corps with Lee, leaving sufficient forces to contain the Union Army in the Suffolk, Virginia, and coastal area of Virginia and the Carolinas. General Longstreet began his movements Northwards, troops, long supply trains, artillery, and attached units. Before General Longstreet could join with General Lee, the Battle of Chancellorsville was fought the first week of May 1863. It was one of General Lee's most significant victories. The Confederacy paid a high price: General "Stonewall" Jackson was seriously wounded and would shortly die. As General Lee reportedly wrote Jackson upon hearing of his serous wound, "You have lost your left arm, I have lost my right."

The defeat of the Union Army of the Potomac at Chancellorsville, and the rejoining of General Longstreet's Corps with their forces, brought to strength with recruits, returning wounded, men on leave, stragglers, and "AWOLS," along with the supplies recently acquired, was now available to General Lee and the Army of Northern Virginia. That offered several options to the South.

First, with the death of General Jackson, the Army of Northern Virginia needed reorganization. The First Corps was to remain under General Longstreet. With the re-assigning of certain brigades into divisions, and the shifting of certain divisions, there was created a Third Corps. Generals Ewell and Hill were selected to command, respectively, the Second and Third Corps.

The Confederate senior military generals and government officials met to discuss the next movement of the Confederate Armies. Among the options discussed: The possibility of re-enforcing the Armies in the West being threatened by General Grant and his movement to capture Vicksburg and gain control of the Mississippi River for the Union. Keeping open communication with the trans-Mississippi area and the supplies from Texas and Louisiana and Arkansas. Would sending large bodies of men and material from Virginia accomplish the mission? Would it weaken too much Lee's Army and leave a threat to Richmond? Another option was to move forces into Southeast Tennessee, defeat General Rosecrans and then move into East and Middle Tennessee into Kentucky and then Ohio. Would this draw off Union forces from both Virginia and West Tennessee and along the Mississippi River? The third option was to make a strategic move northward with the Army of Northern Virginia, move into Maryland and Pennsylvania, threaten Washington, Baltimore and Philadelphia. Would this cause the Union Armies now located in much fought-over areas of Northern Virginia to withdraw in order to protect the Capital, and if the maneuver was victorious, obtain a negotiated peace with the North and the possible recognition of Great Britain, France and other countries for the Confederacy? This was Lee's plan.

The Army of Northern Virginia was in a very high state of morale, flush with victory after victory, and with full confidence in General Robert E. Lee.

The decision was made -- move North -- and as Hannibal said when he crossed the Alps to invade the Roman Empire, "The die is cast." The plan of the campaign was to have the Second Corps move North, down the Shenandoah Valley, driving the Union forces ahead of them, capturing as much material as possible, move into Maryland and thence North into Pennsylvania and onto York and, if possible, Harrisburg, Pennsylvania. Longstreet's First Corps was to go along the east side of the Blue Ridge Mountains, seize and hold the passes, protect the flank, threaten the rear of the Union Army, then cross the lower fords of the Potomac River and rejoin Lee.

The Third Corps was to follow behind, watching the Federal forces as Fredericksburg and that area of Virginia. Once those Union forces moved in the direction of Lee's main force, to follow behind the First and Second Corps.

Stuart's Cavalry forces were to screen the east right flank of the Confederate Army and report significant intelligence, disrupt Union communications and create alarm in Washington. Ultimately, General "Jeb" Stuart rode behind Union lines, and was between the major Union forces and Washington; he did cause concern, but failed to keep General Lee informed with up-to-date intelligence.

To obtain his own intelligence, Longstreet obtained the services of his civilian scout, Harrison, who was to go into Union lines and bring out military information. This part of the discussed "spy" is referred to in Major Moses' memoirs.

When we entered Chambersburg, Pa., we had two spies, Harrison and Schrieber. They used to travel as regularly between Washington and our Headquarters as a mail. They were so successful and regular in their trips that General Lee began to apprehend that they were in the pay of the Union Army, and unfortunately, he lost confidence in them. General Stuart, who was scouting around the Union lines, had not been heard from in about two weeks. One of these spies brought in an exact account of the position of the Union Army and if General Lee had trusted implicitly in the report we could have been between Gettysburg and Baltimore, our objective point, before the Union Army reached Gettysburg, but he doubted their fidelity and we moved from a place near Chambersburg to near Cash Town.

(Note: Historians have heretofore referred to only one spy, Harrison. Moses' reference to two spies, Harrison and Schrieber, may be the name of the second person alluded to in Longstreet's autobiography, *From Manassas to Appomattox*, p. 324, "... while lying near Suffolk a couple of young men dressed as citizens entered my tent one night with letters from Secretary of War Seddon, recommending them as trustworthy and efficient scouts. ... One of them, Harrison, proved to be an active, intelligent, enterprising scout, and was retained in service." Schrieber may well have been the other man, along with Harrison, "the couple of young men" referred to.)

The requirements for a movement of this scale, into "enemy" territory, put a tremendous burden on Corps and Division Quartermaster and Commissary officers. General Lee's orders were very strict and would be obeyed -- purchase what you need -- with Confederate money, of course. The requirements of feeding, supplying, and maintaining equipment of over 50,000 men, plus horses, teamsters, and trains was a major effort. Again, from Moses files and memoirs:

*I think this was on Monday, at or near Cash Town,
which was about nine miles from Chambersburg, and about
eight miles from Gettysburg. We encamped the Army and
remained there the balance of the day, and the next until
about three o'clock, waiting for Ewell's wagon train which
was with his Command at York. Lee had sent for them.
Tuesday afternoon we started for Gettysburg, and on the way
a courier came up with the information that Hill's Corps had
engaged the enemy. We marched on and reached the
neighborhood of Gettysburg that night. These delays I have
never heard alluded to. The report of the information from
the spies was current at Headquarters. The truth of this I do
not know of my own personal knowledge, but I do know that
we could have marched easily from Chambersburg to
Gettysburg, in a day, and been there before the Union troops,
but for our encamping near Cash Town to await the arrival
of Ewell's trains. Col. Freemantle, an Englishman in the
Coldstream Guards, was with us, he shared my tent. I
remember him well, because when he arrived at our
Headquarters his boots were so wet that he couldn't get them
off, and afterwards was afraid that if he ever got them off he
could never get them on again, and for the two weeks that he
shared my tent, but not my bed, I am happy to say, he
remained booted, though not spurred the entire time.*

*General Longstreet did not wish to fight the Battle of
Gettysburg. He wanted to go around the hill, but Lee objected
on account of our long wagon and artillery trains. I
remember in a conversation between Longstreet and
Freemantle the former said after expiating at some length on
the advantages of position which the Confederates had at
Fredericksburg over the Union forces which was very great,
that the Union Army would have greater advantages at
Gettysburg than we had at Fredericksburg, but he was not*

hopeless of our success. I sent a copy of this part of my journal to General Longstreet as I wanted to be certain that I was correct about the spies and I copied his answer, recorded on page 119. [sic p. 297]

*   At the Battle of Gettysburg, I saw Freemantle up in a tree watching the fight, and I was not far from General Lee. I had a splendid view of the grand and disastrous battle. The thunder of the artillery was terrifically grand, the charge of Pickett's division right up along hill in the face of Federal cannon was not exceeded in valor by the charge of the six hundred* [sic: Charge of the Light Brigade, Crimea, 1855]. *But we lost the battle and then came the retreat; the rain poured down in floods that night! I laid down in a fence corner and near by on the bare earth in an India rubber [sheet] lay General Lee biding the pelting storm.*

The all-important Battle of Gettysburg, often referred to as "The High Tide of the Confederacy" has been written on, reviewed, discussed, televised, critiqued, and "what if'd." The summary of this Battle, from July 1 through July 4, 1863, can be summarized by major events of each day:

July 1 - Confederate forces moved toward Gettysburg on the Chambersburg Pike. In a meeting engagement, Confederate forces under Lt. General Hill initially engaged the Union Cavalry force commanded by General Buford. The battle continued to develop as both sides committed their troops arriving in the area in a piecemeal manner. They day ended with the Union Army in retreat to Cemetery Hill and the Confederates holding the town of Gettysburg. The "what if" will always be discussed, should General Lee continued to press the advantage and attempt to drive the Union forces off Cemetery Ridge.

July 2 - Federal forces dug in and continued to reinforce their position on the fishhook-shaped defense lines, stretching from Culps Hill to the Round Tops. Uncoordinated and delayed attacks disrupted the Confederate battle plan. General Longstreet wanted to sweep around the Union far left and placed his forces behind the Union lines and between them and Washington. Lee's orders were to attack the Union left, limited to the Round Tops, with General Hood's Division. It was here that the oft-referred to action of Colonel, later General, Joshua Chamberlain and the Twentieth Maine on the far Union left, stopped the far right Regiment of General Hoods' Division, Longstreet's Corps, that being Colonel Oats and his Fifteenth Alabama Infantry.

July 3 - General Lee believed that he had sapped the Union strength on their right and left flanks and had weakened the center of the defense line in the center and thus ordered the attack which was to become famous as "Pickett's Charge." The Confederates were repulsed with severe losses. General Lee accepted responsibility, uttering, "All this has been my fault." He ordered his Corps Commanders to gather ambulances and wagons and begin sending the thousands of wounded back to Virginia.

July 4 - With the Confederate forces on Seminary Ridge and the Union forces on Cemetery Ridge, each commander expected the other to attack. General Lee then made the decision to withdraw his Army back to Virginia, and on the following day, the Army of Northern Virginia began its difficult journey southward, keeping an active rear guard to hold off the probing attacks of the Federals.

The evening of July 3, 1864, was a time of trial and tragedy for the First Corps of the Army of Northern Virginia. As the shadows of the afternoon cast their light on the bloody battlefield, the stragglers and wounded of Pickett's Charge against Cemetery Ridge made their way back to Confederate lines at Seminary Ridge. General Lee was there to encourage the weary soldiers to keep up their morale. The Corps Commander, General Longstreet, General Pickett and the surviving Confederate officers surveyed the remnants of the once strong division.

The orders were issued late that night that the Army of Northern Virginia would strengthen their positions, await a Union counterattack, and commence the long line of ambulances and wagons to remove the thousands of wounded back across the Potomac River to Virginia. The day had been exhausting. Among those witnessing the battle was Lt. Col. Arthur J.L. Freemantle, of Her Majesty's Coldstream Guards of the British Army. After returning to England, Freemantle wrote a book, *Three Months in the Confederate States*. In this book, he tells of arriving on June 27, 1863, at General Longstreet's headquarters, of being introduced to the staff: Colonel Sorrell and other officers, including Manning, Walton Clarke, Goree, Latrobe, and of his tent-mate-to-be, Major Raphael J. Moses, the Chief Commissary Officer of the First Corps. As Freemantle describes Moses: "He is the most jovial, amusing and clever Son of Israel I ever had the good fortune to meet."

There was, however, another incident not referred to in the Official Records or in Moses' memoirs. It was contained in the correspondence and affidavits contained in Major Moses' military files. The following pages include copies of the original documents, and transliteration of them, of the theft of the Commissary funds the night of Pickett's Charge, July 3, 1863.

Culpepper CH. Va. July 27 1863
Personally appeared before me Raphael J. Moses, Maj. & A&S 1st Corps Army of N.V. who being duly sworn says that on the morning of the 4th July 1863 between 1 o'clock A.M. and 4 o'clock A.M. near Gettysburg, Penn., his tent was entered by person or persons unknown to the department, his trunk taken therefore, carried into a field about two hundred yards in rear of his tent, broken open by cutting the top and bottom out with an axe. The contents strewn upon the ground and a Package of Confederate money containing ten thousand dollars & about seven hundred dollars Confederate money in a broken package making ten thousand seven hundred dollar bills of North Carolina Bank & State Treasury and a pair of Gold Sleeve Buttons belonging to Deponent was taken therefore and carried away. That his clothing and papers scattered about in the fields but not taken away. Deponent further says that his trunk had a tray in the top part and he kept his money under the tray among his clothes and the trunk in his tent where he slept that being the most secure place which he had for keeping it, as the Govt did not furnish iron chests or other means of security. That he had been kept up until about one o'clock A.M. making arrangements for the movement of the supply wagons of the commissary trains prior to the falling back of the Army to Hagerstown. Expecting further orders he laid down in his tent with his clothes on with Col. Freemantle of the Coldstream Guards, fell into a heavy sleep and neither of them was awakened by the removal of the trunk. Deponent further says that the movement of the Army followed immediately after. That there was no person on whom he could fix as perpetrator of the robbing and that he has so far been unable to get any trace of the same.

Sworn & Subscribed before me
this 27 day of July 1863.
Moxell Sorrell   Raphael J. Moses, Major C.O.
          Lt. Col. A.A. Genl

...

Hagerstown, Md. July 8th, 1863
   I, Arthur Freemantle, a Capt. & Lt. Col in Her
Majesty's Coldstream Regt. of Guards, British Army hereby
declare that on the night of the 3rd last [July] I slept in the tent
with Major R.J. Moses, Chf Commissary of Genl Longstreet's
Corps d'Armee near Gettysburg, Penn.

   I went to sleep about 11 P.M., before doing so
observed a trunk inside the door of the tent which I knew
belonging to Maj. Moses. When I awakened in the morning
about 5 A.M. I hear Maj. Moses' servant remark that the trunk
was gone & I could not perceive it anywhere. After a
considerable search the trunk was brought in by two servants
having found in a wood nearby -- the trunk had been broken
open -- all the garments & documents seen brought in
separately having evidently been strewn about in the wet
grass. No money was brought in although to the best of my
belief I hear Maj. Moses remark that a large amount of public
& private money was kept in it.

   I was not woke up by the abduction of the trunk but I
am a heavy sleeper and had been fatigued by a hard day's
exertion.

         Arthur Freemantle
         Lt. Col. & Capt.
         Coldstream Guards

Hagerstown, Md. July 8th, 1863
Personally appeared before me Arthur Freemantle,
Capt. Lt. Col. in her Majesty's Service who being duly sworn
deponent & saith that the facts stated above are just & true.
 Jon D. Keiley, Jr.
 Maj. & QM

     Arthur Freemantle
     Lt. Col. & Capt.
     Coldstream Guards

Monthly Summary
July 1863

Dr.

In Balanceas Due a/c Individual$33,711.18

Officers July Remitted June 14.05
Error 3r Quarterly Arty Lst of Purchases 1862 71.80

$33,797.03

Cr.

Disbursed $640.00

I certify that on the morning of the 4th July, between
1 A.M. & 5 P.M. (sic) [A.M.], being the morning of the night
of the Battle of Gettysburg, my trunk was stolen out of my
tent while occupied by Lt. Col. Freemantle of the Coldstream

Guards, England & myself, we both being asleep. The trunk contained the Corps money belonging to the Confederate Govt $10,700 and $1500 NC bills belonging to myself. That at the same time the trunks of Dr. Barksdale, Capts. Buqor, Campbell, Maybell and chest of Maj. Kirby QM attached to staff of Genl. Longstreet were taken. That they were all carried into the fields adjoining. The trunk broken open and the clothes scattered about & lef. The money above referred & which was in my trunk robbed & carried off. That the Army was then falling back to the Potomac, the movement of the wagons having then commenced and that I have been so far unable to trace any part of said money, or put suspicions on any particular person. The loss occurred without any fault of mine as I will show by affidavit and therefore accept until the Govt can act upon by that portion of the money belonging to the Confederate Govt.

$10,700 $11,340

---------   ---------

$22,457.03

I certify that the above is a true statement of all money I received and refunds by me on account of subsistence money the month of July 1863.

R.J. Moses, Major, CSO

Personally appeared before me Raphael S. Moore Major & Act.
1st Capt. Cavy No V.a. who being duly sworn says. That on the morning
of the 4th July 1863. between 1 O'clock A.m. & 4 O'clock A. m. near
Gettysburg Penad he had was entered by some person or persons unknown
to the deponent, his trunk broken thereupon, & carried into a field
about two hundred yards in rear of his Tent, broken open, of cutting
the top and bottom out with an axe), the contents & scattered upon the
ground and a Package of Confederate Money Containing Two Thousand and 50
Dollars, about Seven hundred Dollars Confederate money in a broken
Package making Two Thousand Seven Hundred Dollars belonging to the
Confederate Government, Fifteen hundred dollars Bills of North Carolina
Banks & State Treasury. and a pr of Gold Sleeve Buttons were taken
therefrom and carried away. That his clothes and papers were scattered
about in the field, but not taken away. Deponent further says that his trunk
had a tray in the top part and he kept his money under the tray among his
clothes and the Trunk in his Tent where he slept. That being the most secure
place which he had for keeping it, as the Govt. did not furnish him Chest or other
means of security, That he had been kept up until about One O'clock A.m. making
arrangements for the movement of the supply Wagons of the Cavalry Division from
the falling back of the Army to Hagerstown. Expecting further orders he laid
down in his Tent with his clothes on with Col. Rosser and the 5th Va and
moved, fell into a heavy sleep and neither of them were awakened by the
removal of the Trunk. Deponent further says that the movement of the Army
moved on immediately after. That there was no person or whom he could fix
the perpetrator of the robbery. and that he has so far been unable to
get any trace of the same

Sworn & Subscribed before me
this 27 day of July 1863.

J. L. Gildersleeve
Lt. Col. A. A. Genl.

R. H. J. Chas. Major C.S.

Hagerstown Md July 8th 1863

I, Arthur Fremantle a Lt Col in Her
Majesty's Coldstream Regt of Guards British Army
hereby declare that on the night of the 3rd July I
slept in the tent with Major R Morey Chf Commissary
of Genl Longstreet's Corps d'Armee near Gettysburg
Penn —

 I went to sleep about 11 Pm & before doing
so observed a trunk inside the door of the
tent which I knew belonged to Maj Morey.
When I awoke in the morning about 5 am
I heard Maj Morey servant remark that
the trunk was gone & I could not perceive
it anywhere. After a considerable
search the trunk was brought in by two
servants having been found in a wood
close by — The trunk had been broken
open & all the garments & documents were
brought in separately having evidently
been strewed about in the wet grass. No
money was brought in although to the
best of my belief I heard Maj Morey
remark that a large amount of
public & private money was kept in it

I was not woke up by the abduction of
the trunk but I am a heavy sleeper
and had been much fatigued by a
hard days exertion

Arthur Fremantle
Lt Colonel & Captn
Coldstream Guards

Hagerstown Md July 8th 1863
Personally appeared before me Arthur
Fremantle Capt & LtCol in Her Majesty's
service who being duly sworn deposeth
& saith that the facts stated above
are just & true.

Arthur Fremantle
Lt Col & Capt Cold Gds

Jno D Keiley Jr
Maj &c

WAR DEPARTMENT
RECORD DIVISION

Moses' ability as a procurer of subsistence and supplies even drew comments in the Brig. Gen. G. Moxley Sorrel's (A.A.G.) book, *Recollections of a Confederate Staff Officer* (Chapter: Gettysburg Aftermath):

> Everything was paid for in our national currency -- Confederate bills! I did get something, however, our good Commissary, Major Moses, managed to secure (by payment of course) a bolt of excellent velveteen. Wearing quite as well as corduroy, indeed, he got some of the latter also, and sent the plunder to our Headquarters, where the stuff went around sufficiently to give me a coat and trousers, which did good service, I think, to the end of things. He also managed to get a few felt hats, and deserved more, for he was grumbling furiously at the ill success of his important requisition for cash, stores and Army supplies: also for the sound rating and liberal abuse he had taken from the irate females in furious rage at his work.

General Lee's Army of North Virginia encamped around Culpepper, Virginia, healing the wounded, gather stragglers, recruiting replacements, and resupplying. The Union Army did not pursue the depleted Confederates after the Battle of Gettysburg. That Army also rested. However, military action in Mississippi and those in Tennessee and Georgia became the focus of attention. Vicksburg surrendered to the Union forces of General Grant on July 4, 1863,. General Rosecrans in Tennessee began his movements southeast toward Georgia.

Chapter 14

September-December, 1863: Raphael's Memoirs and Military Records
(East Tennessee-Knoxville Campaign)

In September 1863, the 1st Corps of the Army of Northern Virginia, General Longstreet's Command, began a roundabout journey by rail to join General Braxton Bragg's Army of Tennessee in an effort to defeat the Union Army of General Rosecrans advancing into Northwest Georgia. As Commissary Officer, Major Moses had the responsibility of subsistence of this command strung out along six hundred miles of railroad, not in the best of condition. This movement which was 10 days of slow movement from the encampments in Virginia through North and South Carolina, into Georgia, then northwest to the Ringgold-Catoosa area. The Division and Brigade Commissary Officers had their respective units all along the trackage. The noble women of the South eagerly awaited each passing train to assist in the feeding of the veteran soldiers of such battles as Chancellorsville, 2d Manassas, and more recently, Gettysburg. They eagerly sought out family and friends all along the route as the slow trainloads of soldiers riding in and on top of freight cars, passenger cars, flat beds, and coal cars eager to hand them the delicacies of the kitchen and cupboard. For the Commissary Officers, this was a much appreciated assistance.

The Battle of Chickamauga, September 18-20, 1863, was a Confederate victory. Part of Longstreet's Command arrived in time to participate in the final crucial last day of the Battle of Chickamauga which the Union forces in a near route escaping into the recently occupied city of Chattanooga. Bragg's senior commanders urged him to continue to the pursuit. Instead, he chose to occupy the high ground surrounding the city -- Lookout Mountain and Missionary Ridge. The latter curved around the city in such a topographic way so as to run from the base of Lookout Mountain, which bordered the Tennessee River, around the east and north of the city to the Tennessee River, on which Chattanooga was located.

With the proper placement of sufficient forces, Bragg controlled the supplies into the city, and any activity in the city. In effect, Chattanooga was under siege. General Longstreet, as the next senior general and one accustomed to the military style of General Lee, realizing Bragg would not attack, urged him to bypass Chattanooga, take most of his victorious Army north to recapture Knoxville, then move either into Kentucky or to reinforce Lee.

The simmering feud precipitated a visit to the area by President Jefferson Davis. Davis cautiously sided with Bragg, attempted to pacify the other disgruntled general officers, but did authorize General Longstreet to act as an independent command to move north to attack the Union forces at Knoxville, under the command of General Burnside. However, valuable time had been lost, as by mid-October 1863, the weather had become cool, and available supplies, equipment, and especially transportation would be at critically low levels.

General Longstreet's Command began its organization in the area of Tyner Station, several miles on the back side of Missionary Ridge, away from Chattanooga. The region had mixed emotions about secession, with local families often in open conflict: some were Confederate, some were Union. The

Campaign in East Tennessee is considered to have run from November 4 to December 17, 1863. It was not a successful campaign, and Knoxville remained in Union hands. The difficulties of obtaining commissary supplies are reflected in this report of Major Moses:

OFFICE CHIEF COMMISSARY, ETC.
Russellville [TN], January 1, 1864.
SIR: I have the honor to report that when we left Tyner's Station for Sweet Water we were without meat rations. I applied to General Bragg's Chief Commissary, and received two days' rations. When we arrived in Sweet Water [TN], four days afterward, our troops had been two days without meat, and no provision whatever had been made for their supplies. The country within our lines was completely exhausted of beef cattle, and the few hogs collected by Major Gillespie, Commissary of Stevenson's Division, had been ordered to the rear. Of 90,000 pounds flour at Charleston [TN], 40,000 pounds had been sent back to Chickamauga. I applied to General Longstreet, and obtained an order upon Major Gillespie for the hogs and flour in his control. But for this order the Army must have suffered intensely. Under the order I obtained from three to four days' rations of fresh pork, and an order on Charleston for two days' rations of flour.

The flour from Charleston, a distance of 14 miles by railroad, could not be got to Sweet Water for forty-eight hours. At Sweet Water the engineer refused to remove it farther. Our troops were then near Loudon [TN], and out of flour rations, except such as could be collected from wheat hauled to the mills, for which purpose no supply train had get been furnished. In order to get the flour to the troops I had to take forcible possession of the road and run the engine with an officer detailed from one of the Tennessee Regiments.

A few days later a supply train of 35 wagons reached me. It should have consisted of at least 70. We commenced hauling wheat and used every possible exertion to ration the troops, but as they were then moving on the enemy toward Knoxville, it was impossible to collect supplies and keep the trains up with the troops.

In consequence of these difficulties, the Army was two or three days without flour rations, and some portions of it more than double that length of time. With every energy in the power of this Department the troops were a day or two in front of Knoxville before they could be regularly rationed, and it was only a day or two before we moved from Knoxville that as much as three days' rations could be accumulated. The Department, on our arrival at Sweet Water, was utterly unprovided for, and its condition as bad as it could be in a country not utterly exhausted.

Respectfully, your obedient servant,

R.J. Moses, Major, and Chief Commissary

Liet. Col. G. Moxley Sorrel, Assistant Adjutant-General, & C.

The reports of the other staff officer of the Corps also reflect the difficulty of movement and supply. Extracted from the report of the Quartermaster's office, Longstreet Corps:

OFFICE CHIEF QUARTERMASTER, LONGSTREET'S COMMAND,

Russellville, Tenn., December 26, 1863.

We reached Sweet Water 30 wagons short of the transportation allowed us, while all our supplies were delivered at the railroad terminus 8 miles off, and opportunities given to make every wagon available by unloading baggage. While at Sweet Water our supplies for men and horses had to be collected and many wagons had to be repaired, which reduced the number available. We had no supply trains for either Division, and were 25 wagons short of the Artillery Ordnance transportation required by General Orders, No. 182. ... While we were numerically short of transportation, the condition of what we had was beyond all question the worst I ever saw; wagons frequently breaking down, mules just able in a large proportion of cases to carry their harness, harness much worn, and many teams without collars of saddles...

Frank Potts
Captain, and Assistant Quartermaster, Longstreet's Corps.
Lieut. Col. G. Moxley Sorrel, Asst. Adjt. Gen.

The detachment of Longstreet's Division was to have a serious impact on the General Bragg's Army of Tennessee. General U.S. Grant was now in command of the area. He replaced General Rosecrans'; effected a supply line, referred to as the "Cracker Line"; strengthened the Union Armies and Grant made plans for the breakout of the besieged forces. Re-enforcements arrived designated as the XX Corps, made up of Units of the Army of Potomac, veterans of Chancellorsville and Gettysburg, who traveled to Chattanooga. These forces were under the command of General Joe Hooker. On November 24, 1863, Hooker's Command assaulted and captured Lookout Mountain in the battle often referred to as "the Battle of the Clouds."

On the other side of Chattanooga, General Grant had General Sherman attack the North end of Missionary Ridge. This attack was stopped with re-enforcements being sent into the fight by both sides. The effect of the departure of Longstreet's Corps was greatly felt by General Bragg, who weakened his center to re-enforce the north end of Missionary

Ridge. The forces attacking the center did not stop with their limited advance and continued on and over Missionary Ridge, soundly defeating General Bragg. The Confederate forces retreated to Ringgold, Georgia, on the Tennessee-Georgia line. By November 26, the major fighting had subsided.

The Battle of Knoxville was fought during this same period of time and the Confederate forces were repulsed. Upon receiving word of Bragg's defeat and realizing that re-enforcements and supplies were not forthcoming from that source, General Longstreet's forces went into winter quarters in northeast Tennessee. There was constant skirmishing with Federal troops during this time. Major Moses, as Commissary Officer, along with Quartermaster and other staff officers, faced a very difficult task in finding supplies for the Confederate troops. This part of the country was rugged, with little forage and food. The independent mountain population was generally pro-Union. Deserters from both armies moved around the region as renegades. To obtain food, Moses had to use various means to find food, known to be hidden in the thickly wooded hills, valleys, caves, hollows, and mountains. Perhaps the most colorful commentary is to quote directly from Major Moses' personal memoirs:

I was again promoted to Chief Commissary of Longstreet's Corps. I kept the Army supplied six months after Longstreet thought he would be obliged to retreat for want of supplies. This was in Tennessee.

I did it by ascertaining that the wheat was thrashed by toll by machines. I got the books of the wheat thrashers and so knew who had wheat and how much. When they hid the wheat so effectually that it could not be found for seizure, we went after the sheep that wandered upon a thousand hills, and at that time in the fall, mutton was not fit to eat, but they (the

Tennesseans) wanted wool for winter clothing. I seized the sheep in flocks and gave receipts for them as commissary. Then I offered two pounds of sheep for one pound of bacon, and this unlocked the secret places in which the bacon was hid, and sheep proving good currency, I got nearly all the bacon necessary for rationing the Corps. Now and then, I would have to give the Brigade "sheep meat" which was in very thin condition, very distasteful to the soldiers, and as a remark of the displeasure a soldier in Benning's Brigade one night cleaned sheep, took the entrails out, then took a cross stick to hold the legs apart, set a candle where the bowels were meant to be, and went about the camp Diogenes like, seeking to find "an honest Commissary." ...

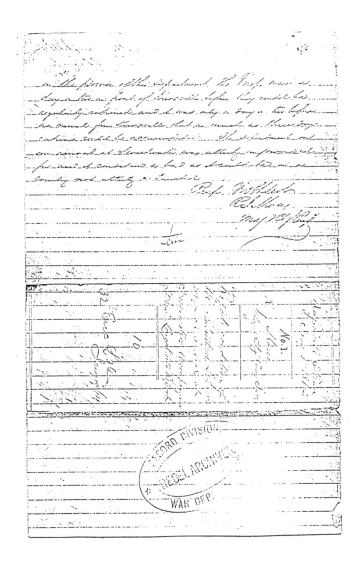

Chapter 15

January-May, 1864: Raphael's Memoirs and Military Records

By mid-April 1864, General Longstreet's forces had crossed the mountains into Virginia and "very happily" to reunite the Army of Northern Virginia.

I remember one night Longstreet came to headquarters at about eleven o'clock p.m. He had been riding all day, through Paris Gap, and reconnoitering other passes of the Blue Ridge. I remarked to him that he must be very tired. He replied, "No, I never have felt fatigue in my life." He was afterwards wounded at the Battle of the Wilderness. I received a letter from him a few days ago [1891]; in it he said: "My arm is paralyzed; my voice that once could be heard all along the lines, is gone' I can scarcely speak above a whisper; my hearing is very much impaired, and I sometimes feel as if I wish the end would come; but I have some misrepresentations of my battles that I wish to correct, so as to have my record correct before I die." What a change! I suppose Longstreet is 69 or 70, and I am nearly 79. In comparison, how much I have to be grateful for, and I certainly am filled with gratitude. ...

The Virginia theater had been relatively quiet during Longstreet's six months absence. However, in early May 1864, the Army of the Potomac, now under General George Meade, but guided by the overall Union Commander, General Ulysses S. Grant, began the year-long campaign to defeat General Lee. The first major battle was the Battle of the Wilderness, May 5-7, 1864. Then, as recorded in Moses' memoirs, began a series of events that set the stage for the "Last Order."

I remained in this position, Chief of Commissary Longstreet's Corps, until just before the Battle of the Wilderness, when the difficulty of supplying the Army became almost insurmountable. Georgia was the chief source of supply and the speculations of the men who were buying food for the Army in Georgia became so intolerable that the farmers refused to sell. It occurred to me that if I could go to Georgia and speak to the people who had sons, brothers, relatives, and friends suffering for food, that I could get supplies; that one coming direct from the Army and having no motive to deceive them would command their attention, enlist their sympathies and unlock their granaries and pig sties. I suggested to General Longstreet to give me a furlough for this purpose. He consented at once, but it required the approval of General Lee. I carried my furlough to Lee's headquarters (signed by Longstreet) which were near by. He had very little red tape routine. He was writing in his tent. When I entered he looked up with a friendly smile and said, "Major, what will you have?" I handed him the furlough. He read it and said, "Major, I would approve it but really we can't spare you." I then explained to him my plans. He hesitated a moment or two and then said, "Well, Major, if you think you can do anything for my poor boys, go and may God crown your effort with success." He approved my furlough and I started for Georgia.

The preceding sequence of correspondence and endorsements came from Major Moses' military files and his memoirs:

Bristol [Tennessee/Virginia], 13 April 1864
To Leut. General J. Longstreet

GENERAL: The return of your Corps to Charlottesville involves the necessity of its entire supply of provisions being drawn from the Depot of Supplies. If the supplies are at the Post the present Acting Chief Commissary can fulfill all duties of the position without endangering the subsistence of his Division.

The source of supplies is now in Georgia and North and South Carolina. I can be of vastly more service in exciting the people in Georgia to the necessity of parting with supplies and in that way contribute more to providing subsistence for the Army than I can by remaining with it! Otherwise notwithstanding the claims of my family are very pressing I should not make this application.

If you will grant me a conditional leave of absence of ninety days to be determined whenever you think the interest of the Corps requires my presence. The Commissary General will temporarily order me to duty in Georgia which will enable me more effectively to serve the government all the same time allow me to give some time to the cares of my family which are indeed very pressing.

Respectfully, Your Obedient Servant,
R.J. Moses, Maj.
& Chief Comsy, O.

Hqtrs, April 20 1864

Respectfully forwarded approved. The supplies for the Command can be obtained without Major Moses, and I think that he may be able to aid in collecting supplies in Georgia to greater advantage than any other officer.

J. Longstreet, Lt. General

Req: forwarded

I have no objection to the granting the application. If any good can be done it certainly is deserved.

R.G. Cole

Apr 20 1864   Lt. Col.

Approved for 30 days with provision to apply for an extension provided it is found Major Moses is not wanted with this Army.

R.E. Lee

20 April 1864   General

The ensuing Battles in Virginia delayed Major Moses' departure and he subsequently made his way to Columbus, Georgia. There, he visited his family and began meeting with people in order to gather supplies and subsistence.

The leave was subsequently extended to 90 days.

Letters Received
A & I G O,

Confederate States of America,
SUBSISTENCE DEPARTMENT.

Richmond Va Mar 27/64

General

I have the honor to request that all of the purchasing State Commissaries now on duty in that portion of the Army occupied by Genl Longstreet's forces be ordered to report to Major E. J. Moses Chf Cs Genl Longstreet's Corps for duty until further orders.

Very respectfully
Yr obt svt
L. B. Northrop
C.G.S.

To
Genl S. Cooper
A&I Genl
Richmond
Va.

Chapter 16

January-May, 1864:
Israel Moses Nunez, Artilleryman

Israel Moses Nunez, the oldest son of Raphael Jacob Moses Israel, was born at St. Joe, Florida, in 1838; raised in Georgia, served as a private in a Virginia Artillery Batter, and shortly after the Civil War moved to Texas where he died in 1905. His life is an interesting story.

Nicknamed "Major" as a child, Israel was the oldest surviving son of Raphael (an older son, Isaac, died in 1850 at the age of 13), and by Confederate law, passed at the outset of the Civil War in 1861 and was exempt from military service. This law permitted a plantation owner with slaves to leave one male adult at home. As the Southern tide of fortune began an irreversible downturn with the defeat at the Battle of Gettysburg in Pennsylvania and the loss of Vicksburg and Port Hudson on the Mississippi River in July, 1863, all available manpower reserves of the Confederacy had to be called to duty. Completing the work at Esquiline on the plantation and of other businesses, Israel headed North to join the Army. Working his way thru western Georgia, past the Union forces occupying Chattanooga Tennessee, Israel arrived at the encampment of General Longstreet's command at Bean Station, Tennessee, near Knoxville, in mid-December, 1863. He enlisted as a private in Parker's Virginia Battery of Artillery, of Longstreet's Corps. Perhaps influenced by his father, Major Raphael Moses, his enlistment was in one of the better known combat artillery units of the Army of Northern Virginia, a veteran unit of the major battles of General Robert E. Lee's command.

Israel joined the Battery at the conclusion of the Battle of Bean Station. The Knoxville campaign of November-December had ended, without success for Southern forces, and Longstreet's command went into winter quarters in Northeast Tennessee. This was a mountainous, rugged area, pro-union, and throughout the region, groups of brigends, deserters from both armies, terrified the isolated farms and villages. These outlaws preyed particularly on Confederate patrols and stragglers-killing them on the slightest pretext of robbery.

Shortly after joining the command, Israel was detailed to corps headquarters. He remained on detached service until the summer of 1864. Israel rejoined Parker's Battery in Virginia in late summer of 1864 and remained with the command until sent on furlough in early 1865. During the period of August, 1864-January, 1865, the battery was positioned along the defense line before Petersburg, Virginia. The section of that defense perimeter was referred to as "The Howlett Line," Parkers' Battery, supporting the 15th and 17th Virginia Infantry on the front line. there were intermittent artillery fire exchanges with Union batteries and gunboats throughout the period. In early May, 1865, Israel Moses Nunez was with his father in Washington, Georgia.

After the Civil War, he and his wife Anna Marie (Moses), whom he married in 1859, lived in Columbus, Georgia. The family moved to Texas, eventually settling in West Texas, where, in 1870, he laid out the town of Stonewall, Texas. The family operated the stagecoach station from their home. Israel and Anna had eleven childrem. He moved his family to Austin, Texas, in 1890, and later retired.

Israel Moses Nunez and his wife Anna Marie Moses Nunez are buried in the cemetery of Temple Beth-Israel, Austin, Texas.

Chapter 17

1863-1865:
R.J. Moses, Jr.,
C.S.N./P.O.W./C.S.A.
Letters and Military Records

Raphael J. Moses, Jr., was assigned to CSS "Georgia," Savannah Squadron, 1862-1863. This latter vessel participated in several actions in the Atlantic Ocean off the European coast and put into a French Port for extensive repairs.

Raphael Moses' service record included: "Service Abroad 1863-1864." He wrote:

> *In March '63, the Confederate Government sent me out under Captain Page as one of the officers to take charge of the Laird Rams being built for the Confederate Government in Liverpool, but the English Government refused to allow the vessels to the Channel. I then went to Paris for a year and was ordered to the [CSS] Alabama, but the vessel was sunk by the [USS] Kearsage just off Cherbourg.*

Returning to the Confederacy in a blockade runner, he wrote:

> *We were then ordered home and I came in by way of Halifax running the blockade at Wilmington, Delaware. After my return to the Confederacy in September 1864, I was sent at the Naval Batteries, known as the Semmes Batteries about fifteen miles below Richmond. I had command of a Battery of*

six, eight inch rifles and we used to have almost daily artillery duels with the Northern forces opposing across the River. During this time, the most exciting events were the laying of torpedoes at night in the River. We had to go with muffled oars in a row boat, pick out a night particularly dark, then tow these torpedoes to the points we wished and anchor them with just sufficient rope to keep the torpedo concealed and as it was concealed from the enemy, it was equally concealed from us on our return trip.

He was captured at Dutch Gap, Virginia, on December 22, 1864.

I had worked my men so hard during the last few months that just about Christmas time, I decided to raid a cornfield I saw on the opposite bank and get enough corn to send to Richmond to buy them a good dinner. This did very well for two or three boatloads, but like the proverbial pitcher, I went once to the well too often and I was captured and sent first to the old Capitol prison in Washington and then to Ft. Delaware.

After several months as a prisoner of war, he was paroled February 27, 1865, and in the final weeks of the war, he was in the Confederate Army. He enlisted in the 20th Georgia Volunteers and assigned as courier to Benning's Brigade, CSA, of General Robert E. Lee's Army of Northern Virginia. He was discharged and paroled at Appomattox Court House Virginia, April 9, 1865. According to his father's memoirs, "He walked home to [Columbus, Georgia]." All this in less than five years after having been admitted as a midshipman in the United States Naval Academy at the age of 15 years, 9 months.

Office of the Provost Marshal,

Department of Virginia and North Carolina, Army of the James.

BERMUDA HUNDRED, VA., _____ 186__

Office of the Provost Marshal General,
Armies operating against Richmond, Va.,

City Point Va

Decbr 28. 186.

Col. T. Ingraham
Pro. Mar.
Washington.

Colonel,

By direction of the
Pro. Mar. Genl. I have the hon.
to forward to you under guard
the following named prisoners of
War —

R. J. Moses   C. B. Navy.

Very Respectfully
Your Obt Sert

Old Capitol Prison Dec 28 [illegible]
Capt & Pro Mar

Chapter 18

July,1864-May 3, 1865: Raphael's Memoirs and Military Records

Confederate States of America
Subsistence Dept.
Richmond July 18th 1864

General S. Cooper
Adj & Maj Genl, C.S.A.
Richmond VA

General

I respectfully request the following may be used as a Special Order.
The leave of absence for special purposes heretofore granted to Major R.J. Moses, C.S. Longstreet's Corps, A.N.V. is extended ninety days.

I am, General, Very Respectfully
Your Obedient Servant,
L.B. Northrop
Comsy. Genl.

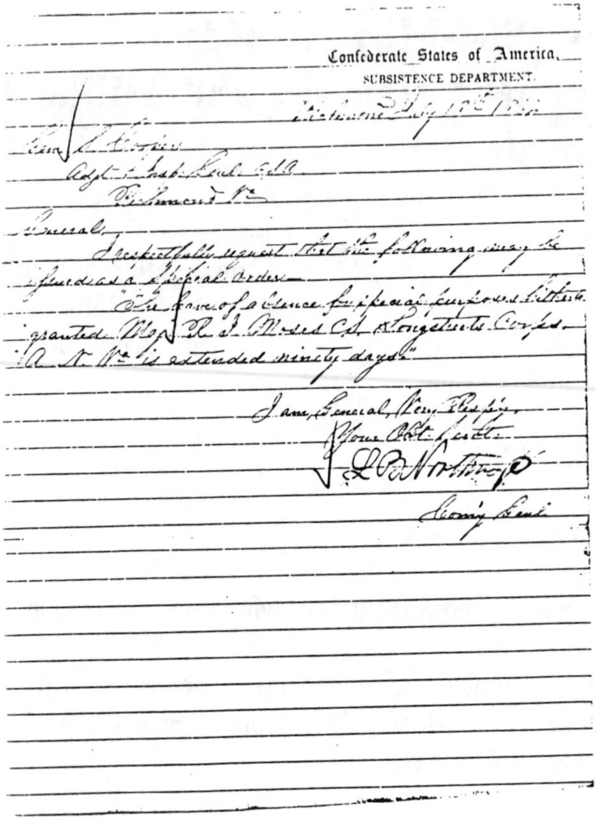

Confederate States of America,
SUBSISTENCE DEPARTMENT.

Richmond [illegible] 186[illegible]

Genl. S. Cooper
Adjt. & Insp. Genl. C.S.A.
Richmond Va.

General,

I respectfully request that the following may be issued as a Special Order —

"The leave of absence for special purposes hitherto granted Maj. R. J. Moses C.S. Longstreet's Corps. A. N. Va. is extended ninety days."

I am, General, Very Resp'y,
Your Obt. Servt.
L. B. Northrop
Comy Genl.

Adjutant and Inspector General's Office,

[Extract.]

Richmond, _July 24_ 1864.

SPECIAL ORDERS, }
No. *172* }

XXXIX. The Leaves of absence heretofore granted the following named officers are extended as follows:

Major R. J. Moses, C.S. Longstreet Corps Ninety (90) days.

By command of the Secretary of War.

John Withers
Assistant Adjutant General.

Major Moses
Maj. C. S. A.

Moses, in his memoirs describes his efforts.

*The first meeting that I called was at Columbus [GA],
in Temperance Hall. There were about thirty persons present.
I thanked them for their presence and stated when I last spoke
in this hall it was to urge the people of Columbus to send
their sons and brothers to confront the hazards of war to
redress their country's wrongs. The house was full from pit to
gallery with patriotic citizens ready for the sacrifices asked.
Now I come from those near and dear to the people here to
appeal to them for bread, for the starving Army, and I am
confronted by empty benches: I must try more fruitful fields.
An appeal to the few that are here could promise no good
results! I thanked those present for their attendance and
closed the meeting.*

*I went from here to S.W. Georgia and was met there
with a very different spirit and had a very successful trip.
While on this trip, Major Locke, the Confederate Commissary
for the State of Georgia, died, and without any soliciting from
me or any such expectation on my part, the Commissary
General, Col. Northrop, telegraphed me from Richmond
assigning me to duty as Confederate Commissary for the
State of Georgia, in which position I remained until the War
closed.*

During his services in south Georgia, military events in
the northern part of the State from May to December 1864
effectively cut off Major Moses from delivering large
quantities of subsistence back to Virginia. General Sherman,
now commanding the three Union Armies, began a major
campaign from Chattanooga to Atlanta. In a series of major
battles; Sherman's forces, outnumbering the Confederate
forces now commanded by General Joseph E. Johnston, drove

the Confederates to the gates of Atlanta. General Hood succeeded General Johnston and attempted to counter the Union advance. He was unsuccessful, and Atlanta was taken by the Union forces, which entered the city on September 2, 1864.

Major Moses and General Hood were well known to each other, Hood having been one of the division commanders under Longstreet. Therefore, while Moses was with Longstreet's Corps in Virginia and Gettysburg and Chickamauga, as Corps Commissary Officer, he would have been in contact with Hood's Division Commissary Officer, Samuel Jonas, who was related by marriage to the Moses family. Hood was wounded at Chickamauga and did not accompany Longstreet to Knoxville and thence to Virginia. Hood was subsequently promoted to Corps Commander in Georgia, Jonas remaining as Commissary Officer of Hood's Corps, now commanded by Lt. Gen. Stephen D. Lee. Therefore, in his new position as Commissary General for the State of Georgia, he would again have contact with those of Hood's Corps.

Samuel Jonas' father, Abraham Jonas of Illinois, had to suffer the anguish of having four sons in the Confederate army and one in the Union army. The families were related, as Abraham Jonas' niece, Rosetta Jonas, of Cincinnati, had married Dr. Montefiore J. Moses of Columbus, Georgia, a relative of Raphael and Eliza Moses. The many stories of brother against brother were not lost on families of Jewish heritage. Dr. Moses was a Confederate surgeon of the staff of Lt. General Stewart (CSA). It was not unusual for the surgeon's wife to assist her husband, or at least be nearby. This was very possible, because in August of 1864, General Stewart's corps was southwest of Atlanta, towards Columbus, with those Confederate forces attempting to prevent the Union army from cutting the rail lines to West Point and Macon, Georgia. That may well have placed Rosetta Jonas Moses in the general battle area. One of the three Confederate brothers apparently had been at the house for several days and hastily had to leave as the situation was very fluid. Rosetta, not having seen her cousins for several years, was shocked and dismayed when a Union soldier arrived at the door the next day. Thinking they were one and the same, she proceeded to berated the "YANKEE" officer as a turncoat, when in fact, it was probably her Union cousin, Edward, whose corps was also operating in the same battle area.

After resupplies and replacements arrived, General Sherman began his famous "March to the Sea," thus cutting Georgia in two. Savannah was enveloped and captured by Union troops during the period, December 6-22, 1864.

The references in the OR's of Major Moses' service during this difficult period from his assignment to Georgia, and immediate post-war period, gave an indication of the drive and the problem and pressure of the office.

OR IV (3) p. 828-829

Subsistence Department
Richmond VA November 17 1864

Major R.J. Moses, Chief Commissary of Subsistence:
    Major: Your letter of 4th instruct has been received. ... regulate impressments ... warrant your making impressments ...

L.R. Northrop
Commissary General of Subsistence

Office Chief Commissary,

Savannah, Columbus Dec 22 1864.

M. C. A. Hopson

Keasons. Va.

Sir:

Your far 16hor. only reached me yesterday the recent break on the road having rendered Communi_____ uncertain and slow

_____ I am inclined to facilitate your views but you approval at will be independent in action

How many gallons per day can you lump or refine?

What quantity of Sugar does a gallon sorghum of average quality yield?

Upon what terms do you propose to refine or to convert into Sugar?

How many Gallons daily could you make the Govt to furnish?

Do you expect the machinery to be transported as Govt Freight, or merely to have the Govt facilitate the transportation as private freight?

Do you expect the Govt to purchase an interest in the establishment or merely to give it patronage to an individual enterprise? Answer these questions and will promote your views as far as they accord with the Govt interest.

Resp,

P. H. Moss Maj

C. Comsy Su

OR 47 (2) p. 1088

Augusta, February 3, 1865

Major R.J. Moses,
        Commissary of Subsistence, Planters' Hotel:
        MAJOR: I am instructed to advise you that Maj. F. Molloy, commissary of subsistence, has been directed to collect without delay at Abbeville, S.C., ten days' rations for 15,000 men; at Washington, Ga., five days' rations for 10,000 men; at Columbia, S.C., thirty days' rations for 20,000 men, and at Augusta, Ga., ten days' rations for 15,000 men, and to ask that you afford him every facility within your power to accomplish this result.
        Respectfully, your obedient servant,
                        George Wm. Brent,
        Colonel and Assistant Adjutant-General.

OR 47(2) p. 1092

Augusta, February 4, 1865.

Major R.J. Moses,
        Chief Commissary, State of Georgia:
        MAJOR: General Beauregard desires that you send to Washington, Ga., all the surplus subsistence stores that you have in this place instead of Columbia, S.C., as heretofore requested.
        Respectfully, your obedient servant,
                        George Wm. Brent,
        Colonel and Assistant Adjutant-General.

        The following dispatch to the Confederate Commissary General reflects the difficult and changing conditions in Georgia in the final days of the Civil War. This letter, dated April 10, does not refer to General Lee's surrender on April 9, 1865, of the Army of Northern Virginia, and apparently not known at the time. Moses' proposals reflect the sound judgement and concern for his attention to duty for the Southern cause.

From Major Moses' military files:

Office Chf Commis ST GA

Genl J.M. St. Johns   Augusta, April 10/65

Coms Genl Danville

Genl: The following read this day from Col. Williams order date 21st March 1865, directed to Maj. L.H. Cranston. "Under a recent decision Secy War, the Comsy Genl directs that you will return to Maj. John McGrady Eng. $50,000, paid to you by him on account subsistence furnished Engineer Employees. You will issue rations to them as to troops not requiring payment only make a separate abstract of each issue." I have just ordered sales on monthly credits to Nitre & Mining Bureaus under your order same date and shall let this order for N & M Bureau stand until I hear further but I presume the principle settle in order War Dept covers the N & M Bureau Q.M. & Ordn Dept. I hope it may be so & that subsistence will be confined to on Bureau in Ga. To do this however we should have means to procedure supplies. If these Depts. would be required to turn over to this Dept. one 4 mule team & wagon to every 500 men that we are to supply so as to enable us to have in tithes it would be a great relief and a source of much economy. If every Dept. is allowed to collect & distribute tithes every Dept. will have its own wastage & want of supervision over that in which they have no interest but abundance. We are pressed for want of cotton goods to Exchange, the manufacture to receive without money & I threaten them with the possibility of the Gov ordering their details to the front they no longer serving our purpose in the factory! But really factories cannot live without money. It occurred to me that I could get capitalists to advance money for the privilege of a position of the mfg at the Gov cost, it would pay them to do it and force factories to deliver. I desire your views before I act in this matter. I wrote you from Columbus that Capt. Cosetter proposed to bring in Ordn and deliver it on Florida coasts accessible to Ordinance Transportations customary blockade freight, payable in cotton on the Apala[latchee], Chattahoochee, & Savh[nah] rivers. He was to have the privilege of carrying out this freight & cotton to make up cargoes in payt of comsy stores brought in, which he could deliver upon terms stated in my letter. Not hearing from you & learning that the matter had been placed in charge of Mr. Hobart Coml Agt Tallahassee. I gave Mr. H.H. Efling banker at Columbus & Capt C a letter to Mr. H recommending them this proposal to his favorable consideration. After my arrival here yr. L/D & Mgs was forwarded to me from Columbus. "Your letters about getting forward supplies received see at once J.J. Noble Columbus Col Baynes Agt, and arrange thru him for immediate operations." I wrote immediately to the parties referring them to J.J. Noble and if no such persons could be found there to Maj. T.J. Noble who was in Montgomery, when my letter reached they had gone to Florida to see Mr. Hobart, Copy has been sent them but I have not heard results. If it accorded with Col. Baynes views I wish I could manage this matter of importing supplies directly & account to him for my conduct so far as it effected his Dept. McDonald, a son of Gov. McDonald, met me in the street & told me he had control of that business on Savh[nah] River to the extent of 300,000 bales cotton & wanted to know what supplies I needed & showed me a pass for Maj Genl P Young to go through our lines with his cargo & two men. I had but little conversation with him as I thought it impossible that he had been invested with such powers & as he seemed on a frolic, I thought much of his authority was imaginary. If he is really an agt. please inform me to what extent I am to contract with him to receive & receipt to him for supplies which he may deliver. I went to Washington, Ga. to see what trans was there and found none. This was on the 8th they expected 80 wagons on the 10th I have ready for shpt meat flour peas & salt to load 250 wagons and we are still accumulating. The Q.M. said during this week he would have 130 other wagons which I have arranged to load but we cannot keep the supplies at Wash until they move off the present supplies. We have to place supplies at Greensboro, Barnett & Washington. I can keep the wagon trains supplied from East Ga. until the RR opens to Atlanta 23/36 April after that my supplies will be accumulating at Atlanta when they are already ordered from Columbus Macon SW Ga. and when the road is once open it is very important (unless military reason prevent it) for the reason stated in a former letter that Augusta should be the point of shipment. When the RR opens all of our supplies which we purchase should be purchased in SW Ga. Not one dollar should be bought on this side until that country is bought out. On this side our reserves should be only thru collected for tithes for those reasons.

We can get more from SW Ga than the Q.M.s will carry. Prices on this side are three times to four times as high as they are in SW Ga. If we buy on this side where prices are high and everything scare we will force prices up and speculation will increase in SW Ga to buy for sale on this side and that will carry prices up there until they are nearly equalized. Now as we have ten times the supply in SW Ga that there is in East Ga. our policy is to prevent inflation of market there as much as we can and buy that out before we begin here, prices this side will then decline. Another thing is if we ship largely speculations [we] can't because we will take up the RR transportation. And if now and then they manage to do so we can impress on that side when the market price slides low, get the supplies & stop the shipment in that way, but to do this we must keep our men out of the market in E Ga for the present. The people must be fed. Whatever the other side and if impressments becomes necessary at high prices all the supplies of SW Ga will already have been Tsy controlled at low prices. But we must have some money if Secty Tsy sells gold we ought to have sufficient of the proceeds to pay 1/2 purchases balance in certif indebtedness. We can spend 20 millions of dollars in a short time, $300,000 in gold will raise it. My own opinion however is that we can do more with 300,000 in gold than we can with 20 mil in Confed. If we had Confed currency to pay out to the extent that taxation demands it. The people very soon discover speculation values and many farmers who don't go to Brokers to exchange would prefer to a certain extent to have coin to provide against contingencies. Every man in the country now recognizes the fact that he may at any moment be placed in a condition when a little gold will be a necessity. I allude to temporary occupation of points by the Federals. We shall lose immensely in sub stores when Mobile is evacuated, as large accumulations have been made there. The danger of this & the loss of Selma with other points threatened creates a general feeling of insecurity and a desire to provide against it. The spirit of the people however is unbroken and they look to final results with confidence.

Very respectfully
Yr Obd Servt
R.J. Moses Maj
Chf Commis c/o Georgia

April 12
A night of reflection satisfies me that there will be
many difficulties in "disbursing" gold which it impracticable.

With the end of hostilities in April 1865, provisions
and rations for discharged soldiers and civilians became a
serious matter. Apparently Moses made a decision to
distribute some of the rations in his presence to Southern
families. With this decision came the following order from the
Commanding General of the Army of Tennessee:

OR 47(3) p. 870

Greensborough, May 3, 1865.

General Allen, or
Commanding Officer,
    Charlotte:
    It is reported that Major Moses, in charge supply train
on Catawba, is disposing of his train to country people.
Ascertain facts, and if true, prevent it.

J.E. Johnston,
General.

The movement of former Confederate soldiers upon
the ending of hostilities left a difficult and confused state of
affairs. The discharged soldiers, some paroled, some

exchanged, some told to just go home, some were stragglers, some deserters, some just bewildered and lost. They moved in every direction, a vast migration of men, mingled with freed slaves and displaced civilians, moving in every direction. Confederate government and senior state officials, and some military officers, fearful of treasons charges and prison terms or worse, sought to find way to reach the coast and leave the country. Their fears were compounded by the assassination of President Lincoln on April 14, 1865.

Chapter 19

1861-1865:
"Oh Death, Where Is Thy Sting?"

The "Lost Cause" took its toll on the immediate family and on the extended family of Raphael Jacob Moses. The Moses family, itself, and through his wife also named Moses, Eliza Moses, was related to most of the Jewish families of the Old South, and to some extent, the North. The families of Harby, Cohen, Levy, Lazarus, Machado and Cardoza, in addition to the Nunez and Luria surnames, all had kinship. These families first arrived in America in the 1700's. Dozens of the extended Southern "family" hastened to the call and entered the Confederate military service.

The soil of the South and the "Lost Cause" is stained not only with the blood of Raphael and Eliza Moses' son, Albert, but with that of their nephews:

Pvt. Perry Moses, Jr., 2d South Carolina Infantry
 Fatally wounded, Malvern Hill, VA, July 1, 1862

Lt. Joshua L. Moses, Palmetto (SC) Artillery.
 Killed in Action, Fort Blakely, AL, April 9, 1865

The monument in the Confederate section of Magnolia Cemetery in Mobile, Alabama, is inscribed:

Lieut. J.L. Moses
Age 25 And three comrades who
fell at Blakely on April 9 1865
He fired the last gun in defense of Mobile
He fought for the cause from its breath and
 refusing to surrender gave his life to die with it.
Oh death, where is Thy Sting?

Another nephew, Lt. David Cardoza Levy, was killed in action at Stones River, Murphreesboro, Tennessee, on December 31, 1862.

The extended family's cousins who gave their lives for the Southern cause include Saul Magnus, killed at Resaca, Georgia, May 14, 1864; Alexander Hilzheim, killed at Kennessaw Mountain, Georgia, June 17, 1864; Gratz Cohen was killed at Bentonville, North Carolina, March 19, 1865; and the deaths of two brothers, Isaac Phillip Goldsmith, at James Island, and Mikel Myers Goldsmith, at Macon, Georgia. Still other family members were wounded or invalided during their military service.

•••

In Memory of Those That Gave Their Lives
Someone Should Say Kaddish

•••

Members of the extended Moses family that had settled or moved to the Northern States served in the Union Military Forces. Septima Marie Levy was a niece, whose brother, Lieutenant David Cardoza Levy, C.S.A., was killed in action at the Battle of Stones River, Murfreesboro, Tennessee, December 31, 1862. Her husband was Captain Charles Collis, and before the Civil War ended, awarded a Medal of Honor and promoted to a Brevet-Brigadier General in the Union Army. In her post-war book, *A Woman's War Record,* she wrote of her late brother, "He lies to-day, God only knows where, without a grave, unknelled, uncoffined, and unknown."

Part III

The Last Order

of

the Lost Cause

May 4-7, 1865

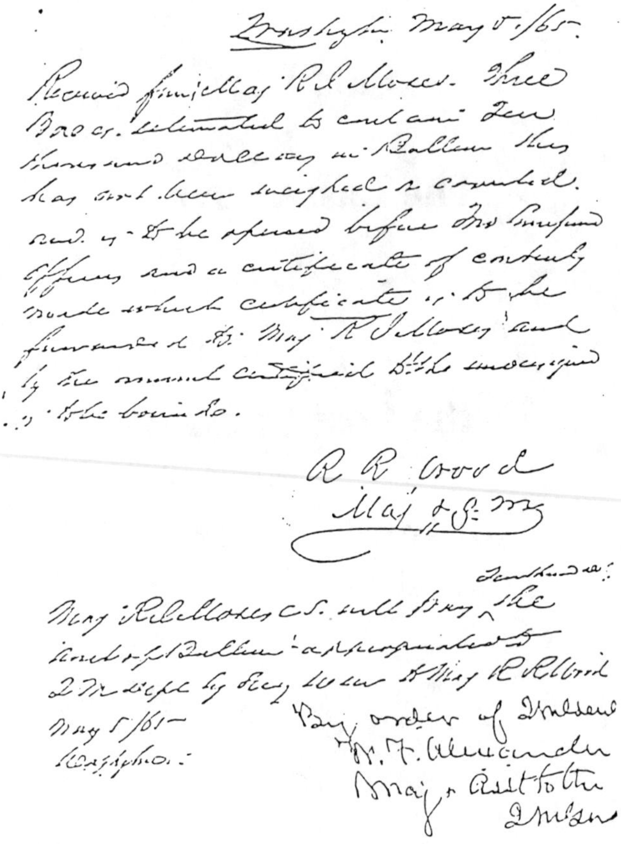

Washington May 5. /65.

Received from Maj R J Moses Three Boxes estimated to contain Ten thousand dollars in Bullion this has not been weighed or counted. and is to be opened before the Commissioned Officers and a certificate of contents to be made which certificate is to be forwarded by Maj R J Moses and by the amount certified the undersigned is to be bound.

R R Wood
Maj & QM

Maj R J Moses C.S. will pay the amount of Bullion appropriated to QM Dept by Secy War to Maj R R Wood
May 5 /65
Washington

By order of President
M. H. Alexander
Maj & Asst to the President

THE LAST ORDER OF THE CONFEDERATE GOVERNMENT,
Given at Washington, Wilkes County, Georgia, May 5, 1865.

Confederate President Jefferson, and his cabinet and aides, after abandoning Richmond, went first to Danville, Virginia, to set up a government. After General Lee's surrender on April 9, 1865, Davis, along with several of his cabinet and aides, moved cautiously through North and South Carolina into northeast Georgia. General Johnston surrendered his forces at Durham Station, North Carolina, on April 26, 1865. On May 5, 1865, in Washington, Wilkes Country, Georgia, he held the final meeting of the Confederate Government. Present, in addition to Davis, were General John C. Breckinridge, Secretary of War; John C. Reagan, Postmaster General; A.R. Lawton, Quartermaster General; I.M. St. John, Commissary General, and Major Raphael J. Moses.

Those final days of the Confederacy were turbulent. Union soldiers were searching for President Davis and former Confederate Government officials. Again, from Moses' memoirs:

I forgot to say that my son, Major (Israel Moses Nunez), was with me in Washington, at General [Toombs'], and one day a cavalry man rode up coming from Breckenbrige and threw over the fence a sack containing $5,000 in gold for [Toombs'] personal use. He [Toombs] handed it to Major and told him to buy corn and provisions with it and distribute it among the returning soldiers as they passed through Washington, GA., and my son did so use it. ...

It was shortly after this that the Government came to arrest [Toombs], and my son Major met the officer between the gate and the house, while [Toombs] escaped out of the back way, mounted his horse, donned blue spectacles and after many hair-breath escapes, fled to foreign parts, where his wife followed and he lived with her some time in Paris.

Major Moses had arrived at Washington, Georgia, some days prior and was at the home of General Robert Toombs when President Davis, with his wife, Varina, and staff arrived on May 4. Davis, along with General Joseph E. Johnston, determined that the supply of unused rations in Supply Depots in various locations, particularly in unoccupied areas of north Georgia and the Carolinas. Major Moses was given "the Last Order of the Confederacy," to obtain the rations by using the funds provided in compliance with the intent of the instructions.

The orders were:

Major R.J. Moses, C.S., will pay $10,000, the amount of bullion appropriated to Q.M. Dept. by Sec. War to Maj. R.R. Wood. By order of Q.M. Gen.

W.F. Alexander, Maj. and Asst. to Q.M. Gen.

5 May, 1865, Washington

Herein begins the odyssey of that "Last Order," from
the memoirs of Major Raphael J. Moses:

Shortly before Johnston's surrender, I was ordered to
Washington, Wilkes County. Soon after, Davis and his
cabinet arrived there. Mrs. Davis met her husband in
Washington. A train containing gold and silver bullion
accompanied the cabinet. It was brought from the Richmond
banks. I was staying with General [Toombs]. Reagan (now of
Texas) also stopped at [Toombs]. We slept together. During
his short stay in Washington, Breckenridge, Secretary of War,
was with Davis. An order was passed paying a cavalry
Company and some soldiers and officers who accompanied
Davis to Washington, $20.00 each in specie. I remember
seeing General Bragg waiting under an oak tree to get his
$20.00. I received an order from General J.E. Johnston to
provide 250,000 rations at Augusta for the returning soldiers.
I had had a few days previous to Johnston's surrender was
known the warehouses were depleted by the citizens in
wagons and every means of conveyance that could be
improvised.

I sent a copy of the order to the Secretary of War
asking for gold to buy rations, based upon an order that I had
previously drawn and had signed by General St. John (I think
was his name) who succeeded Northrop as Commissary
General, and who was also staying with [Toombs], directing
me to draw the gold, carry it to Augusta and there arrange as
best I could with General Mollyneux [Molineux] who then
occupied Augusta with Federal troops, to protect me in
furnishing the troops as they passed through Augusta and to
provide for the sick and wounded in hospitals there. I could
not get the gold and I told General [Toombs] that unless I got
it, I would publish Johnston's order and state that I had made

an unsuccessful effort to get an order from the Secretary of
War or the Secretary of the Treasury (Reagan, I think) for the
means to supply the returning soldiers and in that way relieve
myself from responsibility. He interceded with the Secretary
of War and I received the last order of the Confederacy for
$40,000 in gold, the original of which I gave to I.W. Avery of
Atlanta when he was publishing the History of Georgia, he
having asked me if I could aid him with any interesting relics
of the War. He had the receipt lithographed and it is copied
in his History of Georgia. The receipt is in my handwriting:

Washington, May 5th, 1865.
Received from Major R.J. Moses three boxes estimated to
contain Ten thousand dollars in bullion, this has not been
weighed or counted and is to be opened before two
Confederate officers and a certificate to contents made,
which certificate is to be forwarded to Major R.J. Moses and
by the amount certified to the undersigned is to be bound.

R.R. Wood, Maj. and Q.M.

Major R.J. Moses will pay Ten thousand dollars, the amount
of bullion appropriated to the Q.M. Department by Secretary
of War to Major R.R. Wood.

May 5th, 1865. By order of Q.M. General
W.F. Alexander, Maj. & Assist.
to the Q.M. General

[From Moses' memoirs]
Ten thousand dollars was paid under the order to R.R.
Wood, Maj. & Q.M. for General A.R. Lawton, Q.M. General.

I got this at night on the road out of Washington in front of where General McLaw's family were then staying. It was all bullion in boxes. I returned with it to Washington that night, and then the questions was, "What shall I do with it?" The town was full of stragglers, cavalry men who had just been paid $20.00 each. They had arms but no consciences, and the little taste they had of specie provoked their appetites and like Oliver Twist, they wanted MORE.

[Toombs] gave me the names of ten of the Washington Artillery, all gentlemen well known to him. I agreed to pay them $10.00 each in gold to guard it that night and go with me to Augusta. I then took a squad of them and destroyed all the liquor I could find in the shops. I then got part of a keg of powder and put it in a wooden building that was unoccupied and put the boxes of bullion in the same room, placed my guard outside and around the building and gave out that I had laid a train of powder to the outside, and if the guard was forced the train would be fired. I remained up and about all night, and the next morning had the boxes put on a freight bound for Barnett, a station twenty miles off, where this Washington City railroad connected with the Georgia railroad running from Atlanta to Augusta. The train was made up of a number of open cars filled with about two hundred returning soldiers, and about twenty-nine cavalry men who said they were going to Barnett to get salt. Of course I realized the danger. My specie guard and myself occupied a box car with the door closed. When we got within a mile or two of Barnett the conductor, a nice old man, came to our car and said, "Major, from the talk I reckon the boys are going to 'charge' your car when we reach Barnett." Charge meant to attack it and take the specie and divide it among themselves. I asked him if he could not switch us off and run by Barnett. He said no, that might cause a collision

on the Georgia railroad.

When we got near Barnett there was an embankment for the railroad, about five feet high, and I thought it would be better for our car to stop there than go up to the platform which would be on a level with the car and could be therefore more easily forced, I held a council with my guard, and I told them that if they would stand by me, keep cool, fire (and reload) through an opening we would make in the doors, I thought we could successfully defend the car, but they were not ready to do this, we would be overcome. They consulted together, and I was afraid they would conclude "To join the Cavalry," but they finally said, "We will stand by you as long as there is a chance to save the specie."

I then got out of the car through as small an opening as I could squeeze through, went among the men who were as thick as blackbirds, talked quietly among them, read my orders, told them I had no interest in the world in protecting the bullion except to fulfill my orders, that every dollar of it would be devoted to feeding their fellow soldiers, and caring for the wounded in the hospitals at Augusta; that I should do my best to carry out these orders; that they might kill me and my guard but they would be killing men in the discharge of a duty in behalf of their comrades! That if they killed us it would be murder, while if we killed any of them in defending the bullion, which we certainly should endeavor to do, we would be justified, because the killing would be in self defense and in a discharge of a sacred duty.

Then Shepard, a brother of E.T. Shepard of Columbus (I think his name was Andrew), spoke out and said, "Men, I have got to go as far as any of you. My home is in Texas, I know Major Moses, and I'm sure he would not touch a dollar of the money except to carry out his order."

Then Col. Sanford of Montgomery spoke up pretty

much on the same line as Shepard had spoken, and the crowd
began to disperse and those that were appeased by the
appeals of Shepard and Sanford moved up towards the
platform, but a number remained hovering about the car.

I went back into the car and said to the conductor,
"You had better take us to the platform. All who are satisfied
are there and here I am in the midst of unfriendly
disorganizers." We moved up to the platform and if we could
have gone immediately on to Augusta, we could have had no
further trouble. But unfortunately the Atlanta train was late
and we had to wait at Barnett for more than an hour, and the
billows of the seas rise and fall when disturbed by the winds,
this restless crowd at the depot would surge and press up
against the door of my box trying to get in and I would have
to threaten them and appeal. At last the storm seemed to be
subsiding, when a Commissary whom I knew in Bristol,
Tennessee, said to me, "Major, you think this trouble is over,
but it ain't by a d-d sight. They have just had a talk about
charging the car and some officers are in it. You see that
young man walking up and down the platform, him with the
courtplaster on his cheek; he is leading the men on." He was
a Tennessean.

I thought a moment and then concluded that my only
chance of safety was to take the bull by the horns. I walked up
to the young man and said to him, "You appear to be a
gentleman and bear an honorable wound." I then read my
orders to him, explained my position, and how trying it was
to be forced perhaps to take life and lose my own in the
performance of a duty that I could not voluntarily avoid. I
told him that I had a guard and some friends in the crowd but
we would be outnumbered unless I could enlist men like
himself in our behalf. He seemed embarrassed, but said, "I
don't think you will have any further trouble," and I did not.

We went to Augusta. The most of the soldiers went the other way, but the young Tennessean went to Augusta.

When we reached Augusta, the banks were afraid to take charge of the bullion. I applied unsuccessfully to Metcalf's Bank. I then went to General Mollyneux [Molineux], explained to him my mission, got a guard from him and had the bullion carried to the Commissary's office in Augusta.

The next day I met the Tennessean and told him I was glad he was in Augusta as it would enable me to show him that I had no interest in specie except for the benefit of the soldiers as required in my orders. He went with me to Governor Cummings, formerly Governor of Utah. We met General Mollyneux [Molineux] at his office. He agreed to receive the silver and gold, ration the troops as they passed through, appropriate $2,000 to the hospitals, and at his request I wrote the correspondence on both sides. He signed one in duplicate and I the other, and he faithfully fulfilled his contract. I never knew whether the U.S. Government got the bullion or not. I delivered it to a Mass. Provost Marshal by Mollyneux [Molineux's] order. I tried afterwards to trace it into the Treasury and left all the papers with Jerry Black of Penn. He was, I think, Johnston's attorney general. James Waddell was with me when I delivered the papers but I have never heard anything about the bullion.

As quoted from *Confederate Veteran* [Volume XXXIII, p. 335]:

When Jefferson Davis withdrew from Richmond at Lee's evacuation of Petersburg, the Confederate government was temporarily set up at Danville, Virginia. After the surrender on April 9, 1865, Davis moved South through the Carolinas, accompanied by some of his cabinet and his military aides. At last, on May 5, 1865, he came to the little town of Washington, in Wilkes County, Georgia, and there on that date, was held the last meeting of the Confederate cabinet. Those present were: John C. Breckinridge, Secretary of War; John H. Reagan, Postmaster General; A.R. Lawton, Quartermaster General; I.M. St. John, Commissary General; and Major R.J. Moses. So, at last, in the old Heard house in Washington, on Georgia soil, the Southern Confederacy ceased to exist and passed into history.

History of Georgia indicates the Last Order of the Confederate Government was dated May 5, 1865. Only those listed on the preceding page were still present; the others presumably having departed prior to that date.

Monument in Washington, Wilkes County, Georgia

With the carryout of the final orders, Raphael J. Moses returned to his home place in Muscogee County, Georgia. He had suffered severe financial loss; a son, Albert, killed at Fair Oaks, was buried in the family cemetery at Esquiline Hill, Columbus. He then began the efforts to rebuild his life in Columbus, to strive for reconstruction and reunion of the country, and become a citizen.

Raphael and Eliza, though their hearts were heavy with the loss of their son Albert, were thankful for the return of young Raphael, of their son Israel to his wife and their home, and of their son-in-law to be, Confederate Army Veterans, Lionel C. Levy and William Moultrie Moses. Indeed, they now worked towards a re-united country, and were highly thought of amongst their friends and neighbors. They had fought for the "Lost Cause," and now would give their energies and prayers for the next twenty-five years of Raphael and Eliza's lives, and that of their children and descendants.

Part IV

The Post-Bellum Years

1865 - 1893

Raphael Jacob Moses

And His Family

Chapter 1

1865-1875:
Peace, Reconstruction, Politics and the Family

... And when it ended I had forty-seven free men. All left me except one -- old London, he stayed with me until he died.

The War broke out in April 1861. That put an end to the Northern shipments, and so I went to Virginia and had my fruit shipped there, and I was generally known as the peach man. I sold several thousand dollars of fruit. The currency was good then and I invested the entire proceeds in negroes whose value turned out to be four years service during the War, involving an annual loss.

... When the War closed I owed the State of Jacob I Moses, $15,000 and some $2,000 or $3,000 besides. For this $15,000 Isaac J. Moses as executor had my bonds with interest at 8% payable semi-annually, and a mortgage on my lands and I think my negroes, 47. Moultrie Moses took this $15,000 debt as a part of his portion of his Father's estate, not because he wanted it in preference to anything else, but it was the best he could get, and it certainly was not what would have been called a gold faced security, for my negroes were all emancipated, and at that time it was by no means certain that my lands would not be confiscated. I also had a half interest in about fifteen or twenty bales of cotton with H.H. Epping that I held, and told my son R.J. Moses that

whenever he concluded to go on and get married I would give him fifteen dollars [per bale] and until then I would hold the cotton. He concluded one day to go to Liverpool, and I sold my half interest to Epping, for about thirty-two cents and in about a week after it rose to forty-seven cents or about that, which was about the highest price that cotton ever reached.

I forgot to say that my son Major was with me in Washington, at General Toombs, and one day a cavalry man rode up coming from Breckenbrige and threw over the fence a sack continuing $5,000 in gold for Toombs personal use. He handed it to Major and told him to buy corn and provisions with it and distribute it among the returning soldiers as they passed through Washington, Ga., and my son did so use it. Toombs said he would not defile his hands with any of the damn stuff and I happen to know that at that time he had no money and did not know how soon he would have to go into exile. I know that because at that time I had for safekeeping $2,000 belonging to my cousin, Henrietta Long, out of which I loaned him $500 and a former client of him in Augusta voluntarily loaned him a like amount.

Major not only bought his cotton crop, on the Chattahoochie River, to save it from confiscation, and I sold it for Toombs to Epping and Hanserd. It was shortly after this that the Government came to arrest Toombs, and my son Major met the officer between the gate and the house, while Toombs escaped out of the back way, mounted his horse, donned blue spectacles and after many hair-breath escapes, fled to foreign parts, where his wife followed and he lived with her some time in Paris. When some friends of his were curious to know how he managed to live that he informed them that Mrs. Toombs and himself ate and drank an acre of land a day; meaning thereby that he was living on the sale of his landed possessions. Toombs was never pardoned. He lived and died a rebel and once on visiting Washington, he called to see General Grant, who was then President and told him that it was his practice whenever he visited a foreign country to call on the Chief Magistrate and in pursuance of this custom he had done himself the honor to call. He was certainly a remarkable man. I knew him once to be sent for by Jeff Davis to confer with him upon State matters, and while in Richmond, to be sent for urgently to return to Fairfax Courthouse for consultation upon some military movement. He hated Jeff Davis for his inflexible adherence to old army officers and often said that the War would be a failure, and when the confederacy collapsed History would write upon its grave, "Died of West Point."

While I was with General Toombs at Fairfax C.H., he had a dinner at which he entertained several Generals, including Benning and Joseph E. Johnston. It was given to Col. Preston of Kentucky, formerly minister to Spain. He was the best conversationalist I ever remembered to have met with, and this is saying a great deal coming as it does from one in daily intercourse with General Toombs, who was noted for his conversational powers and brilliant epigrams. Toombs and Wooley and Preston talked and drank Catawba and the Esquiline until after midnight. I had a great deal of trouble to find whiskey and without whiskey it would have been like the play of Hamlet without Hamlet himself! The whiskey that I finally succeeded in getting from a Louisiana suttler smelt more like turpentine than distilled corn, and I really felt ashamed to have it on the table. But I that day saw illustrated the inebriate's axiom, that there is no such thing as "bad whiskey"; there might be better and best, but it was all good, but it went straight to the legs. I saw General Joseph E. Johnston rise to answer a toast and his base line was immense, from the base to the head formed a right angled triangle, and the hypothenuse had to be considerable extended to keep the pyramid from topping from its base. There was a General Thomas there, a Judge in civil times, of the Superior Court of the Northern Circuit of Georgia. He was brimfull of witticisms and good stories. I remember one of his ideas for preserving the peace of the State was to have in each Circuit an election annually to determine who should be hung in that County. The people were to vote and who ever secured a majority of votes was to be hung! The consequences would inevitably be that every fellow who had any qualifications in that direction would quit that Circuit and in this way the State without expense would be purged of villainy.

My son Albert Luria was killed in the battle beyond Richmond, in 1862. He was distinguished for his bravery. At Ewell's point Virginia, in the beginning of the War, a very large shell was thrown in the midst of the men, and Albert seized it and threw it into the water before it could explode. The shell was sent to his Mother by the Company with the inscription, "Sergt. A.M. Luria C.L.G. (City Light Guards), Sewells Point, Norfolk, Va., May 20th, 1861. The pride of all his comrades, the bravest of the brave." I suppose Nina is correct, but I have thought it was as I have written it. It is now at the head of his grave in our cemetery at the Esquiline.

His younger brother, R.J. Moses, Jr., entered the Navy from Annapolis where he was a cadet in high standing. Commodore Tatnall with whom he sailed, told me after the War in Savannah, that he was the coolest boy in danger that he ever met with. He was sent to Liverpool to assist in bringing out one of the cruisers that were being built for the Confederate Government. While in Liverpool he became engaged to a Miss Samuel, whom he afterwards married. When he ceased to have a Navy, he volunteered on Toombs

*Staff, then went into the ranks as a private; fought all through
the War and surrendered with Lee at Appomattox. He was for
a time a prisoner at the old Capitol at Washington. While in
prison he studied Law, and soon after the War was admitted
to practice in Georgia and entered into practice with me. But
I am writing my autobiography, not his, and as a part of mine
I will say that he remits me $50.00 per month to eke out my
limited income and would send more if I needed it. For these
and other things praise be the Lord. And among the other
things I will specify as good an affectionate a family of
children as parents were ever blessed with.*

*I can't altogether leave the War, without stating that
Isabel wanted to be a modern Joan d'Arc, and lead a
regiment. Maria's name was changed to Marie to
commemorate a visit she paid me with her Mother while I had
my Headquarters at Mary's (Pronounced Maree). The name
was afterwards made famous by the assault on Mary's
Heights, at the Battle of Fredericksburg. When she came with
her Mother she was a pretty curly headed little flaxen haired
girl.*

*Nina was at Miss Peagram's school in Richmond. I
wish I had two letters now that I received from her while at
Mary's. One was a calm letter informing me of the rediculous
panic that had seized the girls and their ignominious and
hasty flight from Richmond at a report of an anticipated
invasion by the Yankees. But she wasn't alarmed; no, not a
bit; right there she would stay. About two days laster I got
another letter. I opened it and from the capitals, dashes,
exclamation points, etc., I thought it was a circus bill or some
other spectacular show, but it was neither. It was merely to
inform me not that she was going to leave if I approved, but
that she had ignominiously fled, (I think, but I won't be sure
of this) not even waiting for her trunk, which she always*

regretted -- for the battle of Seven Pines followed immediately. She missed seeing her brother Albert for the last time.

On June 28, 1865, "Nina" Moses married William Moultrie Moses. She wrote of her wedding:

We could not well send to New Orleans for a Minister, on account of the time and expense-Railroads had been torn up and all connections destroyed.

Lea [Raphael, Jr.] went on horseback and told the friends we were to be married just before sundown-the Jewish custom-and about 100 were present: I dressed and went downstairs for the family servants to see and admire the Bride, a short time before the ceremony-my Father had been a Justice of the Peace and could legally marry us, so he did.

Dick Levy, Capt. John Walter Robison, Rynear Moses and my brother Lea were among the Groomsmen-Lea had bought for himself, in Paris, some white kid gloves; Cousin Alice, who sewed beautifully, cut off the ends of the fingers of one pair and sewed them over for the Groom, his hands being smaller than Lea's-Lea had brought a blue silk dress and a purple one and several suits of underclothing for me when he came from Paris, for me because I was a Young Lady, not with any idea of a trousseau-the rest of which I bought in Europe; we were married under a canopy of evergreens and white flowers, made by Cousin F.W. Moise; Mathilde and Joe Woolfolk nominally supported two of the posts, Rosa and John Woolfolk the other two. [Author's note: The four posted canopy is the "CHUPTA," a traditional part of a Jewish wedding service.]

"Moultrie" was a Confederate Army Veteran, having served with theSecond Georgia Infantry, enlisting in 1861. Afflicted with asthma, the hard marches and battles took their toll on his health. In the heavy fighting in Virginia, the summer of 1864, "Moultrie" suffered a severe case of heat prostration. This permanently affected his asthmatic condition. He died in 1878 at the age of 36. He left his widow, Nina Moses, with five sons-referred to, affectionately, as the "Five Books of Moses," ages fourteen months to twelve years.

In 1869, Belle married Lionel C. Levy, a Confederate Army Veteran who entered service at age 15, served first in the 13th Louisiana Infantry and transferred to the well known Fenners' Battery of Louisiana. Fenners' Battery was part of the Army of Tennessee, with extensive field service in battles in Mississippi, Tennessee and Georgia under Generals Bragg, Johnston, and Hood until the end of the Civil War. Lionel died in 1906, Isabelle Moses Levy survived until 1933, and in her later years recalled Dr. Ticknor and his poetry-and, his poem dedicated to her-"Brownie Belle of Esquiline." Perhaps it was the memory of a life long ago-gone with the "Lost Cause" and of her father, Major Raphael Moses who was entrusted with that "Last Order."

After the War, the United States had a law under their reconstruction plan that prohibited anyone from holding office in the States who could not take a certain test oath; and no one could take the test oath who had held office before the War. I was one of the few men in Muscogee county of any prominence as I never held any political office, and for this reason and no other I consented to run. I was elected without any effort, on my part, and was made chairman of the Judiciary Committee, although I did not go to Miledgeville for some days after the organization, and was not desiring any position. But Col. Tom Hardeman, the speaker, appointed me, and when I arrived in Miledgeville and was advised of the appointment I would have declined it but at the Speaker's earnest solicitation I accepted with much reluctance the responsibility of the position.

The immediate post-Civil War period was difficult for the Southern states. The economy was in ruin; railroad lines wrecked; and tens of thousands of families, separated by years of war, waited months to learn the fate of loved ones. Then, too, there were many thousands of freed slaves; the "carpetbaggers" attempted to gain political and economic control of the area, with military officers in control of designated Military Districts. One person, to whom all Southerners and many Northerners looked to for leadership, was the revered General Robert E. Lee. Lee, though offered many positions, elected to become the President of a small college in Lexington, Virginia--Washington College [later, after his death, renamed Washington and Lee (W & L)]. It was his utmost desire to heal the wounds of a divided nation. Lee's activities were restricted by the terms of his federal laws. He called upon prominent men of the South to whom he could rely to direct their efforts to reunite the nation. One of those to whom he wrote was Raphael Jacob Moses of Columbus, Georgia.

Lexington, VA 3 April 1867

Major R. J. Moses
Moses & Garrard
Columbus, Georgia

My Dear Major:

I have read with the attention the subject demanded the article enclosed in your letter of the 23rd, ult. I think there can be no doubt in the minds of those who reflect, that conventions must be held in the Southern States under the Sherman bill, that the people are placed in a position where no choice in the matter is left them, and that it is the duty of all who may be entitled to vote to attend the polls and endeavor to elect the best available men to represent them and to act for the interest of their States. The division of the people into parties is greatly to be reprehended, and ought to be avoided by the willingness on the part of everyone to yield minor points in order to secure those which are essential to the general welfare. Wisdom also dictates that the decision of the Conventions should be cheerfully submitted to by the citizens of each State, who should unite in carrying out its decrees in good faith and kind feeling. As I am relieved from the necessity of deciding how to act, I think it safer to leave to those who have to bear the responsibilities the decision of the questions involved, without embarrassing them with the opinions of those who do not feel this responsibility.

Under these circumstances, and for reasons I am sure you will understand, I have a great reluctance to obtrude my opinions upon the public, and must therefore request that you will not publish my letter which has been written out of my kind regard for yourself.

Very truly yrs.
R. E. Lee

30

Lexington, Va., 3rd April 1867.

Maj. R. J. Moses
Messrs. Barnard
Columbus, Georgia.

My dear Major:

I have read with attention the subject recommended the articles enclosed in your letter of the 23rd ult. I think there can be no doubt in the minds of those who reflect, that Conventions must be held in the Southern States under the Sherman bill, that the people are placed in a position where no choice in the matter is left them, and that it is the duty of all who may be entitled to vote to attend the polls and endeavor to elect the best available men to represent them and to act for the interests of their States. The division of the people into parties is greatly to be reprehended, and ought to be avoided by the willingness on the part of every one to yield minor points in order to secure those which are essential to the general welfare. Wisdom also dictates that the decision of the Conventions should be cheerfully submitted to by the citizens of each State, who should unite in carrying out its decrees in good faith and mind feeling. As I am relieved from the necessity of deciding how to act, I think it right to leave to those who have to bear the responsibility the decision of the questions involved, without embarrassing them with the opinions of those who do not feel their responsibility.

Under these circumstances, and for reasons which I am sure you will understand, I have a great reluctance to obtruding my opinions upon the public, and should therefore request that you will not publish any letter which has been written nor of any kind regard for yourself.

Very truly yours,

(signed) R E Lee

My reluctance from the fact that I had done four years in the War; my mind was entirely occupied with other matters; I had not even seen a Supreme Court decision, was entirely unfamiliar with the laws that had been enacted, and I therefore doubted my qualifications to discharge the duties to my satisfaction. I did, however, by hard work, discharge the duties of the office, satisfactorily to myself and the Legislature. But my business increased rapidly and the necessity for me to repair my fortunes was too great to justify my return.

It was during that session of the Legislation that the Lottery Bill was passed; it was lobbied through the Legislature nominally to establish a Confederate Orphans Home pressed before the Legislature under the auspices of the Masons. I was satisfied that it was a job gotten up by a few men for their individual benifit. I was satisfied of this from the names of the incorporators. I did every thing that I could to defeat it, but when the vote was taken I was satisfied from the sound that the bill was passed, before the Speaker announced its passage. I called for a division, and took from my vest pocket an amendment I had prepared and moved to amend accordingly by striking out the names of all the Corporators except Boyd of Atlanta who got the bill up, and insert in lieu of the men named, the names of four Confederate widows. I made a short speech urging them that if the Lottery was in good faith for the benifit of the Confederate Orphans, the proper custodians of its treasury would be Confederate widows.

I then eulogized their husbands who fell in the defence of their cause, and the vote was taken on the amendment and overwhelmingly carried. And in this way the Lottery Bill passed leaving the original incorporators out of the Charter, all except Boyd. I was obliged to leave one man in or it would have been objected that women could not have carried on the business. I then (after the adjournment of the Legislature) got these ladies and Boyd, who were made Trustees by the Charter to call a meeting of the Trustees at Atlanta and organize. My sole idea was to build a home, provide a place for the ladies as matrons, etc., and pay them a reasonable salary for their services. I went to Atlanta to the meeting as a friend of these ladies, to advise them, when the Trustees assembled. Boyd introduced a Mr. Broadbent, of Baltimore, an adept in Lotteries. I knew that this was the man (Boyd) expected to manage the drawings. I wrote to Baltimore to inquire about Broadbent and the reply was that he was perfectly competent, knew all about Lotteries but was very unscrupulous. I concluded that it would be best to employ him. None of the Corporators knew anything about Lotteries, and if Broadbent was unscrupulous it was best to let him have a reasonable margin for filling his purse until we could accumulate a capital and learn something of the business.

    Broadbent was a man of the world, with very pleasant manners. He talked Lottery like one who knew all about it, and when it was mooted how the ladies and Boyd should be compensated (really for nothing until the home was established). Broadbent said to pay them $2,000 each per annum. This knocked me in a heap. Pay salaries of $10,000 when we hadn't a red cent to pay with! But Broadbent said, "Bless your soul, we'll take in gold by the barrel full, the barrel full, Sir, nineteen thousand dollars is nothing." Boyd and the ladies had to vote on the proposition and as you may judge, it was carried "Nem Con." Then three managers were to be elected, and at my suggested Mrs. Wilson's son, Dr. H.L. Wilson, Mrs. William's brother, John Howard, and an old army friend of mine, Alex Wallace, and another friend of mine, James Waddell, who was clerk of the Legislature when *the bill was passed, were elected managers and agents. They got two thousand dollars apiece, so that gave Mrs. Williams and Mrs. Wilson $4,000 each, and the other Trustees $2,000 each. I think there was another widow lady a Corporator, a niece of Judge Lumpkin, a Mrs. DeLoney. She of course got $2,000 also. Then there was office rent and a salaried bookkeeper, besides commissions for drawing, etc.*

I was very uneasy about the matter of paying prizes in case Capitals should be drawn, but Broadbent pooh poohed and the Lottery was launched, schemes advertised, policy shops opened, etc. Broadbent always came from Baltimore to personally supervise the drawing, never had the least apprehension of being hit for a Capital, had boys blindfolded to take out and unroll the tubes and everything so far as I knew, was fair and square. But I don't think it could have been or we would have some time have been hit too hard.

At all events I felt very uneasy. I think I was nominal manager, without salary except to reimburse actual expenditures. Of course, I could have had $2,000 or any other salary I would have named, but I never had a thought except to run a Lottery for the benifit of the home, and to see that the ladies didn't get into trouble. The salaries were paid to the agents who opened offices in Savannah and Augusta, and the managers who were obliged to attend personally and give all their time to the business in Atlanta. I forget how Broadbent, but he was fully provided for!

I kept a very watchful eye on the management. I knew them all to be honest, except Boyd. But I soon saw that there was too much whiskey drunk by the managers and their friends. The managers drank because they loved it and they invited their friends under the mistaken notion of popularizing the Lottery. After awhile they bought a brick building and opened a school for the Confederate Orphans.

The profits soon began to stop. We sold no large prizes, but the hits on policy tickets at the North, for we had offices in several Northern and Western Cities and the small prizes sold about absorbed all the receipts after paying salaries, etc.

I don't remember now how I found it out, but I discovered that Boyd's son-in-law, the Commissioner, who took down the numbers drawn and recorded them, did not record them as drawn but that he had a book made by Broadbent, with the numbers to be recorded as drawn for a month ahead, and it mattered not what numbers were actually drawn. The numbers on Broadbent's memo book were the numbers recorded and telegraphed to Baltimore, Richmond, etc. I should say here that I put a party in the Atlanta office to especially watch the drawings and see that the proper numbers were recorded. But when this was done the North and West sent numbers from Broadbent's book instead of from the record, and it wasn't long before my young man was short in his account and had to be discharged. I further found that a fellow named English, now a big financier in Atlanta, President of the Chattahoochie Brick Co., lessee of the State Convicts and a prominent promoter of the Georgia, Southern and other Railroads, and who a short time previous to my discoveries was our agent in Griffin, Ga., who then resigned, travelled about the North and West buying prize tickets and hitting us right and left on policy tickets. This was an alarming state of things; I was satisfied of the existence of these things but I could not prove them to a demonstration. So I went North. I had English shadowed and traced him to a Richmond office, where he went several consecutive days, hit us heavily on policy tickets and small prizes; I went to see the agent who described English so that there could be no mistake about him, and who agreed to me that if I could pay his expenses he would come to Atlanta when ever I sent for him, confront English and expose him. I found that Broadbent had men in Cincinnati and New York playing the same game.

I determined to break the thing up and when I could leave the concern in safety I would wash my hands of the whole affair. My great trouble was this: while these fellows were able to rob us, they knew pretty nearly what our receipts were, and they confined their pilfering within our ability to pay. Boyd was in with them, but if they once found out they were discovered they would buy a capital prize, say $30,000, put the tickets in the hands of a third party, burst [sic] us and then when we failed to pay, with seeming indignation and offended honesty withdraw from the concern and leave us to bear public censure. Broadbent knowing the numbers, could buy the Capital prize when ever he chose.

After going to Richmond, New York, and Cincinnati, I went to Baltimore and called on Broadbent. I told him we had an insufficient set of managers, that we were making very little money, and I proposed to give him the whole scheme if he would pay the home annually a sum of money which to him was a mere bagatelle. We agreed on terms which I was to submit to the trustees when I could call them together in Atlanta, and he knew very well that they would do whatever I deemed best. This left me safe from any effort to break the lottery. (This was fighting the Devil with fire, but I could do nothing else and be safe.)

When I got back to Atlanta I stopped the drawings and called the trustees together, sent for the Richmond agent, confronted him with English. English denied, of course. I proved Boyd's complicity; I got some letters of his from Broadbent, I forget them now; had him expelled as trustee, severed my connection with the lottery.

I have often regretted since that I did not moved to

Atlanta on a large salary and give the matter my personal supervision, but at that time I had a very large practice and did not know how much the lottery could well afford to pay.

I am satisfied now that had I undertaken the management I could endowed a magnificent home and the Lottery would have had millions, enough to have prevented the repeal of the charter when it was repealed, but then I would have been censored for drawing too large a salary and suspected of getting a great deal to which I was not entitled, so while my withdrawal was bad for the home, I expect it was best for my reputation.

The Lottery lasted two or three years after I quit it, but its existence was a sickly one.

The ladies that I had benefited were always extremely grateful to me, except Mrs. Pember, whose name I inserted at the request of her brother-in-law, Octavus Cohen. When I had her appointed she wrote me a letter profuse with grateful acknowledgements in giving her a competence when she said she was earning her bread by her needle. Afterwards $2,000 didn't satisfy her extravagance and she got the consent of a majority of the trustees to sell out to Ben Wood of N.Y. In this trade she was to get the lions share. I got wind of it; had influence enough with the other ladies to defeat her plans, and made her my enemy. I have heard of several of her tongue lashings but I have always regarded her enmity as lightly as I did her friendship, and having had her appointed a trustee was always a matter of regret to me.

Perhaps Raphael Jacob Moses was unaccustomed to a woman like Mrs. Pember. It might be said Phoebe Yates Pember and her sister, Eugenia Phillips, were women 125 years before their time. Born Phoebe Yates Levy in Charleston, South Carolina, in 1827, and her sister, Eugenia

Levy, born in Savannah, Georgia, in 1820, were the daughters of Jacob Levy and Fannie Yates. The Yates were a prominent Jewish family in England. The two sisters were among the most prominent and ardent supporters of the Confederacy. Widowed, Phoebe Yates Levy Pember became Chief Matron of the Chamborza Confederate Military Hospital in Richmond, Virginia, during the Civil War. She traveled in the best social circles of Richmond society, could obtain needed and scarce supplies for the wounded soldiers in her wards. Her book, *A Southern Woman's Story,* became one of the best Civil War books written by a woman and has been reprinted on several occasions in recent years. Mrs. Pember was definitely not the stereotypical woman of the mid-19th Century.

Not to be outdone was her sister, Eugenia, wife of Philip Phillips, one of the first Jewish congressmen, representing the Mobile, Alabama, area. Living in Washington, D.C., after her husband's term expired, she too was involved with Southern sympathizers then so prevalent in the nation's capital. Eugenia was known as an outspoken "Rebel lady." A very close friend of the famous Confederate female spy, Rose O'Neil Greenhow, Eugenia, along with her small daughters, was soon placed in house arrest along with Mrs. Greenhow in the latter's residence. Among the accusations against Eugenia was that she and Mrs. Greenhow gave aid and comfort to the Confederate prisoners of war confined in the capital prisons and "had trained her daughters to spit on Union soldiers." Finally, after several months, the family was given safe passage under a flag of truce and passed through the battle lines on to Richmond where she was treated as a celebrity. She moved to New Orleans where she felt family would be safe from harm's way, only to have that city occupied by the Union, and placed under the military rule of Major General Benjamin "The Beast" Butler. Arrested for reportedly laughing while the funeral corteges of Union Lt. Dekay passed under her balcony, she was brought before General Butler. When questioned about the incident, she responded, "I was in good humor that day." Whereupon General Butler issued special order No. 150, dated June 30, 1862, confining Eugenia to a prison on Ship Island, a spit island of sand in the Gulf off the south coast of Mississippi.

Ironically, at this time in 1868, Raphael Moses was probably unaware that the marriage of his son, Raphael Moses, Jr., to Georgina Samuel in 1865 and later that of his daughter, Mathilda, to Robert Samuel in 1882, caused him to be related by marriage to Mrs. Pember and Mrs. Phillips. Georgina and Robert were the great-grandchildren of Samuel Yates of England, who was also the grandfather of Mrs. Pember and Mrs. Levy.

...

In 1868 I was one of the electors on the Presidential ticket for Seymour and Briar and canvessed the 4th district. I also spoke at the celebrated Bush Arbor meeting in Atlanta, with Toombs, Cobb and Ben Hill; it was a very exciting campaign. A.O. Bacon was then a young man and an elector. He has since been very prominent in the politics of the state, but like most politicos his life has been one of excitement and disappointed ambition. He has long been an aspirant of gubernatorial honors, but has never risen higher than the Speaker of the House of Representatives, to which position he has several times been elected. I was with Stevens, Crawford and others of the council for the Columbus prisoners. This was in reconstruction times, when we were surrounded by spies, carpetbaggers, a class of polititions, men without character who came from the North in swarms "seeking whom they might devour." Among them was a man named Ashburn, who like others of the same ilk, were feeding the passions of the slaves who had recently emancipated and urging them to assert their rights to social as well as political equality, the latter having been given to them by an amendment to the Constitution of the United States.

A party of masked men went to his shanty one night ready to tar and feather him. Ashburn fired on the crowd and he was killed. When the news of his death was spread the next day, indiscriminate arrests were made of whites and blacks, principally among the better class of young men of Columbus; without a particle of trustworthy evidence they were arrested, ten or twelve young men, and sent to Fort Pulaski and the Barracks at Atlanta. Two black men, John Wells and Henry Jarvis, were sent to Fort Pulaski, put in sweat boxes until their limbs were frightfully swollen, then taken out, their heads lathered and shaved, and they were placed in front of a cannon with threat of blowing them to atoms unless they would give evidence against the young men of Columbus. But they really knew nothing and refused to put themselves into safety. In this they behaved better than two or three white radicals, Republicans, natives of Columbus who voluntarily perjured themselves.

These inquisitory tortures were fruitlessly inflicted on the two negroes under the supervision of Major Smythe, a U.S. officer, afterwards U.S. Marshall, and now of the "creme de la creme" of Atlanta society.

Joe Brown, the present U.S. Senator, was attorney for the prosecution and his merciless and exhaustive examination of Miss Woody Shephard, a young girl of seventeen, the sister-in-law of Dr. Kirksey, one of the prisoners, brought down upon his head the anathemas of all conservative Southern men, and of none more bitterly than the writer. The trial was protracted until Civil Law was restored, and then the Military Court Martial was dissolved. The evidence for the prosecution was broken down by proving the alibi of a man named Dukes, one of the prisoners whose participation in the killing was proven by all the perjured witnesses of the U.S. It was on this trial and on this evidence that Alex Stevens asked all the witnesses, all who answered affirmatively, "Are you as sure of this fact as of any other that you have sworn to?" Then we proved conclusively by unimpeachable testimony of half a dozen respectable witnesses that on the evening of the night when Ashburn was killed, Dukes was at a blacksmith's shop in Greenville having repairs made to his buggy. We showed that he was in Greenville that night and part of the next day (there was no communication between Columbus and Greenville then by Railroad). This evidence was gotten up from my office. I heard that Dukes was in Greenville at the time, and sent Wm. Garrard to obtain the evidence that would establish the fact. And he did the work ingeniously and so thoroughly that "there was not a loop whereon to hang a doubt." A subscription was raised to pay counsel for the defence, and the prorata allotted to the Columbus attorneys was at my suggestion given to the Democratic Executive Committee or the Democratic Club, what ever may have been the organization at that time.

Not very long after I ran against Buchanan for the Congressional nomination that very Democratic Club, Crawford in the chair, while I was away making a canvas as Presidential Elector, packed a delegation, (A.R. Lamar was the controlling spirit of the delegation). Another was a Columbus person whom I had served without compensation, one Jim Barber, a sort of political tool of the Junta, to go to LaGrange where the Congressional Convention was held, and Troup County, unanimously for me -- to vote against me, and this delegation defeated me, though it was known to it that the

County was for me. But I lived long enough to cry quits with both. I had Lamar defeated through the Jewish folk in his race for Mayor and Crawford when he would not announce himself as a candidate but expected to be chosen as a dark horse in the contest between Parsons and Buchanan. My influence and the speach I made in the convention nominated Harris and he recognized this fact as did his friends and Harris. Afterwards, about two years, when Harris wanted the re-nomination and could not get a two thirds vote and could have had me nominated with a word he allowed the convention to break up without a nomination and announced his candidacy. I was in Atlanta at the time. When I came home I announced myself in opposition, but finding that Parsons had announced and was at work in the Northern part of the district, that I was too late for a conference, and if all three ran Harris would be elected, I came down, promptly made a canvas of six weeks for Parsons and elected him.

I suppose you will want to know why I wanted to go to Congress, if I had no political ambition. Strangers would perhaps doubt me, but my children will believe me when I say race feeling was the predominating motive. I wanted to go to Congress as a Jew and because I was a Jew and believed that I might elevate our people by my public course. I am not a conformist, but I am proud of being a Jew and would have liked in a public position to confront and do my part towards breaking down the prejudice. I don't believe all the Biblical of the Jews but their remarkable career satisfies me of one of two things:

That they are either under special divine protection, or they are the most wonderful people on the face of the earth, to have risen to a position which they occupy despite the prejudice and persecution with which they have been pursued for nearly two thousand years.

In either case to be a descendant of the race is a lineage to be proud of, and I pity the weak creatures who would conceal their origin. I sometimes doubt the purity of their blood and think there must be some unknown admixture with a lower type of being.

Messrs. Benning, Crawford and Lamar Ramsay and others who controlled the politics of Muscogee County were all Democrats and my personal friends. I believed they all liked me personally but they all combined against me when I sought public position in National politics. I would not have been a presidential elector in 1868 if they could have prevented it, but my position in the Legislature of '66, as chairman of the Judiciary Committee, added so much to my reputation in the State that they could not prevent my nomination as Presidential Elector, and I improved my opportunities in the fourth district so much during my canvass as elector that nothing could have defeated me for Congress but these, my personal friends in violating the wishes of the County and casting the vote of Muskogee against me. No candidate can succeed when his own County repudiates him! All these gentlemen had political bees in their bonnets and Crawford was dreadfully stung with the Congressional bee. I always had the vanity to believe that this Junto kept me down because they believed that if I once represented the District I would be very hard to displace, and they all know that I had a will of my own and could never be controlled by them. I am led to this conclusion because our social relations were very close and I can think of no other motive that might have influenced them.

In 1865 and 1866 the controlling men in Columbus were Hampton Smith, Wm. H. Young, Joe Kyle, Daniel Griffin, Lloyd Bowers, Gray Bedell and Hughes and others. H.H. Epping and Joe Hansard were just coming into prominence. Wm. Dougherty was a leading lawyer, and the terror of all stockholders of insolvent banks. He had been pursuing them with "the hunters ire, the hounds untiring hate" for nearly twenty years. Crawford and Ingram did but little. Seaborn Jones with whom Benning was associated, did a leading practice. Peabody and Brannon were just getting into business, they had held bomb proof positions during the War, Peabody had been Solicitor and Brannon was really suffering with a disability in the ankle, so that neither of them had ever heard the sound of a gun until Columbus was taken, if they heard it then, of which fact I am not apprised. Johnson and Downing were in good practice. Johnson had for a short time served as Apothecary in the home troops, (known as Joe Brown's pets) in Atlanta. Johnson was over age for conscription, and a pronounced Union man, afterwards appointed by Andy Johnson Provincial Governor.

These men who did not go to the front necessarily got into some practice while all the other lawyers were in the army. They had the civil field to themselves and as the sun shone for them they took advantage of the opportunity and made hay, which they stacked away instead of consuming. When I write this at the end of twenty-four years Brannon is President of a Bank, and one of the rich men of Columbus; Peabody who early learned "to bend the supple hinges of the knee that thrift may follow fawning", is one of Wm. R. Young's pets, of whom more hereafter. He, Peabody, is a Director in the Eagle & Phenix Mfg. Co., trustee of the public Schools, a leader in the Presbyterian Church, and a leader at the bar. All this has become with very little natural ability, but a great deal of industry, and a keen appreciation of St. Paul's advice, "Being all things to all men." Before the War he studied Law with me and I gave him a nominal interest in my business and the advantage of my name, doing business as Moses and Peabody. I did the same at one time before the War with Wm. A. Laws, Ed. W. Moise, and after the War in fulfillment to a promise made to his father just before he died, I gave Wm. Garrard an interest in the cases in the Bankrupt court, associated him with R.J. Moses, Jr., whom I took in as a full partner under the name of Moses and Garrard.

R. J. MOSES, SEN. ⎫
R. J. MOSES, JUN. ⎬
W. C. GARRARD. ⎭

OFFICE OF MOSES & GARRARD

ATTORNEYS AT LAW.

Columbus, Geo. July 28 1867

Letterhead of the Law Firm after Raphael J. Moses, Jr., joined his father, Raphael L. Moses, Sr., and William Garrard in the firm.

I think they all appreciated my course to them except Peabody, and if he did he deserved a prize for his conservativeness, for he has never in any way manifested the least consciousness of ever having been served by me. But in this as in every other instance where men have failed me, I have squared the account and left a little to my credit.

I might have curtailed some parts of this Journal, had I remembered that these events and some others were more elaborately referred to in Avery's History of Georgia, a copy of which I have just looked over, belonging to my daughter Nina, and while I may still refer to some incidents briefly, I will here cite the pages in the index of the history on which my name is mentioned. - Pages 43, 264, 5, 6, 327, 328, 390,

329, 352, 359, 361, 387, 388, 391, 524 and 595.

The society of Columbus was upheaved and the bottom turned on top by the revolution. The butchers and the bar keepers of 1865 are the "creme de la creme" of '90 and the decendants of what was the best and richest society in '65 are many of them in the humblest positions, nearly all poor, some working in the factories, and I know of one instance where the grand-son of an ancestor, John Woolfolk, who owned three or four hundred slaves and the finest plantation on the Chattahoochie, part of which his mother inherited, died the overseer to a merchant who bought the plantation after the War.

No one except one who has passed through the ordeal can realize the changes of fortune and with the change of fortune generally a like change of position, that takes place in a generation following a revolution. "Money makes the mare go" and few if any stop to consider how the money has been made, or knowing it, care much about the means. In 1865 our immediate neighbor on the Esquiline was Dr. F.O. Ticknor, the Georgia poet. He was a true poet, a true friend and a genial companion. In '65 he had been our neighbor for ten or fifteen years, and our friendship with his family has continued unbroken, although the doctor has been dead many years. His wife was a Miss Nelson of Virginia, and her sisters were Mrs. Carter, and Mrs. Woolkfolk, who lived in the suburbs of Columbus, and our friendship with them has been uninterrupted and a source of genuine pleasure (I think) on all sides. Dr. Ticknor's farm, about a mile from here, is occupied by a negro, but the change in tenancy is more respectable than some that have occurred. When in the Legislature I made a great effort to relieve Bank Stockholders from the severe penalties of personal responsibility, but without effect.

The prejudice against insolvent State Banks was so strong that no allowances could be interposed where Banks broke from the effects of the War. This prejudice has been lost as to State Banks. Since the 10% tax fixed on State Banks by the U.S. -- the U.S. Banks have driven them out of existence (the prejudice) is new directed against National Banks, while the clamor is now for State Banks freed from 10% tax coupled with visionary schemes for Farmer's Loans which will inevitably break any bank that has to pay specie in redemption of its bills, when the bills are issued in the shape of long loans to farmers on the security of land. This will prove disastrous for many reasons, but one is enough: no Bank can exist and pay expenses and dividends if its issue are only equal to the specie in its vaults. A Bank is obliged to make short loans so that its circulation is frequently returned by the payment of loans. A bank is considered for this reason justified in circulating three times as many bills as it has specie in its vaults, but if it issues bills beyond the specie payable on demand in gold or silver, and puts this excess in circulation on long loans secured by land or any other security, the bank must necessarily fail, for its liabilities are due on demand and its assets are not due for a long time. On the other hand capital would not be invested in Bank stocks if they could not issue more bills than the specie capital paid in, because it would be impossible for a bank to lend its capital out at legal interest, even if it made no losses, and paid its stockholders a dividend equal to the legal interest recovered, and pay out the expenses of fixtures, rent, officers salaries, printing bills, etc.

If, however, the public pressure should result in the re-charter of State Banks to aid Farmers, a few years will fill the country with broken Banks, the old prejudices will be revised and with no class will they be more intense than with the very Farmers who caused the failures!

During the latter part of the War Wm. H. Young came to the army when we were just about to move from New Market. Any one who has ever been in the army can realize the position of an old man so deaf that he couldn't hear or make his way or wants intelligible, arriving in the army under such circumstances. His object was to meet a son in the cavalry, then many miles away. I knew that the cavalry were under orders (or would be before he could reach it) to make rapid movements. I could not disclose these facts to Mr. Young, but I brought him to our headquarters and made him comfortable; through Osman LaTrobe, then acting as adjutant, I managed to get his son leave to come and see his father. His son was nearly barefooted. Young's money could not buy shoes, but my influence could get them. I had him shod, took care of Young until the army movement began and then carried him with us until he could be safely sent back to Georgia alone. My recollection is that his son was killed shortly after. I have an idea that I got him a furlough afterwards to come to Georgia, where he saw his Mother before his death, but the events occurred so long ago, and so much has happened since, that I am not distinct about this last circumstance, but I am very clear about the others. I well remember that I contributed to Mr. Young's amusement while at our headquarters by loaning him "What will we do with it?" and I never saw any business man more absorbed in a book than he was in this novel; and this man is my only enemy that I know of!

I had been his attorney before the War, both in Columbus and Apalachicola, where we had both lived some years before, so that when the War closed, it was natural that upon the failure of the Bank of Columbus, in consequence of its large investments of Government bonds, etc., Mr. Young

should employ me to draw up the assignment for the Bank,
and also employ me to represent him as a stockholder and
director. DeWitt Wilcox was made assignee, Mr. Young's
liability, for the redemption of bills was either $130,000 or
$160,000. At all events it was enough to ruin him, if he had
it to pay. By my advice he purchased bills enough, at ten and
twelve and one half cents, to redeem his liability. The old
dicisions [sic] had established the rule that when a
stockholder was sued if he could plead and proffer in defence
that he had redeemed the amount of bills for which he was
liable, his liability was thereby discharged.

It remained unsettled whether a stockholder who had
redeemed bills to discharge his liability could participate with
other stockholders in receiving his pro-rata of the assets of
the Bank.

I had two duties to perform as attorney for Wilcox, the
assignee; I had to protect him from liability and see that he
made no mistakes in the discharge of his duties.

I had to defend Mr. Young as a stockholder and
protect his interest. To do the latter it was necessary for him
to collect as much as possible on his bills.

I had no duties in conflict with these. For protecting
Wilcox and drawing the assignment I received a fee of
$5,000. This amount was fixed as a proper sum by Alex
Stevens, Robert Toombs and Ben Hill and Linton Stevens, all
of whom I consulted as to what I should charge.

I made no contract with Young about fees but I
thought if I succeeded in clearing him in liability and
collected from him out of the assets all that he had paid for
his bills so that he would be relieved from his ruinous liability
without the cost of a dollar, either in payment of liability or
of one dollar out of his pocket, in payment of fees he would
have been delighted to have made it, because I had not then

any idea that I should affect any such result, and I went on working for his safety and profit without any contract trusting, yes, not for a moment doubting! that he would pay me reasonable fees for my services, judging by what might be the result of my labors.

As I have already said, it was undecided whether a stockholder who purchased bills to relieve his liability would be allowed to share in the assets of the Bank.

To provide against this contingency with Mr. Young's full knowledge I divided his bills into separate parcels, say 50 or 100, I don't remember now, and I took Dunn's register and altering names a little I filled my notices within the six months as required by assignment as attorney for these several names.

This could hurt no one except speculators on Bank Bills represented by Dougherty, John King, Peabody and Brannon, Russell Smith and Alexander and other attorneys, and this made it appear that the bills presented to the assignee were more than were really presented, by the amount of Young's bills, because they were twice represented, once by his claim as director, and again by my claim as attorney for diverse fictitious persons. This part is important to explain matters.

The circulation of the Bank by which the liability of stockholders was fixed was a little over $880,000. The only trouble possible in entering bills in duplicate was that it might appear that there were more bills presented than the total issues, but I risked this on the reasonable certainty that in the long existence of the Bank, and four years of the War, many bills had been lost or destroyed and that many would not be presented within six months. I was right in this because the amount of bills presented up to 1869 was less than $600,000, inclusive of those apparently held by directors.

Before I could safely let the assignee make any payments I had to make a case raising all the points involved, and I did make such a case and we agreed that the assignee might pay out 12½¢ of all bills presented within six months except by the directors who were to withdraw their bills. And they did give a formal notice of withdrawal, all in good faith except Young, because he knew that I could draw for him on his bills entered in fictitious names, 12½¢. There may be a question as to his obligation to his company directors, but more as to mine. I owed them nothing and all directors represented by me were protected the same as Young was.

I took no action in this matter until the case was decided at December Term 1869, and then I made this trade. I agreed with Dougherty that if he would sign an agreement to accept 20¢ which was about what the fund would pay, I would allow him ten cents additional out of my fees. This was contingent on my success. I knew if Dougherty took 20¢ and quit the fight any one else would and in this I was right. John King, a Banker signed off about $160,000; Jim Russell who represented Belcher, claimed 50¢ which I agreed to pay him because Belcher had taken the bills for value before the War, and the decision of the Supreme Court was that they were to draw a pro-rata on the cost of bills. This was the reason Dougherty and John King came in, their bills were all bought on speculation, costing $10.00 and $12.00.

When I went to see Young to fix on my fees and draw 12½¢ on his bills entered by me as attorney for fictitious persons, I suggested a settlement as to my fees and proposed to him to allow me $10,000 not out of the 12½¢ that I would then draw but out of the excess that I would draw on final distributions. He wouldn't hear of this talked about the $5,000 that the Bank paid me and proposed to allow me a balance of $900.00 or $1,000 that I owed him on a balance *of accounts between us.*

There we quit and quarrelled and he couldn't draw on his bills as director for he had withdrawn them on the record. He couldn't draw on the names under which I had notified, because I was the attorney notifying, but he concluded that as these names were fictitious there would be a surplus after all the bill holders under my contract with them had drawn their 20¢ and that his bills would yield him 30¢ or some $40,000, but he didn't know his men. I bought bills from some of the directors, I bought bills through brokers in New York, Baltimore and Charleston. With their bills I drew for nearly all the names I had entered, some of them cost me as high as 20¢, some more. But Young kept watching the balance in the hands of the assignee, making daily visits! Towards the end I suggested to Blanford that he could make a good fee by filing a bill and enjoining the directors from drawing until the County and some other depositors represented by him were paid.

Young became very much outraged, wrote me a letter charging me with being at the bottom of the injunction and threatening to expose me. I wrote him back to go ahead, that I had not a cent of interest in Blanford's fees -- and I had not and if I had ever advised him to file a bill and ask for an injunction, it was in the line of protecting the assignee who was the only client that I had who had a particle of interest in the distribution of the Bank funds; I ought to say here that after Dougherty signed, and King and others agree to take 20¢ and release the stockholders, all other bill holders signed, and I made a contract with all the principal stockholders to pay them 10¢ for their bills, and they were to allow me as fees and for what I had to pay Dougherty and others for signing the release, whatever excess I might receive on final distribution.

Young finally got about $8,000 on his bills, If he had paid me a fee of $10,000, as he should have done, he would have drawn from the fund, about $40,000; that would have left him $30,000 instead of which he got $8,000, difference $20,000 or thereabouts. For this he has pursued me ever since, but I have stricken back for every blow that he has made.

Chapter 2

1875-1880:
"You Call Me a Jew, You Honor Me."

I have no doubt that I have lost money in the end by my controversy with him [Young], for his Factory [industry] influence is very great. He has with his friends pretty much controlled things in Columbus, and very naturally, for his energy and foresight has built up the manufacturing interests without which Columbus would have been a dead town. I have had other suits against his factory interests (his old factories) and after hard contested fights have invariably whipped him out.

Since writing this Journal, Young has been turned out of the factory as President and the stock has fallen to 30¢. If I were vindictive I could say "Vengeance is mine," but I really sympathise with him in his loss of power and money.

He became the residuary assignee, had with his own stock the majority of the stock, controlled by his influence and inflexible will power, to approve all of his reports. I cost him about $20,000 in two or three suits, one of which lasted until about 1880. He slandered me basely in the Bank suits; I sued him, forced him to cover his property up, then submitted to arbitration of Governor Smith, and Young's attorneys in defence of the libel suits M.J. Crawford and Col. Chappel. Report not only exhonerated me fully, but praised my skill, ingenuity and good faith to the Stockholders, but it *white washed and excused Young and fixed my fee at $1,000 when Smith had previously acknowledged to me that $10,000 to be paid out of the assets of the Bank was not unreasonable. Crawford fixed it up, Smith assented and Chappel was out voted but thought properly that the main point with me was my professional integrity, and as the report was full and clear and favorable on that point, that the mere question of fees was unimportant.*

But I remember Smith's bad faith and in 1877 when he was a candidate for U.S. Senator, vs. Benjamin Hill, I ran for the Legislature. They put up Reese Crawford against me, a son of M.J. Crawford, and in the primaries the whole influence of the factories, Young, King, Salsberry and their tools, were against me. I never moved in the canvass personally, was nominated by the primaries and of course elected! In one of the precincts, Nances, all of Young's influence was concentrated to beat me and would have been successful except for a gentleman named Griggs whom I did not know but who had a great admiration for me, it seems, and had the packed vote taken over when they had packed it, and reversed the voice of the precincts. I would have been nominated without that precinct, as it turned out, but I have always been grateful to Griggs and would serve him any way in my power, and he knows it -- in fact, I have served him.

John King, a clerk in the Bank of Columbus, and a bombproof, a personal friend of Peabody, Brannon and Salsberry, was started by Lloyd Bowers as a Banker. Bowers made him and Bowers broke him in 1875. He, Bowers, was and is a wild speculator in cotton. A Jew named Koernecker went to King's Bank while they were drawing the assignment in the back room. Peabody was the lawyer and Salsberry the assignee. The Bank was then broke, but the fact not know to outsiders. While this assignment was being drawn up,

Koerneker who had saved a thousand dollars to visit his Mother in Germany, applied at the counter for a check on New York. The teller stepped to the back room where King and his counsel and assignee were closeted, returning to his place as teller, receipted Koerneker's $1,000 and sold him a check on New York that they knew was not worth a cent. Concequently, Koerneker had to abandon his trip. King went into bankruptcy. I opposed him and had no hesitancy in saying on the streets that if King had purchased a check from Koerneker, a Jewish Banker, under the same circumstances, the Jew would have been hung to a lamp post. After thinking the matter over I was satisfied that King was less to blame than his counsel and his assignee. He was a weak man, in great trouble at the time that Koerneker applied for the check, hardly knew what to do and was governed by his counsel and assignee. I became satisfied after a very thorough sifting of his schedules that he had made a full surrender of all his property, and finally in behalf of creditors, represented by me, enough to make a majority, I consented to his discharge. His friends afterwards purchased for him the Columbus Enquirer, which was always bitterly opposed to me, so by pursuing an independent course, I had arrayed against me the cliques that controlled Columbus.

I had two purposes in running for the Legislature in 1877; one was to convince my enemies that they could not defeat me, the other was to defeat Smith in his candidacy for U.S. Senator. Benjamin Hill and Tom Norwood were his opponents. In order to use my influence against Smith it was necessary that I should have the sentiment of the County against him, for much as he had wronged me in bowing to what he supposed was a stronger combination, I would not have misrepresented my constituency to redress a personal wrong. I told Ben Hill so, and suggested to him to come to

Columbus and address the people. He was a very able and remarkably eloquent man. Altogether Smith's superior in his qualifications for Senator. Hill came to Columbus, addressed the people at the Opra House, made a grand speach, enthused the people and became at once Muscogee County's favorite for the Senate.

I was selected in the Legislature to nominate Hill, and did so; his opponents were Norwood and Smith. Smith failed to develop any strength, the contest was really between Hill and Norwood. The latter had with him seven or eight votes less than enough to elect him, Smith had only eighteen votes. His votes thrown to Hill would elect him. We had a caucus that night. I was chairman of the caucus. Smith's friends proposed that if we would give him a vote that would enable him to withdraw respectably he would withdraw and his eighteen votes would come to Hill, on the next ballot, and elect him. Our caucus was willing to accept but he trouble we had was that none of the Hill men were to vote for Smith and so be apparently against Hill. I said to the caucus that in the army when they wanted to send out a forlorn hope, the call was made for volunteers, and the most devoted men came forward. And in an effort to serve a friend under unpleasant circumstances, the same feeling ought to prevail. I therefore made a call for volunteers, and led with offering myself. We soon mustered some fifteen or twenty, and the next day when the balloting began after one or two ballots, and fifteen of twenty left Hill for Smith, the Norwood men were exhultant, and Hill's friends who were not in the secret were proportionally despondent. Smith received about forty votes and (soon after perhaps two ballots more) according to the contract withdrew. Then Norwood's friends were jubilent, they were sure he would be elected on that ballot, but as the names of the Hill deserters were called, they came back to Hill. And as the Smith men were called, they almost without exception voted for Hill and we had a reserve of four negroes, fixed by R.L. Mott who all through had thrown their votes off. They voted for Hill on this ballot, and he was triumphantly elected. It was on this occasion that Grady, who was of a very emotional nature, rushed up to me, almost embraced me and wept like a child.

Hill was ever after my steadfast and faithful friend.

I have just received the following letter from General Longstreet, to whom I sent a copy of my remarks, on page 76 [sic p. 188], relative to the battle of Gettysburg.

Gainsville, Oct. 12th, 1890.

My dear Major Moses;

Your interesting letter of the 7th is received and carefully noted. My recollection in the main agree with yours, but was it not Greenwood where we halted after leaving Chambersburg and rested the night of the 30th and marched next day as soon as Ewell's wagon train passed to give us the road? I am not sure but think it 25 or 30 miles from Chambersburg to Gettysburg. You put it Early's trains instead of Ewell's. The latter commanded the second Corps. We started for Chambersburg the same day as A.P. Hill and could have been with him at the first opening of the fight if we had not been halted at Greenwood. I am sure now it was at Greenwood that General Lee halted us early on the 30th, and after calling to arms on the first ordered us to await the passage of Ewell's trains before taking up our line of march. The scout Harrison came to me the night of the 29th, and was sent over to General Lee who was camped near us.

Was amused at your account of Freemantle, of the Cold Stream Guards and remember now of his mention of his trouble with his boots. The fight of the first was four miles

west of Gettysburg, we could have been on the ground on the first in time for the opening if we had not been delayed by General Lee's orders. Early was in the fight on the 1st and Rhodes of Ewell's Corps. Johnsons division of that Corps, cut in with Ewell's train in front of us. Pickett of our Corps was left at Chambersburg as guard to General Lee's trains.   *Yours*
                                                        J.L.

This agrees substantially with my account; the main fact was the information regarding the spy Harrison and the delay. The letter confirms the place may have been Greenwood but I said a place near Cashtown, and I presume Greenwood is near Cashtown. I say we could have been between Gettysburg and Baltimore but for the delay. Longstreet says we could have been there with A.P. Hill, in the battle of the first; that Hill left Chambersburg the same time we did on the morning of the thirtieth. according to Longstreet's letter, the scout brought the information the night of the 29th. Now if Hill met and fought the enemy the afternoon of the first when I know only part of the enemy's forces had arrived, of course if Lee had placed implicit confidence in the scout's report and moved the night of the 29th, as he would have done but for his doubts of the scout, this additional nights march would certainly have carried us and Hill beyond Gettysburg somewhere between that point and Baltimore, and no one can tell who would have had the advantage of position, or who would have been forced to make the attack, and it may be to this mistake that General Lee magnanimously referred when on the battle field of Gettysburg after we had lost the day, he said, "This is all my fault."

When I went to the Legislature in 1877, A.O. Bacon,

who was elected Speaker of the House, offered me the Chairmanship of any committee that I desired, but particularly wanted me to be Chairman of the Judiciary Committee. He excepted the Chairmanship of the Finance Committee, which he had promised to Dr. Carlton, the present representative to Congress from the Athens district. But I declined the Chairmanship of any Committee. He then offered me second on the Finance Committee, on which committee I pretty much controlled matters. There is no doubt but that I was generally acknowledged as the leader of the House. I had a severe contest with Turner, the present member of Congress from South West Georgia. Our contest was on giving State Aid to the North Georgia Railroad, and I succeeded in obtaining State aid for what is now considered the most important railroad for developing the mineral resources of the State. It was flattering to me, and of course gratifying to see the members from that section huddle around me while I was speaking and to see so many hard fisted men from that section in tears when I made some of my appeals to the Legislature to assist in opening up a section that for the want of communication was almost entirely cut off from the rest of the State.

I also defeated a powerful and almost successful effort to buy for a mere pittance the Macon and Brunswick Railroad, which then belonged to the State, and was afterwards sold by the State under a bill passed at the session for a very large sum I think considerably over $1,000,000. In short, there was no important presented to that Legislature (and there were several) in the passage of which I did not take a conspicuous part, either to defeat or pass, and my positions were always in the interest of the State. Not withstanding all this, the Enquirer of Columbus, then controlled by the cliques against me, never passed a single *favorable comment on my course!*

In the Georgia United States Congressional race of 1878, the opposing candidates for office were a Mr. Tuggle and a Mr. Harris. There had been some discussion that Raphael Moses would be a candidate; he, however, chose to advocate and campaign for Harris. Tuggle, however, chose to make Moses' religious heritage an issue. In an open letter, written August 28, 1878, Raphael Jacob Moses, in no uncertain terms, responded to Mr. Tuggle's attack.

I have taken time to authenticate a report which I heard for the first time on the evening of the last day of the convention.

At West Point [GA] during your congressional campaign, and in my absence, you sought for me a term of reproach, and from your well-filled vocabulary, selected the epithet of Jew.

Had I served you to the extent of my ability in your recent political aspirations and your overburdened heart had sought relief in some exhibition of unmeasured gratitude, had you a wealth of gifts and selected from your abundance your richest offering to lay at my feet, you could not have honored me more highly, nor distinguished me more gratefully than by proclaiming me a Jew.

I am proud of my lineage and my race; in your severest censure you cannot name an act of my life which dishonors either, or which would mar the character of a Christian gentleman. I feel it an honor to be on of a race whom persecution can not crush, whom prejudice has in vain endeavored to subdue; who, despite the powers of man and the antagonism of the combined governments of the world, protected by the hand of Deity, have burst the temporal bonds with which prejudice would have bound them, and after nineteen centuries of persecution still survive as a nation, and assert their manhood and intelligence, and give prof of the divinity that stirs within them by having become a great factor in the government of mankind.

Would you honor me? Call me a Jew. Would you place in unenviable prominence your own un-Christian prejudices and narrow minded bigotry? Call me a Jew. Would you offer a living example of a man into whose educated mind toleration can not enter -- on whose heart the spirit of liberty and the progress of American principles have made no impression? You can find it illustrated in yourself.

Your narrow and benighted mind pandering to the prejudices of your auditory, has attempted to taunt me by calling me a Jew -- one of that peculiar people at whose altars, according to the teachings of your theological masters, God chose that His son should worship.

Strike out the nationality of Judea, and you would seek in vain for Christ and his apostles. Strike out of sacred history the teachings of the Jews, and you would be as ignorant of God and the soul's immortal mission as you are of the duties and amenities of social life.

I am not angered, but while I thank you for the opportunity which you have given me to rebuke a prejudice, confined to a limited number, distinguished for their bigotry and sectarian feelings,

of which you are a fit exemplar, I pity you for having
been cast in a mould impervious to the manly and
liberal sentiments which distinguished the nineteenth
century.

You are not created without a purpose;
nature exhibits her beauties by the contrast of light
and shade; humanities illustrates its brightest and
noblest examples by placing its most perfect models
in juxtapositions with the meanest specimens of
mankind. So that you have the consolation of
knowing that your mind has been thus deformed in
the wisdom of the Great Architect, that you might
serve as a shadow to bring forth in bold relief the
brighter tints of that beautiful picture of religious
toleration engrafted in the Constitution of the United
States by the wisdom of our fathers.

I have the honor to remain, sir,
Your most obedient servant,
Raphael J. Moses
Columbus, Georgia
August 29, 1878.

In the decade before and after the Civil War, non-Jews
quite often referred to the Jewish people as Hebrews or
Israelites. It was not uncommon, either, for Jews to call other
Jews their "Hebrew Brethren" or "Israelite Brethren." In the
Civil War period and post period, the expression "Jew" most
often was used in a derogatory sense.

*At the next election, and the only instance before or
since, from 1865 to the present time, the Democratic
Executive Committee in the interest of Louis F. Garrard,*

declined to make any nomination. They knew that I would be nominated by the party and they also knew that I would not enter into a scramble for an office that I could not fill by making a sacrifice in my business. I did not become a candidate and Garrard and some one else were elected to the succeeding Legislature. The new members were boomed by the Enquirer, and Garrard at the next session was elected Speaker. Since 1877 I have not taken any active part in politics except in the contest for Governor between Colquitt and Norwood. Soon after that Sol Levy of Philadelphia insisted upon the payment of $4,000 that his Father in his life time had very kindly loaned me, knowing that I expected to pay it out of some $7,000 fees that I would receive on the termination of case that I had against the Eagle & Phenix Mfg., Co., in the receipt of which I had been delayed from time to time by there immense influence through their money power over the juries of the County. Not by direct use of money, but by their growing power to reward or punish jurors who decided against them by giving or withholding employment. The debt of D.C. Levy was safe beyond peradventure. I wrote Sol Levy that if he persisted in his demand for the money in October, he should have it, but that I would have to pay it at a sacrifice much greater than the whole debt, for landed property in this Country was terribly depressed at that time. He insisted on the payment, and although his father had the oldest lien on my estate in a judgement yet I did not wish to have my property sold under execution, levied at the instance of my brother-in-law's estate. To avoid this I had to make a voluntary sale, and to make good titles under a voluntary sale, I had to pay off every incumbrance on my property.

The Georgia Home Insurance Co., had a mortgage younger that D.C. Levy, judgement for $3,000, Toombs had

*a mortgage for $2,500 also younger, so that too pay $4,000
I had to sell property enough to pay about $10,000. I had too
much pride to admit that I had to sell property to pay debts
and this necessity was forced by a nephew, so that I
determined to move to Atlanta and make my move the
ostensible reason for the sale. I did so. The first property that
I sold was some city lots for a little over $600.00 that five or
six years after and now are worth as many thousands. I sold
everything except 1100 acres of land which was a part of my
home on the Esquiline, and of course as I had notified my
pressing nephew I sacrificed more than the whole $4,000 by
paying the debt at that time.*

*The mistake I made was in not appealing from my
nephew to his mother, who really owned the debt; she, I am
sure, would have waited on me, but as her husband as
voluntarily loaned me the money at six percent I felt that
when ever it was absolutely demanded, I ought to pay it if the
payment was insisted on after I had fully explained the
sacrifice I would have to make. And I did pay it, principal
and interest. I would have preferred not to have referred to
this matter, but it was necessary to explain why I left
Columbus after having lived here about twenty-nine years
and move to Atlanta, an entirely new and untried field, when
I was nearly sixty-five years of age.*

*I remained in Atlanta between two and three years, at
the end of which time I had gained a case vs. the Eagle &
Phenix Mfg. Co., and had money enough to pay all my debts,
put my home in good order and have enough to support me
with economy for sufficient time to draw something from my
farm, and then I had a surplus of over $2,000 which by
advice of the President of the Columbus factory, a client of
mine whom I had faithfully served for many years and in
whose judgement I had great confidence, I invested in*

Columbus factory stock. The $2,000 turned out to be a total loss. I then invested another $1,000 in a new company, organized to buy property under its bonded debt of $50,000. The same property when I first invested was capitalized at $300,000. The new company has never been able to do anything with the property and it wold not surprise me if most of the last $1,000 would have to be added to the first loss of $2,000.

My move to Atlanta was not successful. I found a strong Bar, utterly devoid of courtesy, envious of any one who might enter the legal field with a prospect and inroad on their receipts. That standard of the Bar in professional etiquette was one that I have never practiced and was entirely unwilling to adopt. They drummed up cases and sought clients with as much avidity as a Chatham Street clothier would seek customers. Every obstruction that could be thrown in my way was placed there by the Bar; except Ben Hill, Lochraine and Van Eppes, no member of the Atlanta Bar ever did any thing to aid me, but on the contrary did every thing to retard my progress, so that when I brought my Eagle & Phenix Mfg. Co., cases to a successful close, I determined to return to Columbus rather than risk becoming involved there in expenses. If I had been a younger man I would have fought the battle to the end and I think with a vigor and resources that I could have commanded twenty years before, that I would have eventually succeeded in establishing a lucrative practice.

Shortly before I left Atlanta I entered into an active canvass in the contest between Colquitt and Norwood, for the Governorship; in this contest I canvassed most of the State and my canvass was considered a most successful one. One of the issues against Colquitt was his appointment of Joe Brown for the Senate, which I defended as judicious. For

*particulars see Avery's History of Georgia on the pages
referred to. Before I left Atlanta I was employed by Colquitt
to assist the Attorney General in some State cases, and I was
associated with Ben Hill in the defence of a case vs. The
Western and Atlantic Railroad, of which Joe Brown was
President, and with this start I think I could have succeed
even in Atlanta. But I was growing old fast, I was where I
could live with economy at home, and if I should fail in my
effort in Atlanta I would soon exhaust my little capital and
with increasing years, probably be unable to recuperate, and
I was actually afraid to take the risk.*

*After my return to Columbus, I did not resume the
practice of law. I applied to Governor McDaniel, to appoint
me judge of the City Court at a salary of $1,200, but I failed
to get it although I was recognized as altogether better
qualified than the appointee, but he had preceeded me in time
and had committed the Bar and the members of the
legislature from this County to his recommendation and this
controlled the appointment.*

*I never practiced law after my return. For some time
I made some fees as Master in Chancery and Auditor, but the
emoluments were too small and I resigned the position.*

*When I quit practicing I felt quite competent to
continue and think I could have made a good living in
Columbus, but I was afraid that if I did not quit then I might
not realize my failing faculties and then the Bar would
enquire, "Why lingers he superfluous on the stage?" And I
preferred to quit then and rather have them ask, "Why I had
withdrawn from practice."*

*Some four or five years since I ran for County
Treasurer at a salary of $500.00. I would have preferred to
have earned the $500.00 in that way to receiving $600.00
from Lea [Raphael J. Moses, Jr.] as a gratuity, though I knew*

it was freely given. I announced myself as a candidate and made not other single effort to secure the place. (I believe I did speak at one of the country precincts). A young man by the name of Cook who belonged to various societies opposed me successfully. He made a thorough personal canvass of the County. I made no personal canvass, asked no man to vote for me and staid at home on the day of the election. I rested my claims entirely on my record, and was beaten. An instance of how soon past services are forgotten when the power to grant present favors has departed.

I can say with truth I have never regretted retiring from the Bar, losing the appointment of Judge or being defeated as County Treasurer. Of course, I would rather not have offered as I should not have done if I could have foreseen the result; but I have been troubled nearly ever since my return from Atlanta with a disturbance in the circulation arising from a thickening of the valves of the heart. This would soon have compelled me to discontinue my practice and would have materially interfered with my discharging the duties of Judge of the City Court, and in all probably would have shortened my life several years. I suppose I could have continued to discharge the duties of County Treasurer but it would have been at considerable inconvenience, it would not have added one dollar to my income, in fact it would have reduced it $100.00, for if I had been in receipt of $500.00 salary I should have insisted on stopping Lea's allowance to me, and while this would have made me more independent, he would have been deprived of what I know gives him sincere pleasure, the contribution of $600.00 per annum to the comport and pleasure of his aged parents.

Chapter 3

1880-1890:
Raphael, Eliza and the Family

The absence of any public office or business of any kind away from the Home Farm enables me to gratify my tastes without hindrance of any kind. For several years, in the Summer we went North to see Lea's family in New York, and Maria Levy in Atlantic City. The winters we spent here on the farm.

For the last three or four years we have abandoned our Northern trips and live entirely on the farm with my dear Isabel, Lionel and their children, all of whom are as affection and attentive to us as we could possibly desire them to be. And with Nina and her boys in Columbus, all of whom we often see here, and occasional visits from Lea, Marie and Mathilde, our lives (Eliza's and mine) have been a picture of ideal happiness. The mind of man cannot conceive a more contented old age than we are passing. Content and peace is all that is left to declining years.

With more than the usual share of health allotted to our years, devoted children and occasional gathering of grand children and friends coming now and again, "like angels visits few and far between," what more can we ask? My wife employs herself writing and receiving letters, keeping things in order, contributing in every way in her power to our comforts, and I finding intense pleasure in the culture of my

*flowers and garden, with no memories of wrong done to my
fellow man to disturb me, and many memories of benefits
conferred to cheer me, with a Home to live in full of
pleasurable associations and beautiful in its natural
surroundings which it is my pleasure to cultivate and
improve, it seems to me that it would require a very fervid
imagination to picture a calmer sunset to a some what
checkered and stormy life, than that which may be witnessed
daily at the Esquiline.*

*For these and all the other blessings from a grateful
heart I say, "Praised be the Lord."*

*We are now just at the end of a visit from dear Lea
and at the beginning of one from Mathilde which promises us
much pleasure. We had hardly hoped to meet her again. She
brings Marion back to her Mother's heart; no, she has always
been there, I should have said, back to her Mother's arms to
nestle until some robber hand shall snatch from her the jewel!
Perhaps it will continue to adorn her home corner until Eliza
and I are gathered to our Fathers!*

*I suppose I have omitted many incidents that might
have been of interest, but I have written this in the last six
weeks, at odd times, without notes or memoranda of any kind,
and I think I have written enough to show that my life had
been a little stormy at times and that I have never turned my
back on an enemy that was attacking me, or failed to forgive
one as soon as he cried for quarters. I can also say that I
never deserted a friend or pressed a debtor, charged a fee to
a needy widow, in defending their rights or ever reduced my
charges to a client one dollar from the price fixed unless on
the plea of poverty. I adopted this rule because to take less
than I charged for services (on any other ground but poverty)
would be an implied admission that I had endeavored to
extort in the first place, and further that I never prostituted*

my limited ability by taking a fee from the prosecution in a capital case. No man's blood ever stained the current coin received in my practice.

All these things have contributed to the peaceful and happy closing of a not altogether uneventful life. The writing out of this sketch at the earnest request of my children will have accomplished its purpose if it interests my decendants and will cause them to avoid the errors and follies of my life, and emulate its better points. If I think of any thing of moment that I have omitted I will insert it here after in an addenda.

R.J. Moses

October 16th, 1890.
Esquiline Hill, near Columbus, Ga.
When I die if any announcement is made let it be, "Died at the age of _____ at his home near Columbus, Major R.J. Moses, late Commissary of Longstreet's Corps, Army No. Va. He entered the Army at the beginning of the War comparatively rich and left it at its close decidedly poor. During his term of service he oppressed no citizen, neglected no soldier's just claim, and received the commendation of his superiour officers, Generals Lee and Longstreet, for having faithfully performed his duties." (Put nothing else in the papers.)

I find that I have made no mention of the fact, that of a painful chapter in my life's history. I had to perform the burial service for my Mother, Father and Uncle. They died in Florida where we were about the only Jews, and again I performed the burial services over Percy Levy, brother of my son-in-law, to whom I became much attached. This was done at his request.

I also omitted to mention that I was in 1847 a delegate

from Florida in the Presidential Nominating Convention in Baltimore, when Case was nominated. It was a very stormy convention. The slavery issue was even then the bone of contention, Yancy of Alabama and myself tried by correspondence to commit Cass to the right of Southerners to carry slaves into the North West territory. Failing to commit him we endeavored to incorporate in the Democratic platform a recognition of that right, and failing there, William L. Vancy for Alabama and I for Florida addressed the Convention, protested against the platform, refused to endorse the nomination and with our delegations withdrew from the Convention.

I wrote the manifesto to the people of Florida, advising them to be neutral in the election and received a very handsome letter form John C. Calhoun, of South Carolina (to whom I sent a newspaper copy), commending my course. No man who has not been through such a scene can realize the embittered feeling of wild excitement of a Convention of political partisans against delegates who have nerve enough to refuse to endorse a nomination and withdraw from the Convention. Of course our States voted for him "under protest." I could never exactly tell what that meant, or who, but themselves, they protested against.

It may interest some that I should shortly sketch a visit I paid to Alex Stephens, at Liberty Hall, with my friend James Waddell.

Liberty Hall in Talliferio County, Georgia, the residence of Stephens, was an old fashioned white wooden house, with a broad porch, setting about a hundred and fifty yards from the road, with a grove of the original forest between the house and the road; no lawns, just the natural rugged and untrimmed grasses with a smart sprinkling of weeds interspersed as if to show that nature was but little interfered with; the house on the first story had a wide hall with two rooms on either side (the same on the second story) and back of that on the first floor a covered piazza between the hall and his library. A part of this piazza or addition was used for a dining hall, and always at every meal had a table spread for ten or fifteen persons though the house was occupied permanately only by Mr. Stephens and an old friend of his about eighty, who had from time immemorial been Clerk of the Court. Every room in the house but one, and if I remember correctly there were eight, had large double beds in them. Crawfordville, where he lived, was a railroad station, and as regular as the trains arrived Stephens' servant would be at the railroad inquiring if there were any passangers or baggage for Liberty Hall.

At meal times anybody from the County around who happened to be in Crawfordville, knew that a table was spread at Liberty Hall for chance comers and that none ever came without a welcome from the hospitable and distinguished bachelor host.

His old servants lived in the lot, and one of them, a man of about fifty with a broad black forehead, and a countance of more intelligence than you often see in the colored race, Mr. Stephens told me paid taxes on $30,000 worth of property. I think he ran two plantations. His secretary, if we may so call him, was a young colored man, whom he had educated and with whom he joked as though the Ethiopian had succeeded in changing his skin, even if the leopard had been compelled to retain his spots.

I made a speech in Crawfordville which this young colored man attended and when he got back to the house Stephens inquired of him how he liked the speach and which part the people seemed to like the best, and what part struck him most forcibly, etc. Mr. Stephens was himself educated by some ladies belonging to some Church Association (Presbyterian, I believe). He was educated for the Ministry but was carried away by the fascination which politics have for some men.

I expect I would be within bounds if I were to say that a hundred young Georgians were indebted to his bounty for their education. He was a man of broad charities, a statesman of great foresight, and had a wounderful hold upon the people of the State. His habits were very simple. Except reading, his principal amusement was a game of whist, which he played when ever he could muster four hands, himself and the old Clerk playing partners. If I know myself, I am a very poor player, and I don't think Waddell who visited Stephens at the same time played much better, but we were bantered for a game and like two fools proverbial for luck we held the good cards and beat the experts a robber, much to our surprise and their disgust. I will not attempt to describe Stephens' cadaverous anatomy; he is too well known as the only rival physically of Calvin Edson, who exhibited as the living skeleton in some of the museums, but I will tell an anecdote that may not be generally known, and that will not certainly do down to posterity except when preserved in this way.

During the 1st year of the War, an effort was made through some prominent men North who were anxious to preserve the Union and restore the Country to an early peace, to bring about a meeting between Abraham Lincoln and some of his cabinet, and the President of the Confederacy or in preference some prominent Southern citizens as citizens; to meet these views Mr. Davis appointed peace Commissioners to meet Lincoln at Fortress Monroe.

Stephens was one of these Commissioners, and as they passed through an avenue of soldiers on of them, on seeing

Stephens, remarked, "There's a man dead and dug up but he don't know it!"

That remark condensed in a few words a fair photograph of Stephens' personal appearance. The meeting of the Commissioners did not result in any thing. Stephens was opposed to the War in the beginning and although he was Vice-President of the Confederacy, the general opinion was that his feelings in the cause were never ardent. There was certainly between his views and Davis' policy.

On the twelfth of October my son R.J. Moses, Jr., and his sister Mathilde and our Granddaughter Marion Levy returned from Europe. Our son only stayed until the sixteenth, when he returned to New York, with our Grand daughter Hannah and her two children. This visit was a source of great pleasure to us, Mathilde is till with us and I hope if we all live that she may be persuaded to remain until after the 22nd of January, or fifty-seventh wedding day. But if she goes before we shall be thankful that we have lived to see her once more. Marion, as I have before noted, is permanently at Home.

October 18th [1890]

Today is Saturday. We have with us Marion, Lionel, Belle, Arthur and Walter, Grand children, and Wilfred, a great-grand-child; also Belle and Mathilde our daughters. Clarance, Marion and her Father have gone to Columbus. We have had our usual Saturday prayers, and now will follow the daily routine, ramble around the grounds plucking a flower here and there, admiring the evening sunset, and then after a family chat sleeping the sleep that rewards a clear conscience and good bodily health. The history of one day is pretty much the history of every day of our quiet and waning days.

* * *

I have corrected most of the typographical errors, and having done so, with a feeling of relief, I bid farewell to this crude and imperfect effort.

(Signed)   *R.J. Moses*

August 31st, 1891.

Esquiline Hill, Ga.

Chapter 4

1890-1893:
Letters and Travels
"Dear Stanford...you come from a race..."

With the conclusion of writing his all too brief memoirs, Raphael Jacob Moses and his wife, Eliza, now both near eighty years of age, took great pleasure in the visits of their large and extended family. Raphael, Jr., and his wife, Georgina Samuels, had settled in New York. Israel Nunez, and his wife, Anna Moses, had settled in Austin, Texas. The daughters had all married well and they, too, lived in various parts of the United States, and on occasion, in Europe. Raphael engaged in extensive correspondence with family and friends. His letters were affectionate, and spoke of his sense of patriarchical obligation, about the beauty of life and moral obligation.

The following letter was written to his grandson, Stanford E. Moses, son of Raphael and Eliza's daughter, Penina, and her husband, William Moultrie Moses, who were married in 1865. As will be observed, the Moses family was inclined to marry persons with the same surname of Moses. Moultrie Moses died in 1879, when Stanford was seven years old. The young widow was left with five small children to support. Thus, for a period in his youthful years, Stanford lived with his grandparents at Esquiline Hill. There developed a close relationship between the young boy and his grandfather. He was attended to as a child of their own. When he was sixteen, Stanford entered the United States Naval Academy at Annapolis, Maryland. He was one of the ten members of the Raphael Moses family to enter the hallowed ground of the Naval Academy -- the first, being his uncle, Raphael J. Moses, Jr., the Confederate Naval officer, and continuing onto classes entering in the mid 1920's. This at a period of time when service academy appointment were difficult to gain. In the summer of 1891, prior to entering his senior (first class) year, Stanford visited his grandparents at the family home in Columbus, Georgia. The Naval Academy program at the time was for the senior midshipmen to graduate and then spend two years at seas before receiving their Naval commissions. Thus, as Stanford explained to his grandfather, it might well be three years before they would meet again.

      Stanford E. Moses retained his grandfather's letters throughout his thirty-five year Naval service, retiring as captain, USN, in 1927. This warm, affectionate, paternal letter sets forth the deep feelings of a man, now eighty, whose life transcended the 19th Century.

Esquiline Hill
Sept 23, '91

Dear Stanford,
    I thought I would drop you a parting line before you go, as the chances are we shall never meet again on this side, three years at 80 is a very long time, more of earth than one can wisely wish for, but ere the ship sails is a very good time for a little advice gathered from a long experience, and it may be better said in a few familiar quotations than otherwise.
    'Be just and fear not. Unto thine own self be true, for

thou canst not be false to any man!' "Let all the ends thou aim'st at be thy Country's, God and truth."

These with Polonious' advice to Laertes in the play of Hamlet contains all the law, which a man should want to steer by and be assured of coming safe to port, the compass is not truer to the pole, than are these trite quotations to the moral and social duty of man.

In your case these maxims especially the second come to you like Duncan did to McBeth 'in double trust.'

Money in millions can alone secure life's comforts and honor when they are required and used at their best. Your Country guarantees you both, the salary assures the first and every step in the path of duty is on the direct road to the second.

Is this not much, very much to be grateful for, does it not in itself fix deep the roots of patriotism. If the poor devil who knows his Country only by the locality of his birth can stir its latent depths until he is ready to seek death at the cannon's mouth when the exigency of his Country demands it, what sacrifices ought you not to be ready to offer who receives so much? And then beside this love of Country, you have the pride of Race to battle for. You come from a Race who without a nationality of its own is a great integer in many other nationalities and a source of jealousy and fear in the rest. The apprehension lest they succeed to well (more than religion) is the true source of prejudice.

You can point to your ancestry and show the wisdom of Solomon, the poetry of David, the music of Miriam and the courage of the Maccabees. Who can excel you in your past and let the question in the future be who shall excel you as it unfolds its Silyl leaves?

Follow the maxims I have referred you to and you may defy the adverse winds of fortune, let the billows roll

ever so high you are safe from ship-wreck. Good-bye. God be
with you and if we meet again let it be with no regrets for lost
opportunities.

Yr aff
Grand Father
R.J. Moses

Re-read that letter! Grasp the power and sincerity.
Advice as to life, from Shakespeare's *Hamlet;* advice as to the
future as a Naval officer; advice as to his Judaic heritage, "the
wisdom of Solomon, the poetry of David, the music of
Miriam and the courage of the Maccabees." The flow of
words from the heart of an eighty-year-old who has witnessed
success and failure, life and death, war and reconstruction, can
be said to all persons regardless of race, regardless of creed,
regardless of ethnic origin.

Read the letter yet a third time. Stanford never again
saw his grandparents, but continued to receive letters from
Raphael. Subsequent letters speak of family members, and of
how proud they were of the accomplishments of children and
grandchildren, now lawyers and businessmen. In particular, he
wrote of Albert Luria Moses, namesake of the son killed at the
Battle of Fair Oaks. Albert Luria Moses was a brother of
Stanford and had suffered with an extreme asthma condition
as a child. Albert lived six years on a ranch in Texas, probably
with his great uncle, Israel Moses Nunes, then residing in
Stonewall, Texas. Albert eventually settled in Creede,
Colorado, where he became a highly respected member of the
Colorado Bar, and a District Judge.

In another letter to Stanford, written seven months
after the death of his beloved wife of sixty years, Eliza Moses,
Raphael wrote:

Esquiline Hill,
Jan'y 22, '93

Dear Stanford,
        I was very much gratified to receive your letter on my 81st Birthday. It reached me on the 21st.
        I did not suppose that you had forgotten me but I certainly did not expect a letter from you, while you were in the midst of so many new and interesting scenes. I received several letters, but under the circumstances I can truly say that I did not receive one which gave me such a real pleasure, but your attention in this instance is quite consistent to the whole tenor of your life towards your sainted Grandmother and me.
        This is a sad day. I miss her so much, it would have made 60 years of our happy married life, but I can but remember that after her attack of Grip about 18 months before she died, she was always, though uncomplaining, more or less a physical sufferer, and if ever a beautiful life on earth earned a blissful immortality, hers earned the crown! Still I am obliged to miss her sweet companionship.
        Your Mother, Mrs. Willie Swift Mont and Lionel Belle were here from 12 to 3. Train time. I appreciated their coming as I know they hoped to divert my thoughts from sad memories -- but really I would rather be alone!
        Belle is in bed with something like the Grip and Arthur has been kept from school for the last week, he is quite unwell.
        We have had more snow and ice and the severest spell of weather that I ever remember, there is great suffering among the poor and considerable sickness arising from unaccustomed cold, among all classes, but none of it dangerous. I suppose it will thin out old people who cannot

hug the fire as I do, but I am glad to say I am as well as I have been in 20 yrs in some respects (heart trouble for instance) better, but I am obliged to avoid sudden changes from warm room to cold air! Of course we must be reconciled to whatever befalls us, but my hope is that I will not outlive my health for a single day!

Old age has but few attractions for me anyway, and certainly without health it would have none and health may reasonably ask a furlough after over 4 score years of faithful service. Whatever of life may be left in me, be assured that my heart beats will always be in love for you and wishes for your happiness and welfare.

Yr loving
Grand Father
R.J. Moses

My daughter Nina wishes me to state that when she married Wm. Moultrie Moses I, as Notary Public, performed the marriage ceremony; such is the fact. I cannot remember now why this was done, but my impression is that the officiating Rabbi, whose name I do not remember, was a man for whose moral character I had less than respect. He had never been in my house; I never intended that he should be a visitor there, and I, being a Notary Public, was qualified to perform the ceremony, which I did in the presence of a number of friends who were invited to the ceremony. This was the 23th of June, 1865, soon after the War when every thing was still disorganized.

R.J. Moses   March 1st, 1893.

Yet another letter to Stanford, just before Raphael sailed for Europe for a vacation with family members, again expresses his pride in this grandson, and of his emotions on the loss of Eliza.

Esquiline Hill,
June 11, 1893.

My dear Stanford:
 I recd yr affectionate letter last night. I hope to return North with Marie, but not in time to see you before you sail, and perhaps I may be "weary of waiting" before you return, but here or there and I think I will still be somewhere, you will always have the love you have so well deserved from your GrMr and myself by your uniform affection.
 Run your flag high in Honor's field, determd to sink or swim with its folds around you. Honor from Duty well performed is all your profession offers, seek it sedulously and your will find it.
 I am as well, yes better than you would expect me to be in my loneliness, but I can't close my eyes to the fact that yr GrdMother lived a beautiful life for over four score years, died a peaceful and painless death and as one of us had to bear the blow, I rejoice that it fell on me.
   With my blessing and best wishes
   Yr aff. GdFather
   R.J. Moses

 Prior to his departure for Europe with his daughter Mathilda and her husband, Robert Samuel (whose sister was Georgina Samuel Moses, wife of Raphael J. Moses, Jr., the Confederate Naval officer), Raphael received a series of letters of introduction to the American ambassador for the countries he was to visit. These letters were written by John B. Gordon (General, CSA) who was the senator from Georgia. The text of each of the similar letters, written in September 1893, to the U.S. Ambassadors to Belgium, France and England spoke high praise of Moses.

September 1, 1893.

My dear Mr. Bayard:

This will introduce one of my best friends as well as one of the most prominent citizens of the State, Honl. R.J. Moses of Georgia.

Maj. Moses goes to Europe on a pleasure trip and I am sure it will give you pleasure to meet him. You will recognize him as a gentleman of culture and intellect. He is a Lawyer of the highest reputation and a leading Democrat in our political councils.

Any courtesies shown will be most worthily bestowed and appreciated by

Yrs Sincerely
J.B. Gordon

Aboard the ship, Raphael wrote this letter to his daughter Marie (Mrs. James A. Whyte) and asked that she pass it on to members of the family. Again, Raphael Jacob Moses, now 81, shows his mental alertness and feelings.

Oct 1, '93
U.S.M.S. Paris

My dear Marie,

Amazement sits upon my brow as I realize the present surroundings and take a retrospective glance at the long ago.

The sea has not so far been rougher than it was on our trip from Savannah, but so far away from either shore one is differently impressed. I wish I could transfer to paper the emotions that move me. When I compare this palatial steamer with the little craft of my boyhood dependent upon

*wind and weather and see this Leviathan of the deep
propelled by an engine with a steel shaft 200 feet long and
about 8 feet in circumference a speed of 18 miles an hour I
am impressed with the progress of Science and the progress
of man.*

*When I look upon the limitless waste of waters resting
in its great basins as quietly as childhood in the innocence of
sleep, and think if the Ruler so wills it, ere I finish this letter
a raging sea might toss this wonder of Mechanism like a
feather and grind it into impalpable powder, I am reminded
of the littleness of Man and the Omnipotence of God, for the
sea and the earth of this planet is but a speck of the boundless
Universe and Man but an Atom on the speck, thence comes
the thought of my favorite poem,*

> *'Whence came I here and how?*
> *So marvelously constructed and conceived?'*

*Followed by the mental inquiry whither shall I go and
when?*

*Where the mountains are steadfast and the earth and
its colossal buildings are firmly fixed, while one even then
realizes his dependence on a Supreme Being it does not come
home to our hearts as it does here, where we float upon a
moving surface with only a plank between us and Eternity.*

*Robert has just come to say the Titanic is in sight, we
left within ½ an hour of each other and we have steamed over
the trackless sea four days and here we are together, thus
man with his science and progress again asserts himself.*

*The present I enjoy and the future is full of hope for
me. Thanks to a loved and revered Mother who impressed
upon my youthful mind a firm reliance on an immortal future
where the severed shall again be united. I am not according*

to creedists a religious man, but I am endowed with a reverence and dependence on a Supreme Power that few feel, or know in not feeling what a support and comfort they miss. I fear that neither you or Lea inherit this feeling which is worth all else in life.

We all keep well, not of us are ever seasick, our appetites are good and we sleep the sleep of the just with pleasurable anticipation of waking on the morrow.

We have a library of about 1000 vol. I have read the "Revolt of Man" by Walter Besant.

Sunday - I am summoned to church, will finish this later.

Church is over and the substance of the sermon was we must walk by Faith illustrated by the alleged fact that we did everything by faith ... 'Only this and nothing more.' I can't say that I was very much edified by the sermon, but I was touched by the assemblage and the anthems that were lifted to God in acknowledgement of our helplessness and dependence on his Omnipotence.

Give my love to Gina and Lea and all the family, to Hannah and her boys, to Jamie and Kate, to Belle Wilkins and last but by no means least to Louise and through her to her mother and Aunt and cousins of course, and if I have omitted anyone for whom I care or who care for me, furnish them out of your abundant store and I will make it good. Everybody, except me, is counting on what time we will arrive on Wednesday, I really don't care, if the weather holds, whetter it is Wednesday or Wednesday 2 weeks.

I have read "Recollections of Fifty Yrs" by Walter Besant, "A House Party" by Ouida and in the Sep. ben. Sketches of Defoe, author of Rob. Crusoe, and Salvini.

I am having as good a time as is anywhere in the Bill of Fare for 82.

Yr affectionate Father,
R.J. Moses
Pass this on to Hannah, to Nina, Belle and let them give my
love to Mrs. Swift and Nona Sarling.

A final letter dated October 13, 1893, and written to Stanford's brother, Mont, and to his mother, Raphael's daughter, Nina from Brussels, was to be passed on to family members. After dinner on the 13th, Raphael Jacob Moses laid down for a nap to rest, and this remarkable person passed into eternity.

As a man, he left his mark on his family and his country and his heritage.

Brussels. 13 Oct. '93

Dear Mont and Nina:
(To Lea, send this to Marie and Hannah)
We arrived last night and received your letters of the 28th Sept. I miss you all and have no doubt you miss me, but it is what must come in the not far distant future, and perhaps it is as well 'that I should grow small by degrees and beautifully less.' This is a dull day and i have not been out in Brussels, but I have been all over Robert's House, down down into the kitchen -- it is all beautiful as if the Wand of the Fairies had touched it.

The Rose Garden is hardly ½ as large as our Dining Table. I counted 11 Bushes in it, and M says several have been taken out of the Center of the Bed, a microscope would I suppose disclose the space from which they were taken, but the Garden about twice the size of our Parlor is really beautiful, the Brick walls enclosing it are covered with Ivy. There is an oval Bed in the centre of the plot and the paths around the oval Bed from of course a Bed all around the Wall which has beautiful Flowers, Chrysanthemums, Dahlias, &c., and all beautifully kept, and a Birdseye view of it from the Conservatory upstairs is "a thing of beauty" and if not a joy forever, affords intense pleasure so long as you gaze upon it or carry it in your memory.

Everything from the Garret to the Cellar is in perfect order, and could not be bettered in any way that I can think of.

We had a lovely day to come here 2 hours by RR from London to Dover, a little over an hour from Dover to Calais, a Bright sun and a smooth sea made the trip delightful, then about 4½ hours to Brussels, so that we travelled by Land about 200 miles in all of which there was not a mile (altogether) that was not thoroughly cultivated in vegetables, Hops, Fields of Beets, small pastures, &c. I saw Beet tops by the acre piled in cones 3 or 4 ft high and in rows as straight as an arrow -- and on the way, a train of cars filled with Beets to be manufactured into sugar. My fellow passengers did not think it interesting because the country was flat, but I did -- for although the finger of God had not done much for the Landscape the hand of man and his thrift compelled by necessity has developed the capability of the soil, and made beautiful what with us would have been a barren waste. Necessity is a hard task master, but it is a great developer. Agnes told me when I left Calais on the cars 'to go to sleep, there was nothing, nothing to be seen.' I expected to take her advise and continuously waited for the uninteresting plateau, until night overtook me, and nothing rested on the vision but the electric lights of the Factories and other Industries in the Suburbs of Brussels. When we reached Brussels at 7:25 p.m. it was quite Dark but the Darkness did not shut out as warm a welcome as you could have desired for us all. Nina Samuel and Laura Weiner were at the Depot and I was welcomed with open arms and tender kisses.

What more could a man expect at 82 or ask for with the figures reversed to 28. At the House we found Mrs. Wyvekens waiting for us, a Lady who Mathilde says knows everything from the making of an Omelette Souffle to the Transit of Venus, otherwise that she is practical Likewise agreeable and charitable in short as she says a combination of Nina, Mrs. Carter and Mrs. Woolfolk. I have had very little conversation with her as the Dinner Table was very full last night and beautifully arranged with Flowers that had been sent to welcome Mathilde's coming! Oh, before I forget it, for Arthur's benefit the two dogs Marquise and Comtesse are the prettiest Dogs I ever remember to have seen. They have long Silky Hair nearer Slate color mixed with Brown and some white spots, and very black noses. They are very fat about ½ the size of Lea, understand French perfectly and Bark with a French intonation.

I think it would pay Arthur some day in recess to run over and see them, but I am doubtful if he could get here in that time, it's a very long way.

I don't know whether I wrote you that a Miss Orgill (about 35) very much like Lulu in size, face &c came with us on a visit of 2 or 3 weeks to Mathilde.

One of the wonders of London is a cousin of Nina Samuel a Mr. Magnus he is about the size of old Mr. Rogers with a fresh English complexion, 87, very fond of Flowers has potted over 100 Pansies for his winter conservatory, has a Grape trained under the Glass roof which is about 15 ft high, he has a ladder, trains it himself and will not allow anyone else to touch it.

He appointed a night to return my visit but the weather was so inclement he sent an apology. A Gentleman congratulated him on his fine health and hope "he would live to 100."

Why do you limit me to 100 Sir? said he, something like Porter Ingram who says he can hardly get through his little odd jobs by 100, and wanted more time. His, Magnus' wife is 84 -- married 58 yrs.

I lunched at Mr. Orgill's in London, everything was in fine style and good taste, we were admitted by a Liveried Footman and received in the Hall by a stout gentleman in Black who I took to be the Prince of Wales, and was puzzling my Democratic Brain for the proper way of meeting him, when he very politely advanced and took hold of my overcoat sleeve, and pulled it off.

"Thinks I to myself thinks I" now I've put my American toot into it, I ought to have taken off my overcoat before I entered into the presence of the Prince of Wales, but I was all right as he turned out to be only the Prince of Butlers. There was a looking Glass in the parlor about 9x12 I think. Marion would have delighted in it.

Tell Alice I know perfectly well that they are all alive and I love them all. I really consider my letters as much to one member of the family as another and suppose my Love to all is understood whether mentioned or not.

Yr aff Father and GrandFather,
R.J. Moses

The body of Raphael Jacob Moses, Major, CSA, was brought home to lay at rest along side that of his wife, Eliza, at the family cemetery on Esquiline Hill in Columbus, Georgia.

Raphael had already indicated the simple funeral he wanted. He did, however, set forth the most beautiful of inscriptions to be set on the headstones of his and Eliza's graves. They are at rest amongst family and servants.

Part V

The Family Heritage

of

Raphael and Eliza Moses

The Ascendants of
Raphael Jacob Moses and Eliza Moses

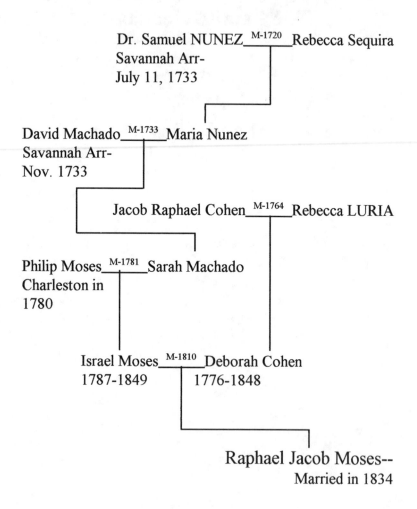

Dr. Samuel NUNEZ__M-1720__Rebecca Sequira
Savannah Arr-
July 11, 1733

David Machado__M-1733__Maria Nunez
Savannah Arr-
Nov. 1733

Jacob Raphael Cohen__M-1764__Rebecca LURIA

Philip Moses__M-1781__Sarah Machado
Charleston in
1780

Israel Moses__M-1810__Deborah Cohen
1787-1849   1776-1848

Raphael Jacob Moses--
Married in 1834

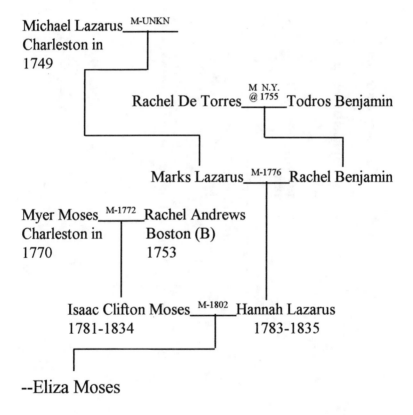

Michael Lazarus ᴹ⁻ᵁᴺᴷᴺ
Charleston in
1749

Rachel De Torres ᴹ ᴺ·ʸ· @ ¹⁷⁵⁵ Todros Benjamin

Marks Lazarus ᴹ⁻¹⁷⁷⁶ Rachel Benjamin

Myer Moses ᴹ⁻¹⁷⁷² Rachel Andrews
Charleston in   Boston (B)
1770   1753

Isaac Clifton Moses ᴹ⁻¹⁸⁰² Hannah Lazarus
1781-1834   1783-1835

--Eliza Moses

First American Jewish Archives
By Dr. Malcolm Stern

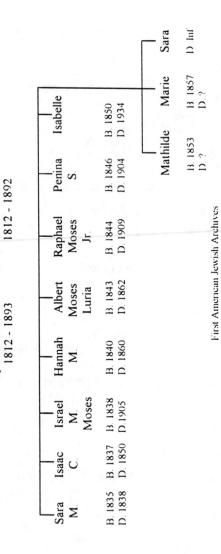

**The Immediate Family
of
Raphael Jacob Moses**

Raphael Jacob Moses (M) Eliza Moses
1812 - 1893   1812 - 1892

Sara M.	Isaac C.	Israel M. Moses	Hannah M.	Albert Moses Luria	Raphael Moses Jr.	Penina S.	Isabelle	Mathilde	Marie	Sara
B. 1835	B. 1837	B. 1838	B. 1840	B. 1843	B. 1844	B. 1846	B. 1850	B. 1853	B. 1857	D. Inf
D. 1838	D. 1850	D. 1905	D. 1860	D. 1862	D. 1909	D. 1904	D. 1934	D. ?	D. ?	

First American Jewish Archives
By Dr. Malcolm Stern

The Descendants
In
Chronological Order

---

1. Sarah Matilda MOSES   (B) Feb. 22, 1835

2. Isaac C. MOSES   (B) Feb. 6, 1837

3. Israel Moses NUNEZ   (B) Oct. 24, 1838

    (M) Anna Marie Moses (June 1, 1859)
    They had eleven children:
    1 - Charles Brown   (B) Apr. 9, 1860
    2 - Albert Luria   (B) June 23, 1862
    3 - Ammie   (B) Feb. 28, 1864
    4 - Rosa   (B) Aug. 15, 1866
        (M) Albert Luria Moses (Feb. 24, 1885)
             (son of Penina Moses and Moultrie
             Moses)
    5 - Raphael M.   (B) Nov. 4, 1868
    6 - Cecila Maria   (B) June 16, 1871
    7 - Frank   (B) Dec. 25, 1873
    8 - Dulce   (B) May 25, 1875
    9 - David Ezra   (B) Aug. 23, 1877
    10 - Clifton Moses   (B) July 11, 1880
    11 - Williamson Moses   (B) Jan. 17, 1883

4. Hannah Maria MOSES   (B) Mar. 24, 1840

    (M) Isaac I. Moses (June 24, 1856)
    They had two children:
    1 - Isaiah   (B) Oct. 29, 1858

2 - Rebecca Hannah   (B) 1859

5.   Albert Moses LURIA   (B) May 8, 1843

6.   Raphael Jacob MOSES, Jr.   (B) Dec. 11, 1844

(M) Georgina Samuel (Dec. 14, 1865)
They had seven children:
1 - Arthur S. LURIA   (B) Jun. 24, 1867
2 - Raphael Henry   (B) Aug. 2, 1868
3 - Lawrence H.   (B) July 6, 1870
4 - Rose Georgie   (B) March, 1872
5 - Albert Raphael   (B) Apr. 29, 1873
6 - Percival Robert   (B) Nov 10, 1874
7 - Nina Blanche   (B) Oct. 5, 1877

7.   Penina Septima MOSES   (B) Aug. 29, 1846

(1M) Wiliam Moultrie MOSES (June 28, 1865)
They had five children:
1 - Albert Luria   (B) Aug. 2, 1866
    (He married his cousin, Rose Nunez.)
2 - William Moultrie, Jr.   (B) Jan. 20, 1870
3 - Montefiore Jacob   (B) June 7, 1871
4 - Stanford E.   (B) Aug. 20, 1872
5 - Lionel Bel   (B) April 3, 1878

(2M) Alexander ROBISON (Dec. 22, 1881)
They had one child:
1 - Walter   (B) Jan. 15, 1883

8.   Isabelle Adeline MOSES   (B) Apr. 22, 1850

(M) Lionel C. LEVY (Dec. 15, 1864)
They had four children:
1 - Lionel Clarence   (B) e 1871
2 - Reynold Johnston   (B) Jan. 7, 1873
3 - Marian Frances   (B) 1874
4 - Arthur Crawcour   (B) Dec. 27, 1880

9.   Matilde Eliza MOSES   (B) July 5, 1853

     (M) Robert SAMUEL (Nov. 7, 1882)
        (a brother of Georgina Samuel Moses)

10.   Marie Luria MOSES   (B) Nov 25, 1857

     (M) James A. WHYTE (June 29, 1882)

11.   Sarah (D-Infant)

12.   (D-infant)

First American Jewish Archives
By Dr. Malcolm Stern

From these descendants came the following very significant contributions to the United States Armed Forces:

(1) Grandson Lawrence H. Moses graduated the United States Naval Academy, with the Class of 1890. He retired as Colonel, USMC.

(2) Grandson Stanford E. Moses graduated the United States Naval Academy, with the Class of 1892. He retired as Captain, USN.

(3) Great-grandson William Jacob Moses graduated the United States Naval Academy with the Class of 1902. He retired as Lt., Cmdr., USN.

(4) Great-grandson Edward S. Moses graduated the United States Naval Academy with the Class of 1906. He retired as Lt., Cmdr., USN.

(5) Great-grandson William Moultrie Moses graduated the United States Naval Academy with the Class of 1920. He retired as Captain, USN.

(6) Great-grandson Lionel Bel Moses, Class of 1923, attended the United States Naval Academy; he was honorably discharged in his senior year for physical disability.

(7) Great-grandson McDonald Moses entered the United States Naval Academy with the Class of 1930, graduated with the Class of 1931. He retired from the Navy in 1934 as Lt., Jg.

(8) Great grandson Walter Cecil Moses, Class of 1930, was

separated for academic deficiency, but entered the United States Naval Service and retired as Commander, USNR.

The descendants of Raphael Jacob Moses and his wife of almost 60 years, Eliza (Moses) Moses, families in America date from the Pre-Revolutionary War period, indeed as far back as 1733. Through their descendants have come military officers, lawyers, judges, and business people. Indeed, they are Americans-Americans who have a heritage to be proud.

He left a legacy that transcended the 19th Century. He left a family that extended to succeeding decades "L'Dor V'Dor," from generation to generation.   Q.E. D.

The Household and Plantation Family

[Census as of June 1, 1860]

NUMBER	AGE	SEX	COLOR
1	70	M	B
2	62	M	B
3	55	M	B
4	58	M	B
5	65	M	M
6	50	M	M
7	45	M	B
8	50	M	B
9	28	M	B
10	21	M	B
11	18	M	B
12	22	M	B
13	41	M	B
14	23	M	B
15	17	M	B
16	24	M	B
17	17	M	B
18	20	M	B
19	21	M	B
20	22	M	B
21	24	M	B
22	28	M	B
23	21	F	B
24	24	F	B
25	1	F	B
26	2	F	B
27	3	F	M
28	1	F	M
29	6	F	B
30	17	F	B
31	24	F	B
32	6	F	B
33	4	F	B
34	1	F	B
35	6	F	B
36	9	F	B
37	17	F	B
38	17	F	B
39	41	F	B
40	32	F	B
41	13	F	B
42	12	F	B
43	26	F	B
44	9	F	B

When the war began [April, 1861], I had 47 slaves.
When the war ended [April, 1865], I had 47 free men.

Esquiline
Columbus, Georgia
"A March Back in Time"

ESQUILINE CEMETERY
Columbus, Georgia

Sacred to the Memory of
RAPHAEL J. MOSES
C.S.A.
Husband of Eliza M. Moses
Born in Charleston, S.C. Jan. 20, 1812
Died in Brussels, Belgium Oct. 13, 1893
"And if these lips should ever learn to smile
With your heart far from mine.
T'would be for joy that in a little while
They would be kissed by thine.

A little while! And now the day dawns sweet
On high midst realms of bliss
Safe in the sunlight of God's love we meet
With the celestial kiss!

Sacred to the Memory of
ELIZA M. MOSES
Born Charleston, S.C. Feb. 17, 1812
Died June 4, 1892

A little way to walk; with you my own
   Only a little way!
Then one of us must weep and walk alone
   Until God's day!

A little way! It is so sweet to live
   Together, that I know
Life would not have one withered rose to give,
   If one of us should go.

This bombshell with its fuse
burning fell into camp at
Sewell's Point

He went into the field
prepared to meet his God

ALBERT LURIA MOSES - 1843-1862
Esquiline Cemetery
Columbus, Georgia

RAPHAEL JACOB MOSES, JR.
C.S.N.
1844-1809

He tried to serve, he loved his fellowman.

Esquiline Cemetery
Columbus, Georgia

ISRAEL MOSES NUNEZ
CSA
1838-1905
Temple Bethel, Austin, Texas

ESQUILINE
Columbus, Muscogee County, Georgia

ACKNOWLEDGEMENTS

I am deeply indebted to several persons, some living, some long deceased and to the kindness of the staffs of several libraries and archival depositories who made the book possible.

To Raphael Jacob Moses, himself, who at the age of seventy-nine, at the request of his family, penned a 138 page memoir of his life. To his grandson Stanford E. Moses, Capt. USN (Ret.) (USNA-1892) who seventy years ago began collecting memoirs, letters, etc. to begin the task of transcribing the material. To the fourth and subsequent generations of descendants of Raphael and Eliza Moses who were kind enough to share their material: Meredith Nunis of Austin, Texas; Lee Di Cesare of Endicott, New York; and especially to Raphael Jacob Moses, great-grandson and the third to bear the name, retired attorney of Boulder, Colorado, who located documents essential to this manuscript. To all of these, I am most grateful.

The cooperation of library staffs who diligently looked through old files for documents and put me "on the trail" of still more persons and papers. Chestatee Regional Library, Gainsville, Georgia; Southern Peaks Public Library, Alamosa, Colorado; Bradley Memorial Library, Columbus, Georgia; Chattanooga-Hamilton County Bicentennial Library, Chattanooga, Tennessee-"Job Well Done." I cannot but mention the cooperation of Yvonne Parker of the Alumni Office of the United States Naval Academy; Peggy Fox of the Confederate Research Center, Hillsboro, Texas; and above all, the staff of the American Jewish Archives, Cincinnati, Ohio; the research of the late Rabbi, Dr. Malcolm Stern and his genealogical research. To the support of the David and Fela Shapell Foundation for their interest in the American Jewish History, my heartfelt thanks!

My gratitude goes to my secretaries (and former secretaries) Deborah Butler, Carol Gilliland, Barbara Burch, and Debbie Culpepper who read my scribblings and deciphered them to readable pages. Finally, to my typists, Julie Johnston Van Valkenberg and Jane L. Brown who put this book in final form. Julie was spurred on because her ancestor, Confederate General Joseph E. Johnston, played a part in this story.

To my wife of thirty-eight years, Sonia gets the Award of Merit for having to be alone while I sat in my office going over documents, making telephone calls and writing and rewriting.

To my friends who encouraged me-Thanks, and to Laurette Rosenstrauch of Columbus, Georgia, who guided me to the Esquiline Cemetery and gave me family descendants to contact. We did it!

If I have left anybody out, it was unintentional. When you read the book, you will know the part you played in making this possible.

Mel Young
Memorial Day
May 29, 1995

Bibliography

Primary Sources

American Jewish Archives, Cincinnati, Ohio (AJA)
-Manuscript of Raphael Jacob Moses (As copied @ 1900)
-Family Pictures, Memos, and Diaries

Official Records of the Union and Confederate Armies in
the War of Rebellion (126 Vol) (OR)
   of the Union and Confederate Navies...(30 Vol) (ORN)
U.S. Government Printing Office-

National Archives, Washington, D.C.
-Service Records:
   Raphael Jacob Moses, S&F
   Albert Luria Moses, 23rd North Carolina Inf.
   Raphael Jacob Moses, CSN
   Israel Moses Nunez, Parker's Virginia Artillery
   William Moultrie Moses, 2D Georgia Infantry
   Lionel Levy, Fenner's Battery (Louisiana) Artillery

United States Naval Academy, Annapolis, MD
-Records of Acting-Midshipman Raphael J. Moses-CL 1864
-Moses Men Attending USNA

I.W. Avery. *History of Georgia.* 1850-1881-pub. 1890

Chestatee Regional Library, Gainsville, GA
-Draft manuscript of Stanford E. Moses, handwritten @
1926-34 with parts of RJM manuscript, extracts of letters to
SEM

Malcolm Stern (Dr, Desd.). *First American Jewish
Families 1654-1988, Third Edition*

Young, Mel. *Where They Lie*. UPA, 1991.

Moses Family Descendants:
-Pictures of family members
-Extracts of journals and letters of Albert Moses Luria
-Extracts of the diary of Eliza Moses
-Letter of Raphael Moses Jr. (1906)
-Various documents, newspapers, memos, poems, etc.
-Extracts from reminiscences and the diary of Penina Moses

<u>Secondary Sources</u>

Confederate Veteran Magazine. Vol. XXXIII, No. 9,
     1925.

Krick, Robert. *Parker's Virginia Battery, CSA*. 1975.

Longstreet, James, Lt. Gen. *From Manassas to Appomatox*. 1896.

Sorrell, Moxley, B. Gen. *Recollections of a Confederate Staff Officer*. 1905.

About the Author
Melvin A. Young

Mel Young is a native of St. Louis, Missouri, and a longtime resident of Chattanooga, Tennessee, site of the Battles of Chickamauga, Lookout Mountain and Missionary Ridge. He is a 1952 graduate of the United States Military Academy and served as an infantry officer during the Korean conflict. He is a past president of the Mizpah Congregation and is a past president of the Jewish Community Center. He also served on the boards of numerous professional, civic and cultural boards in the Chattanooga community and the State of Tennessee.

Mel Young has been married to Sonia (Winer) of Chattanooga since 1957. Their daughter, Melanie Young, resides in Manhattan. The subject of his next book will be about the family of Abraham Jonas, who had sons in both armies, and brother fought brother.

A West Point graduate, Mel Young has spent nearly a decade researching old books, newspapers and historical records seeking the names of Jewish soldiers in the War Between the States for his first book, *Where They Lie*. That book (UPA-1991) documents the stories of more than 500 Jewish soldiers of the Civil War...where they fought, how they were honored and where they lie.